Cyberpolitics

People, Passions, and Power: Social Movements, Interest Organizations and the Political Process
John C. Green, Series Editor

This series explores the people, activities, and institutions that animate the political process. The series emphasizes recent changes in that process—new actors, new movements, new strategies, new successes (or failures) to enter the political mainstream or influence everyday politics—and places these changes in context with the past and the future. Books in the series combine high quality scholarship with accessibility so that they may be used as core or supplementary texts in upper division political science, sociology, and communication studies courses. The series is consciously interdisciplinary and encourages cross-discipline collaboration and research.

Titles in the Series

Forthcoming

⟪Cyberpolitics⟫

Citizen Activism in
the Age of the Internet

KEVIN A. HILL

and

JOHN E. HUGHES

ROWMAN & LITTLEFIELD PUBLISHERS, INC.
Lanham • Boulder • New York • Oxford

ROWMAN & LITTLEFIELD PUBLISHERS, INC.

Published in the United States of America
by Rowman & Littlefield Publishers, Inc.
4720 Boston Way, Lanham, Maryland 20706

12 Hid's Copse Road
Cumnor Hill, Oxford OX2 9JJ, England

Copyright © 1998 by Rowman & Littlefield Publishers, Inc.

British Library Cataloguing in Publication Information Available

Library of Congress Cataloging-in-Publication Data

Hill, Kevin A., 1966–
    Cyberpolitics : citizen activism in the age of the Internet /
Kevin A. Hill and John E. Hughes.
        p.   cm.—(People, passions, and power)
    Includes bibliographical references and index.
    ISBN 0-8476-8742-2 (cloth : alk. paper).—ISBN 0-8476-8743-0
(pbk. : alk. paper)
    1. Political participation—United States—Computer network
resources.   2. Political planning—United States—Computer network
resources.   3. Lobbying—United States—Computer network resources.
4. United States—Politics and government—Computer network
resources.   5. Internet (Computer network)—United States.
I. Hughes, John E., 1968–   . II. Title. III. Series.
JK1764.H55   1998
323'.042'0285—dc21   98-10407
                                                              CIP

ISBN 0-8476-8742-2 (cloth : alk. paper)
ISBN 0-8476-8743-0 (pbk. : alk. paper)

Printed in the United States of America

∞ ™ The paper used in this publication meets the minimum requirements of American
National Standard for Information Sciences—Permanence of Paper for Printed Library
Materials, ANSI Z39.48–1984.

Contents

Tables and Figures

Tables

Figures

Acknowledgments

In chess, the person to move first has the advantage. This is not so in writing. We have greatly benefited because others have cleared the intellectual paths before us. We cannot single out the many scholars whose works have contributed to our knowledge and ideas, or provided inspiration but we do wish to offer them a collective word of thanks. Of course, we also hope to break some new ground of our own and so we invite the students and scholars who read this to build upon what we hope will prove to be a stable foundation of knowledge. We look forward to your help in trying to understand this relatively new field of study.

There are, however, some people we wish to thank personally. Naturally our wives head the list. They have had to put up with late nights and sleepy husbands, busy phone lines, Saturdays at the office, and worse. More professionally, we thank the many people at the Pew Research Center for the People and the Press, particularly Mark Cottrell and Sarah Fulton, for their assistance in analyzing their data. Both authors thank Doris Graber, the editor of the journal *Political Communication,* for offering us a venue for an earlier version of the ideas we have developed in this book. She is a pioneer in the field of political communication. Hill thanks the political science faculty at Florida International University for recognizing that, yes, this really *is* political science we are talking about here. Hughes would like to thank M. Margaret Conway for her support and encouragement, as well as Monmouth University for the release time he received to complete this work. We also wish to acknowledge the many people who use the Internet for their political enjoyment and edification. They are true inspiration for this subject. Finally, we would like to note that if there are any errors or omissions in this work, it is certainly the other author's fault. Each author fully blames the other for any errors in data collection, interpretation, and spelling.

Introduction

The Internet is one of the most talked-about topics of this decade. As such, it may seem mere opportunism to write a book about Internet politics. After all, why not jump on the bandwagon of a current fad? For two primary reasons, however, we believe this subject is important enough to merit a balanced, empirical study. First, many people have suggested that the Internet and related technologies will revolutionize world politics. Through increases in information storage and retrieval capabilities, these people claim, the Internet will destroy the monopoly of knowledge that governments too often hold. Secondly, the Internet, in some form, is going to be around for a long time to come. The precise method of transmitting and representing data for the user will change but there will still be some form of computer-based communication and therefore some type of computer-based political communication. This book is an effort to understand one aspect of computer-mediated political communication.

Communication is a broad term and a broad field of study. Communication takes place within families, organizations, and governmental agencies, between elites and the masses, and among regular citizens. As a field of study, researchers have examined the content of communication, how it is used or not used, its consequences, and much more.

Obviously, we cannot hope to cover even a fraction of those topics. So we limit ourselves and this work to just one of the potential topics: *How regular citizens use the Internet to discuss politics*. This book is not a primer on how to use the Internet politically, nor is it a study of whether politicians and leaders respond to Internet communiqués or how the mass media have adapted to this new demand for information. Instead, we want to understand how and why Jane and John Q. Public talk about politics on the Net. When they go on-line, where do they go? When they chat about Congress, what do they say? Moreover, what do Mr. and Mrs. Public do in other political areas? Do they vote and, if so, for whom? In short, our purpose is to understand just who are the citizen activists on the Internet and what are they doing there.

Computer-Mediated Heaven or Hell?

How is the Internet going to affect society? Reading through the growing number of works related to computers and politics, we see that most answers fall into one of two camps. Probably the larger camp belongs to the utopians, those who see computer networks as ushering in a new age of democratic politics. The other camp, naturally enough, has just the opposite prediction—computer networks will create a new age of conflict and misinformation. At the risk of oversimplifying their positions, we summarize below the basic ideas and beliefs of each camp.

For any democracy, information is an essential resource. On the one hand, one of the major failings of democracy is that so few people actually take part in the democratic process. In 1996 less than one-half of the eligible adult population voted in the presidential contest, and far fewer are involved in activities such as campaigning, writing letters, or circulating petitions. One of the reasons many pundits think the public fails to participate is that they lack sufficient information about the political process. Without basic knowledge about the government, how it works, and who runs it, people simply tune out. On the other hand, we have the simple fact that democracy thrives on information. Democracy requires leaders and, hopefully, the populace to discuss ideas and policies affecting the society. But deliberative, thoughtful discussion requires knowledgeable and informed discussants.

Enter the information superhighway. For utopian visionaries, the promise of nearly unlimited information delivered to your monitor in mere moments is the promise of a better democracy. The Internet, they contend, can help to make all of us more active and knowledgeable about government. In fact, these technologies make it possible to hold national town hall meetings in which the nation (or some sizable portion) meets possibly to debate and certainly to decide the issues of the day. For example, it is technologically possible (though currently prohibitively expensive) to attach a keypad to everyone's television so that during a televised "issues convention" we could each simply log our position—pressing 1 to vote yes, 2 to vote no. An even more sophisticated vision would be an on-line equivalent to CNN's "Talk Back Live," where the public watches the debate and e-mails, faxes, or calls in their opinions or questions. The experts and local audience discuss the comments and then a vote is taken. Either way, even today the technology is available to make such interactive democracy possible.

This potential for computers to aid in democratization has been noted by several people. One of the strongest proponents of this idea is Howard Rheingold. Speaking from his experience with The Well, one of the pioneering bulletin board systems (BBS), he concludes, "If the BBS isn't a democratizing technology, there is no such thing" (1993: 131). He believes that a BBS can be used to exchange ideas, debate issues, and mobilize the public. Michael Hauben (1996) echoes Rheingold's beliefs in a chapter of his "netbook" aptly titled "The Computer as a Democratizer." They both believe that computers will make it possible for more people to be more active in governing through town hall meetings or through the instant communication of electronic mail. And they are not alone. Wayne Rash, while more restrained, suggests that the Internet will open the political landscape to new parties, new interests, and new ideas (Rash, 1997). Less content with predictions, Schwartz (1996) offers something closer to a manual for activists, showing them how computer-based technologies can be used to make Rash's prediction come true. The current Speaker of the House of Representatives, Newt Gingrich (R-Ga.), in an introduction to *Creating a New Civilization* by Alvin and Heidi Toffler, has accepted the idea that computers will revolutionize politics, and mostly for the better (Toffler and Toffler, 1994: 13–18). In short, there is a lot of support for the idea that computer technologies will improve our democratic processes.

There are, however, a few voices offering warnings instead of hope. Abramson, Arterton, and Orren (1988) consider the idea of instant electronic voting for public policies and find it wanting. Plebiscitary democracy, they argue, is not democratic deliberation but simple head-counting. One problem, they assert, is that passive participation is far different from active and thoughtful consideration. Watching and registering one's vote is a far cry from the town hall ideal of debate and persuasion. Moreover, the position that wins is most likely to be the largest and not the most accurate. Finally, electronic democracy runs the risk of dividing a nation into smaller and smaller factions as broadcast media begin to "narrowcast" messages to specific groups. With media sending messages to just those suited to hear them, we become shielded from ideas that we may find distasteful but should hear nonetheless.

In his book *Data Smog,* David Shenk (1997) offers an even more critical assessment of electronic voting. He believes that the Internet will flood users with so much information that it will become impossible to sort the legitimate from the illegitimate, the good from the bad, and the accurate from the inaccurate. This position is based upon two central facts. First, the Internet is indeed full of information, perhaps too full. While utopians see this as liberalizing, Shenk's view is that this is constraining. After all, if a person cannot find the information he or she is seeking but instead finds false or misleading information, what good is the Internet? In fact, Shenk argues that the utopian idea of pure democracy through an electronic town hall is not only unworkable but also dangerous. The ninth of his thirteen "laws of data smog" reads, "The electronic town hall allows for speedy communication and bad decision-making" (1997: 137). He sees the public as uninterested and intentionally uninformed. People are ignorant, he contends, because they do not care. And giving more power (via a town hall) to people who do not care about or understand the policies they debate is likely to be counterproductive. In short, those less optimistic about the effect of new media, including the Internet, see a world in which technology enables us to substitute data entry for thoughtful discussion and passive viewing for active participation.

Leaning Left or Right?

We need to address one other major aspect of computer-mediated political communication (CMC). Technologies may be neutral in and of themselves, but that does not mean their consequences are neutral. For example, computers do not care about rifts between labor and management, but it is clear that computers alter the need for and the definition of labor in our modern economy. Similarly, CMC need not help or hinder a particular ideology, but that remains a possible outcome.

In addition to criticizing electronic democracy in general, Shenk asserts that these technologies are, in fact, politically biased. "Cyberspace is Republican," Shenk declares with his thirteenth law of data smog (1997:174). He argues that the culture of the Internet is particularly attractive to libertarians and some Republicans. The Internet is decentralized and unregulated. Cyberspace is a virtual society governed and policed by its members, not some governmental agency. For many, it seems to offer a virtual taste of the kind of world in which they would like to live. We have already mentioned that Newt Gingrich is an ardent supporter of using technology in political processes.

Others have also found other types of new media to be dominated by conservatives and Republicans. Diana Owen (1996) concludes that talk radio listeners have a strong tendency to be Republican and conservative. Further, whether Democrat or Republican, talk radio listeners tend to be more ideologically extreme than non-listeners.

Do political activists who use the Internet also tend toward conservatism and ideological extremism? If so, why? We see three potential causes of ideological bias on the Internet. First, the Internet is largely the playground of highly educated, upper-income males. All three of these characteristics tend to promote a conservative ideology. Second, the Internet is an alternative to mainstream media, which are often perceived by Republicans as being biased against conservatives. Third, libertarians, as Shenk points out, find the culture of the Internet particularly appealing and so they, and those with similar beliefs, are over-represented on the Internet. We examine each of these explanations in chapter 2, where we explore the political characteristics of Internet users in detail. What we find there, coupled with our observations about the political content of the Web, the Internet's Usenet newsgroups, and real-time "chat rooms" is surprising. As will be seen in chapter 2, people who use the Internet for political activity are actually more liberal and Democratic than the public at large. Paradoxically, the actual *content* of most of the political areas of the Internet is dominated by *conservative, libertarian,* and *anti-government* ideas. How do we explain this disjuncture between individual use characteristics and the social artifacts that Internet users create? One of the major tasks of this book is to figure out why and how conservatives, who are a significant minority of Internet political users, dominate the actual content of the Net.

Questions to Answer

Is the Internet going to usher in a new age of democracy in the United States and throughout the world? Is the Internet dominated by libertarians and ideological extremists from both sides? Do flames dominate political discussion? What about other types of communication such as recruitment and information sharing? Obviously, the research described above will suggest certain answers to these questions. We will see that other new media are ideologically extreme and dominated by conservatives. We will also see that antisocial behaviors are typical of computer-mediated communications. Finally, we will learn that the computer-mediated discussions tend to be friendly to non-mainstream points of view. Consequently, we expect political discussion on the Internet to be:

> *Hypothesis 1: dominated by Republicans, conservatives, and ideological libertarians*
> *Hypothesis 2: confrontational, including a tendency toward ad hominem attacks*
> *Hypothesis 3: more open to non-mainstream groups and points of view*

The chapters that follow elaborate on each of these hypotheses. Since each chapter examines a different aspect of political communication using the Internet, each chapter tests different aspects of these three hypotheses. In addition, at the end of each chapter we consider the implications of our findings for the utopian and dystopian views of Internet politics.

The Plan of the Book

Chapter 1: Internet Leviathan

Chapter 1 sets the stage for the work to follow. Like any good lead-in, this chapter prepares the reader for the information that follows. In particular, chapter 1 meets two important needs. First, we define the Internet and trace its history. This not only provides some basic terminology, but also introduces the various aspects of the Internet such as Web pages, Usenet newsgroups, and chat rooms. Second, chapter 1 describes the major findings of past research on computers and communication. Especially important are the two views of how the Internet will affect democracy here in the United

States and abroad. We also summarize the results of previous studies on how computers affect communication in general. Throughout the book, we will expand on and clarify the answers to these questions, as well as the ones we have presented in this introduction about ideology, utopianism, and dystopianism.

Chapter 2: Internet Activists

This chapter focuses on two questions. First, how do Internet activists differ from other Internet users and the general public? Second, in what political activities do these people engage? To answer these questions, we first need to understand the three groups of people being examined in this chapter. Despite its tremendous rate of growth, the Internet remains a tool used by a very specific group of people: approximately 15–20% of the American public. So the first distinction we need to make is between on-line and non-on-line users. Since most of the public today does not use the Internet for any purpose whatsoever, how do Internet users differ from non-users? Some differences are easily noted: Internet users are more highly educated, they have higher incomes, and they tend to be younger than the average citizen. However, if we wish to understand how the Internet is used for political purposes, we have to make one further distinction. Not everyone who uses the Internet uses it for political purposes, but a significant portion does—approximately 10% to 25% depending on the specific activity. We refer to people who use the Internet politically as "Internet activists." Thus we have three groups to be compared: the non-Internet general public, Internet users, and Internet activists.

This chapter examines the political makeup of Internet users as well as their political activities. The data come from two Pew Center surveys. In 1995 the Pew Center surveyed approximately three thousand people, with a special over-sample of one thousand Internet users. In 1996 the Pew Center repeated its survey with an emphasis on the 1996 election. Together, these surveys provide the best demographic data available on Internet users. Other studies have used on-line surveys that ask Internet users to describe themselves, but since these surveys are not random but self-selected, they contain serious measurement errors. The Pew surveys avoid this by conducting a random sample of the general public with an over-sample of Internet users.

Included in these surveys are several questions related to political activity both on and off the Internet. This enables us to answer two key questions. First, how do Internet activists differ from typical Internet users and how do they differ from citizens who do not use the Internet at all? Second, what types of political activities do people engage in while using the Internet? In summary, we found that Internet activists—those who specifically use the Internet for political activities and discussion—are more liberal and Democratic than the general public. This is a direct challenge to Hypothesis 1, and we assess the implications of this finding for the rest of our research. Thus, at the end of this chapter the reader will get an overview of both how politically distinct Internet users are as well as their level and types of political activity.

Chapter 3: Building Political Communities in Cyberspace

This chapter examines one form of *asynchronous* discourse on the Internet. Communications using the Internet fall into one of two broad categories—synchronous and asynchronous. Synchronous means that two or more individuals are communicating in real time. That is, they are both able to communicate at that same time, as with a telephone call. Most Internet communication, however, is asynchronous. Asynchronous simply means that the people communicating are not doing it at the same time, such as when writing letters. If a person sends a letter, the sender does not know when it is received or read. The person receiving it chooses when to read and when to respond.

E-mail, Usenet groups, and Web pages are all forms of asynchronous communication. The Usenet is a worldwide bulletin board to which people write comments and respond to those posted (written) by others. This chapter examines three aspects of Usenet communications as they relate to American politics. First, we document the extent of Usenet political activity and find that about 12% of all messages posted to the Usenet newsgroups are political in nature. Second, we examine the political content of Usenet messages, and present evidence that political discussions about the United States in these newsgroups is heavily conservative. Finally, we discuss the partisan bias found in Usenet messages, especially in light of the fact that Internet political users, as seen in chapter 2, are themselves more liberal than the public. Reconciling the liberal ideology of the plurality of Internet activists with the unabashed conservative dominance of the Usenet is one main theme of chapter 3.

There are several thousand Usenet groups (topics) to which several million messages are posted each year. Of these we estimate 12% are overtly political. Ratings of Usenet groups show that political groups constitute 7% of all Usenet groups but over 12% of all messages. This works out to an estimated 5.5 million or more political messages per year.

To address our second goal—understanding the content of Usenet messages—we read and recorded over 5,000 messages for their political content. We found that Usenet users behave in ways similar to people in more traditional small groups. That is, Usenet groups, despite being asynchronous and electronic, demonstrate the same kinds of characteristics as normal face-to-face organizations. In chapter 3 we expand on this to demonstrate that these groups provide forums in which meaningful political communication occurs.

Our final goal is to understand the ideological orientation of this communication. Because Internet activists differ so much from typical non-users (see chapter 2), we would expect that their messages would differ in content as well. Our suspicion that there is a strong right-wing or anti-government tilt to Usenet messages is confirmed in our analyses. The remainder of this chapter is devoted to demonstrating and, it is hoped, explaining this bias. Taken together, this chapter demonstrates that the Usenet is a method of meaningful political discourse and that this discourse is dissimilar to that found in more typical or mainstream methods of communication.

Chapter 4: Is the Internet an Instrument of Global Democratization?

This discussion of Usenet newsgroup use turns its focus to non–United-States-oriented discussion groups. As such, this chapter is similar to the previous one, in that our interest is in the political use of newsgroups. However, the analysis in chapter 4 is not based on left versus right-wing usage of these bulletin boards. Rather, we hypothesize that people in less democratic nations will use the Usenet newsgroups devoted to those countries as a relatively "safe" form of political discussion and even protest. We do find evidence for this proposition, since as the level of democratization in a country increases, the level of anti-government messages in that country's subject newsgroup decreases. Further, we expect that nationals of those countries living overseas will use these newsgroups to more openly discuss politics in those nations than they could otherwise do so, though we find less-than-overwhelming evidence of this.

Before turning to our content analysis of the messages posted in non–United States Usenet groups, we must first quantify both the number of these groups and the level of political discussion in them. Currently there are over 150 newsgroups devoted to individual nations, or one newsgroup for almost every country on the planet.

In fact, some larger and more diverse nations such as India have multiple groups devoted to them (*soc.culture.india, soc.culture.india.tamil, soc.culture.india.keral*, etc.). These newsgroups differ in the number of messages posted to them every week, from an average of five for *soc.culture.haiti*, to over fifteen hundred for *soc.culture.singapore*, a true outlier given that city-state's small size and population. In fact, this is the most active *soc.culture* group devoted to a single country on the Internet, something that originally gave us the idea that people in less-than-democratic nations such as Singapore would use the Internet as a relatively safe vehicle for political discussion. Further, *soc.culture.cuba* has by far the highest number of political messages of the Latin American-oriented newsgroups, and over 80% of these messages are explicitly political. This chapter quantifies the international usage of the Usenet as a first attempt to find some patterns in this usage that may be politically motivated. After all, if the Internet is to become the vaunted "global village" and source of "grassroots democracy" that many pundits have imagined, one would expect and desire to find evidence of its positive political impact outside the United States.

Having established the quantity of newsgroup usage, the chapter turns to actually examining the content of these messages using a methodology similar to that used in chapter 3 on American politics. How many messages in these groups are explicitly political? Of those, how many are messages in opposition to the current government of the nation in question? How many messages are pro-government? Do these messages primarily serve as alternative sources of news? Are they attempts to recruit people in the subject country and around the world into some sort of political action? Are richer nations more likely to have higher levels of discussion in their newsgroups than poorer ones? These questions of content in these political newsgroups are the subject of this chapter, with our full expectation that less-democratic nations' newsgroups will contain more political and specifically anti-government discussion than the newsgroups of fully democratic countries.

Chapter 5: Instantaneous Political Discussion: America Online's Chat Rooms

In contrast to Usenet groups, chat rooms and IRCs (Internet Relay Chat) are the two primary methods of synchronous communication on the Internet. Both chat rooms and IRCs work in the same way— people type messages and respond to messages in real time. These messages are usually limited to one or two lines of type and thus the discussions can be disjointed but in exchange, they gain an immediacy not possible with the Usenet.

To contrast the Usenet and chat rooms, we must address several questions. First, how do chat rooms differ from Usenet groups in terms of their political content? Do chat rooms/IRCs have more current-event discussions or less use of outside references? Are people more or less likely to "flame," or insult, each other? In other words, what kind of political communication occurs within chat rooms and IRCs? These questions are important because an increasing number of people are likely to engage in this kind of on-line political discussion, and so we must understand how the method of communication, that is, chat vs. Usenet, shapes the content of the message.

The data for this study come from recordings of chat room sessions on America Online (AOL). This service is not the only place providing chat rooms, but it is the largest commercial on-line service in the world. Moreover, it has a chat room devoted specifically to the discussion of politics. Over a period of three months, we recorded the discussions taking place in

AOL's politics chat room ("The Cloak Room"). We coded the content of these discussions in order to answer the following questions. First, what is the general content in terms of topics and ideological direction? Second, how do real-time chats differ from bulletin boards such as the Usenet? In summary, we find that America Online's political chat room is even more thoroughly conservative than the Usenet newsgroups devoted to American politics. Further, the political discussions in The Cloak Room are much less deliberative than their newsgroup counterparts, but are not more likely to consist of ad hominem attacks. Still, these chats are again dominated by conservatives, while the average Internet political user is more liberal than the American public. Reconciling this gap between individuals and the social aggregates they construct is another theme of this chapter.

Chapter 6: Web Sites, Interest Groups, and Politics

Perhaps the most compelling aspect of the Internet is its unconstrained nature. Anyone with a computer and an Internet provider can create a Web page. The Web pages can be indexed by major search engines and found through keyword searches. Internet searches will report pages from authorities such as the United States government right along with pages by sixth-grade students. Because any Web page can look official when reported by a search engine and because anyone can create a page, Web publishing is bound to attract the attention of groups outside the mainstream of a nation's political culture.

This chapter examines some of the Web pages produced by non-mainstream or fringe organizations. Our first goal is to examine the content of these pages. How do these groups present themselves on-line? Are they explicit about their goals and purposes, or do they tone down their message? Do they try to recruit new supporters or is this a service provided for current "believers"? In short, chapter 6 finds that Web pages vary substantially in their content and technical sophistication. Some pages are multimedia powerhouses that include many graphical elements and even animated text and video. We find that Web sites from mainstream conservative organizations are the most likely to be graphically "flashy." On the other hand, mainstream liberal sites tend to include more hypertext links to other sites on the Internet, and as such engage in more of a community-building enterprise than do their conservative counterparts, whose flashy pages are more geared toward recruitment and advertising. Similarly, we also examine the ways in which these pages are advertised. Are these pages regularly indexed by major search engines or are they found primarily through other pages with similar content? Are pages that are indexed by search engines different from those not indexed, i.e. more moderate? Again, chapter 6 presents evidence that conservative and neutral sites are more widely known on the Internet through search engine indexing and their sheer sizes than are Web sites maintained by liberal organizations.

What about "extremist" groups on the left and right? How do their Web sites differ from those of their mainstream counterparts? One important question is this: Do patterns of Web page use and construction vary between mainstream and extremist groups? Do these types of interest groups use the Web in different ways, or are they both using similar methods to get their messages out, recruit new members, and maintain organizational functions? Previewing the analyses in chapter 6, we can say that fringe pages from the left and right are less technically sophisticated, smaller, and less well known through Internet search indexes than mainstream sites. However, the fact remains that groups and individuals existing on the fringes of American political life sometimes produce Web sites that rival their mainstream counterparts in sophistication and effectiveness in delivering political messages that are largely ignored in the traditional media.

The next important question is just an extension of the analyses in the preceding chapter: Are there more conservative than liberal mainstream groups with Web pages? Do conservatives and liberals have Web sites of differing levels of political sophistication? The findings in chapter 3 about right-wing usage of the Usenet would predict a concomitant conservative dominance of the Web. One of the main purposes of this chapter is to establish whether or not conservative dominance of the Usenet political newsgroups extends to the realm of World Wide Web sites. As chapter 6 details, the numbers of liberal, politically neutral, and conservative Web pages are approximately equal. Here, at least in sheer numbers, we do not find the same conservative ideological dominance in Net use that we do in chapters 3 and 5. However, a full 22% of the pages we examine in chapter 6 are outside the liberal and conservative mainstreams of American political life. Thus, one in five cases in our sample of Web sites is an ideologically extreme site.

The main focus of our analyses here again is two-pronged. First, how many liberal and conservative Web pages are there? This is easily established though the various Web search engines that index pages by keyword. Second, what do these Web sites look like? What do they say? Are they interlinked somehow? In the end, this chapter continues the flow of our investigation: Is the Internet (in this case, the Web) being used for mainstream political purposes? If so, do conservative groups hold the edge in quantity and quality of production here that they do on the Usenet and in extremist Web pages?

Chapter 7: The Internet and the Future of Political Communication

The last chapter summarizes our findings and offers our conclusions. Because anything written about a technology as new and dynamic as the

Internet risks becoming dated quickly, we offer our conclusions with a note of caution. Even so, we do believe our research advances our current knowledge of politics and the Internet and will, we hope, serve as a foundation for future research. Is the Internet a right-wing playground? Is there any reason to believe that the utopians' view of the Internet as a savior of democracy is true? How do we reconcile the liberal nature of the Internet's political users with the largely conservative *content* of the Net? Conversely, are there any kernels of truth to the dystopian claim that the Internet is creeping Big Brotherism? In the end, we present the first major empirical study of the Internet as a political venue, and find that not all political ideologies benefit to the same extent from its existence.

Internet Leviathan

On Rhetoric, Hyperbole, and the Greatness of Sliced Bread

The Internet is the biggest celebrity on Earth today. As with any flesh-and-blood celebrity, this interconnected series of computer networks is adored, hated, mistrusted, idolized, stereotyped, and misunderstood. It has the power to offer up vast amounts of information literally anywhere in the world where there is a working telephone line and electricity. A remote village clinic in Zaire can use a satellite up-link, a gasoline generator, and a simple computer to access vital World Health Organization databases in Geneva—a feat that could easily save the lives of dozens of people in the village. On the other hand, a small group of terrorists using the same technical setup and any freely available encryption software could maintain an undetectable worldwide network for years. With the good comes the bad, as with any new technology or human endeavor.

Almost anything people can do through the mail, over the phone, or face to face, they can do using the Internet. People have met spouses in America Online chat rooms. They have bought hard-to-find motorcycle parts from someone on the other side of the nation who posted a classified ad in the Internet newsgroup *rec.arts.motorcycles.for-sale*. They have constructed Web pages devoted to highlighting human rights violations in obscure countries. On the other hand, while many people find spouses through chat rooms, a few child molesters have stalked potential victims this way. While many people can find good deals on items to purchase though on-line classified ads, others post solicitations for money that are scams. Finally, for every Web page concerned with human rights, there is probably another devoted to advancing a white supremacist cause.

These juxtapositions of acceptable and unacceptable, profane and sublime, legal and illegal, ethical and unethical, left wing and right wing, are all consequences of such a freewheeling, impossible-to-regulate communications medium as the Internet. Pundits, academics, and Internet users alike have remarked on some of these juxtapositions. For example, as the Web has made databases easier and easier to access by millions of people around the world, lawyers and Internet users have fretted about privacy concerns. Second, as the number of sexually oriented Web sites and Usenet newsgroups proliferated, the United States government passed the Communications Decency Act of 1996 in an attempt to protect children from exposure to such easily available materials. Immediately civil liberties groups filed suit against the law, and ultimately the Supreme Court unanimously declared the law unconstitutional. Third, investors have taken to the Internet like fish to water, owing to the ease with which one can research companies and their stocks on-line. At the same time, scam artists have arisen in chat rooms, in the newsgroups, and on Web pages, much to the bane of the FBI, the Secret Service, and state attorneys general.

What about politics? If there is a flip side to all the other activities on the Internet, how could politics possibly be immune? Viewing recent ads for Internet service providers and hardware manufacturers, not to mention several recent "how-to" books on the subject, one could easily believe that the Internet is inevitably going to bring all people together in harmony, make politicians more accountable to their constituents, and advance the causes of human rights and social justice generally. Certainly this is a possibility, but how is the Internet any different than fax machines, telephones, and door-to-door canvassing? Is e-mailing a complaint to one's congressperson any more effective than sitting down and writing a letter to her? Further, if the Internet is going to make it easier for human rights and citizen activist groups to organize, recruit members, and petition the government for redress of their grievances, does not the same logic apply to white supremacist groups, violent anti-government militias, the Ku Klux Klan, anarchists, communists, cults, and any single "nut" with an agenda? After all, it is just as easy for the Klan to put together a Web site as it is for the American Civil Liberties Union, the authors of this book, or an eight-year-old. Anyone with $149 Web page creation software can construct the slickest Web site one could imagine.

Many people would like to believe MCI's recent commercial—that on the Internet there are no races, there are no genders, there is no age, and there are no disabilities. Maybe the Internet will bring about an era of unprecedented human cooperation, as some people would like to believe. But logic and even a cursory use of any Internet search engine will illuminate parts of the Web, newsgroups, and chat rooms that are specifically devoted to advocating actions that are injurious to certain races, genders, ages, and disabilities. True, the Internet does carry with it the potential to create a global community that can influence politics for the better. But it also carries just as large a potential to tribalize the world. Many pundits worry that the Internet will create a world of people who do nothing but sit at home in front of their computer screens chatting away with people they will never meet. To these pundits, this is a gigantic step backward in human relations. The same thing applies to politics: many people believe the Internet will create a political utopia, or at least a sliver of utopia. Others worry that the Internet will make it easier to look up instructions for how to blow up federal buildings, make parcel bombs, and find the time and place for next week's Klan rally.

Politically, the Internet not only has the potential to create utopia and dystopia, it is doing so at this very moment. Because the Web, newsgroups, and chat rooms leave printed and graphical records of themselves, we can empirically study their effect on all types of political activity. That is what this book does. First, in this chapter we define what the Internet is and how other researchers think the Internet will affect society. Next, we will determine how citizens use the Internet for political activities. One of the crucial differences between the Internet and face-to-face, broadcast, and print communication is that Internet political communication is unmediated and impersonal. When communicating via computer you cannot see or hear those with whom you are communicating. Equally important, on the Internet there is no "gatekeeper" like ABC, the *New York Times,* or a panel discussion moderator to get between participants and their subjects of conversation. Indeed, since anyone with access to a computer, a modem, and an Internet service provider can create a Web page that can be read by millions of people worldwide, Internet political communication is not only unmoderated; it is the antithesis of moderated communication. So, not only can anyone post to an Internet newsgroup, join in a political chat room discussion, or create a Web page, but anyone with *any sort of idea, no matter how offensive to the great majority of people,* can do so.

Technically then, the most "respected" news organization, the president of the United States, and Billy Bob the white supremacist all have the same means of communication, and the same extremely large potential audience. This fact is a major theme running through this book. If the Internet can make it possible for people to more effectively communicate with their government, organize politically, and educate each other about political issues, it can do so for anyone holding any extremist political idea just as easily as it can for the most mainstream political party or interest group. Short of blatantly unconstitutional and logistically impossible government censorship of the Internet, we have to take the useful with the useless, the sacred with the profane, and the sublime with the banal as part and parcel of electronic political communication. This book's main task, then, is to quantify and describe this juxtaposition of types of political discourse in cyberspace.

What Is the Internet?

The answer to the question What is the Internet? is not as easy as it may appear at first blush. This is because the answer depends on the question. As with so many social phenomena, the word Internet can be a noun, a verb, or an adjective. Starting with the noun form of the word, the problem gets even more complicated: the Internet is often described as a thing *and* a place. Originally, the word defined a thing—a series of inter-networked computers communicating with each other in a common language. Today, this definition is still technically correct. However, in the popular culture and even among computer scientists, we often talk about the Internet as if it were a place like Ft. Lauderdale, Florida, or Bentonville, Arkansas. The phrase "Find us on the Internet at *www.gop.com*" means the same thing functionally as "Call us at 1-800-GOP-1996" or "Please write to us at GOP, Washington, DC 20002." Even Senator Bob Dole got into the act in his second debate with President Clinton in 1996 by giving out his Web "address." Throughout this book, when we speak of the Internet, we will often be using this place-name definition.

And it does not stop there. The word "internet" can also be the verb "to internet." When someone says, "I am going to internet these computers together," he or she is also technically correct. In fact, the first time the word "internet" ever appeared in history was in 1972, when the networking protocol TCP/IP was invented, allowing widely dispersed computer networks to be "internetted" together. Today, one may well hear an e-mail-savvy colleague say, "Well, Jim, just hold on. I will internet you those schematics at the end of the day." So, this word has become to the late 1990s what Federal Express was to the earlier part of the decade. Indeed, in 1990, that same colleague may well have said, "Well, Jim, just hold on. I will Fed-Ex you those schematics at the end of the day."

Confused yet? Finally, the word "Internet" can also be an adjective modifying another noun. Who has not received an advertisement from a bank, an insurance company, or a book club stating that the lucky recipient can now enjoy "Internet banking," "Internet convenience," or "Internet shopping from the privacy of your own computer"? Our point in this section is not to overly complicate the issue by playing word games with our subject. On the contrary, we point out all these word forms to indicate that the "Internet" is many things, places, processes, and qualities.

Uses of the Internet

The Internet is many things simultaneously. First, it is a new broadcast medium. The simplest way to see this is to look for the analogs of the traditional media on the Internet. ABC, CBS, NBC, FOX, CNN, and C-SPAN all have Web sites that either regurgitate their broadcasts in written and visual form or, more common today, enhance the material available via traditional means. For example, CNN may broadcast a news report about the Senate's campaign finance hearings. Of course, even CNN, a 24-hour news network, can only devote so much on-air time to one story. So an interested viewer can log onto CNN's Web site at *www.cnn.com* to read the text of this story. Further, that same interested viewer may find links to witness testimony transcripts, biographies, or even the actual text of the campaign finance laws under scrutiny. In this way, CNN has used its presence on the Internet to add value to its traditional television broadcast. Still, in this case the Internet is just another extension of the traditional broadcast media. Of course, the print media can use the same broadcast metaphor. Web sites like *www.washingtonpost.com* or *www.herald.com* are Internet extensions of the *Washington Post* and the *Miami Herald,* respectively.

Second, the Internet (as a place) is a gigantic bulletin board. Everyone is familiar with the concept: a church, a university, a professional meeting, or a condo association puts up a cork board with thumbtacks so that people can post notices or even exchange messages with one another. People use the Internet for the same reasons, except that the potential audience is now greatly expanded beyond just the people who may walk by and physically see the bulletin board. Now, anyone with a Web page can post notices that anyone in the world might see if they log onto the site, either by directly typing the Web address into their browser or by finding the site using one of the dozens of Internet search engines. For example, the National Rifle Association may post its concerns about a gun control bill on its site at *www.nra.org*, where the content of the message may be viewed by all 40 million people who are connected to the Internet. The Web as a bulletin board has enormous implications for political organizations, as described in chapter 6. Still, this is *not* some totally new social phenomenon, but merely an extension of the bulletin board or soapbox concept that has been around in one form or another since the invention of writing and oratory.

Other parts of the Internet, most notably the tens of thousands of Usenet newsgroups, are also *interactive* bulletin boards. Here, someone may post a message about President Clinton in the newsgroup *alt.politics.usa* or *alt.fan. bill.clinton*. Then anyone with newsgroup-reading software (which is built into the two major browsers, from Netscape and Microsoft) can not only read the message, but also reply to the message by posting their own thoughts in the same newsgroup. A written, public conversation starts that may go on for weeks and be joined by dozens of other people and viewed by thousands. The Internet becomes a community forum or bulletin board with a world-wide audience and worldwide participants.

Third, the Internet is an enormous collaboration tool for businesses, governments, non-profit groups, and political organizations. Using the previously mentioned bulletin board methods can allow a company to communicate with its customers more effectively and cheaply than a toll-free telephone number. It can also put citizens into contact with government agencies. Indeed, at tax time many of us may need that obscure form from the Internal Revenue Service. Unfortunately, we have probably waited until April 14 to fill out our tax returns and the Post Office does not have the form we need. If we call the IRS telephone number, we will never get the form we need in the mail on time. However, the Internet-connected customer (notice the adjectival use of our magic word here) can point her browser to *www.irs.gov* and download and print an on-line version of that obscure form, fill it out, and actually get her tax return in on time. In a similar fashion, political groups like the American Civil Liberties Union can use their Web site at *www.aclu.org* to coordinate member petition drives on behalf of a civil liberties case.

Finally, the Internet is a huge post office. Almost everyone with even the most rudimentary knowledge of computers has sent or received electronic mail at some time in his or her recent life. E-mail is cheap, convenient, and useful. If one wants to communicate with a friend or colleague in Zimbabwe who has an Internet account, then one merely types an electronic mail message to that person which, barring network problems, will arrive at its destination in a matter of minutes. Further, if a person wants to send the same memo to fifty-eight coworkers or relatives, all of whom have Internet access, then he or she merely types the message once and has his e-mail software send the message to fifty-eight separate accounts. This type of collaboration is certainly possible without the Internet, but the time and economic costs are exponentially higher without Net access.

Thus, the Internet is a venue for one-to-many communication (broadcasting), one-to-one communication (e-mail), and many-to-many communication (Web pages and Usenet newsgroups). How did things get to be this way? Perhaps a little history is in order.

A Brief History of the Internet

The Internet as a series of widely dispersed linked computer networks started as an idea in 1962. That year, JCR Liklander wrote a paper on "wide area networking," which is the concept of linking geographically dispersed computers to each other (Liklander, 1962). Leonard Kleinrock had sketched the basis of this technology out in the previous year with the idea of "packet switching." Basically, packet switching involves slicing the data that flow between two computers over a network into chunks, so that any one part of the data that was garbled or lost could be easily resent, without having to resend the whole piece of data. The modern Internet is based on this concept of packet switching. Anyone who has seen the text part of a Web page displayed almost immediately, only to wait for the graphical components of the page to creep slowly into being, has experienced packet switching.

This method of cutting up data into discreet chunks has had profound implications for the development of wide area networks (WANs). Imagine a

WAN with fifty sets of computers attached. If five of the networks malfunction, the other forty-five will not also crash if they are using packet switching, since they can send these chunks of data to each other without having the whole WAN functioning. The concept is similar to the improvement of the old Christmas tree light strings that would not work if only one bulb was burnt out. A network based on packet switching is more like a new string of lights that will still work if five or six of the bulbs are not present or are broken.

This decentralized nature of a WAN based on packet switching appealed greatly to the U.S. Defense Department and the defense industry, since a strategically important network based on packet-switching technology could largely survive even if several computing sites were blasted out of existence by a nuclear device. In 1969, the Advanced Research Projects Agency Network (ARPANET) was founded, based on packet-switching technology. Backed by the Defense Department for both military and technical academic use, ARPANET would evolve into that vast collection of interconnected computer networks we know today as the Internet. That year, packet switching network protocols connected the campuses of UCLA, Stanford, the University of Utah, and the University of California at Santa Barbara. Electronic mail made its way into ARPANET in 1972, making collaboration between academics at these widely dispersed campuses easier, and laying the seeds of the subculture of cyberspace that is the subject of this book. That same year, the word "Internet" first made its way into computing, when a new packet-switching technology called Transmission Control Protocol/Internet Protocol (TCP/IP) was introduced to allow internetting of computer networks. Over 25 years later, TCP/IP is still the language by which "internetted" computers speak to each other, from the biggest mainframe to the most humble PC. This protocol is now built into major PC operating systems such as Windows 95 and Macintosh System 8, and has been a major technological component of the explosive growth of the Internet and its penetration of the overall culture in the United States and other nations.

The growth of the Internet in the 1980s led to the development of the Domain Name System (DNS), in which Internet-connected computer networks, known as domains, are each assigned a unique name and address. No longer did users have to memorize some arcane numerical address when they wished to contact a colleague via e-mail or remotely log into a computer system. Now, one only had to supply the proper address based on a domain name. This technological development contributed to the commercial and popular viability of the Internet. This is why a user can now type *www.gop. org*, rather than some bizarre string of numbers, to access the Republican Party's Web site. Further, this has allowed Web sites to considerably personalize themselves and market their sites for only the $100-per-year domain name charge. For example, if one is interested in Toyota vehicles but does not know the address of the Toyota Web site offhand, it is a good bet that typing *www.toyota.com* into one's browser will bring one to the correct site (it does). Without this Domain Name System, the exponential growth of the Internet, particularly for commercial and small political group use, would surely have been curtailed.

In 1983, the old ARPANET split into a new ARPANET for academic use and MILNET for exclusive military use. Around the same time, the National Science Foundation (NSF) started funding the physical infrastructure for the growing Internet (building on what started out as ARPANET). In another move that practically guaranteed fast Internet growth, NSF made all its funding to universities for Internet development contingent on that technology being made available to the *entire* campus community. So even if it was the physics department at a university that actually won the NSF grant for networking hardware and software, access to the Internet had to be made available campus-wide. Further, NSF encouraged Internetted universities to enter into agreements with local commercial networks to share the costs of networking, thus laying yet more groundwork for the commercialization and popularization of the Internet outside the halls of academia.

Starting in the early 1990s, commercial services like CompuServe, Prodigy, and America Online began to offer their subscribers limited access to the Internet, primarily e-mail, Usenet newsgroup access, and access to data and programs on the Internet through the File Transfer Protocol (FTP) system. Then the development of graphical browser software for the World Wide Web truly began the Internet explosion in about 1993. Programs like Mosaic, which was free for personal use, now put a friendly multimedia face on the Internet. These browsers, combined with the Domain Name System, now allowed non-sophisticated computer users to access the growing number of Web pages, Usenet newsgroup bulletin boards, and FTP sites that had previously been the realm of tech-heads using arcane language typed on a command line. As the Internet began to fully spread beyond colleges and universities, media organizations and companies rushed to put up Web Sites, and the Age of the Internet was born.

Table 1.1 illustrates the dramatic growth of the Internet between January 1993 and January 1997. The table presents the number of unique Internet domains in existence every six months in that time period. For example, in the Web address *www.cnn.com,* "cnn" is the domain. Likewise, in the e-mail address *president@whitehouse.gov,* "whitehouse" is the domain. Beginning with 21,000 domains in January 1993, this number more than doubled by July 1994, doubled again several months later, doubled again between July 1995 and January 1996, and has settled into a pattern of 100% growth every six months. Almost all of this growth has been in commercial, network provider, and non-profit organization sites (Web sites and e-mail addresses ending in ".com," ".net," and ".org," respectively).

TABLE 1.1
The Growth of the Internet, 1993–1997

Date	Domains	Six Month Growth Rate
January 1993	21,000	
July 1993	26,000	23.8%
January 1994	30,000	15.4%
July 1994	46,000	53.3%
January 1995	71,000	54.3%
July 1995	120,000	69.0%
January 1996	240,000	100.0%
July 1996	488,000	103.3%
January 1997	828,000	69.7%

Source: Internet Domain Survey, January 1997, Network Wizards: www.nw.com.

In April 1995, the National Science Foundation finally pulled the plug on their direct funding of Internet infrastructure, turning the Internet backbone over to private network providers. What had started as a small collection of academics and military users, and then developed slowly across college campus computer science and engineering departments, was now finally and squarely in the mainstream of American life. Today, the Internet boasts over forty million users with no end to this growth in sight.

The Internet and Politics

So what does this interesting technological history have to do with politics? This is a fair question. After all, while the Internet was still the realm of the pocket-protector crowd, even if they did discuss politics among themselves, this would explain next to nothing about any broader social phenomena. But now the Internet has over forty million users worldwide, a very large percentage of whom live in the United States. While describing Net users will be the main focus of chapter 2, we still need to know up front what makes political communication on the Internet unique.

As a starting point, we need to understand that communication is an essential part of politics. Nothing in politics, especially in a democratic society, is possible without some form of *communication*. Standing on a soapbox shouting tirades against the government, placing political advertisements on radio and television, sending people targeted direct mail or faxes, and writing a letter to one's elected representatives are all standard means of engaging in politics. Indeed, even casting a ballot is a form of indirect communication to the government and to one's fellow citizens of political intentions and wishes. Given that politics is dependent on communication, anything that affects how people communicate will ultimately affect politics as well.

Political communication almost always involves four main actors: the public, the print and broadcast media, the government, and interest groups. Further, since most citizens do not get one-to-one contact with politicians or major political events, they rely primarily on the media or social networks for their news (Beck, 1991; Chaffee, 1986). Therefore, the media establishment has always played a crucial role in the process of political communication, and traditionally this has been through the broadcast metaphor of one messenger communicating with many receivers. Thus, the flow of political information between the media and the public is usually a one-way process (Bonchek, 1996).

The Internet, of course, has the potential to change this flow of political information and thus revolutionize the process of political communication. Anyone with an Internet access account, some space on a server, and Web page creation software can now become a "broadcaster" with a potential audience in the millions. As mentioned earlier, the traditional media outlets themselves have already established comprehensive Web sites and user feedback e-mail addresses on the Internet. Still, the open, almost anarchic nature of the Internet allows any small group with a political bone to pick to become a broadcaster of information. Further, this putative political group can just as easily broadcast information that the mainstream media has ignored. So, the Internet can (and does) remove one layer of filtering of political information—the gatekeepers of the mainstream media (Graber, 1992). As we discuss below, the political groups in society that most likely benefit from the lack of media gatekeepers on the Internet are fringe and extremist groups on both the right and left. In the end, one of the truly revolutionary aspects of the Internet is that *everyone* is a potential broadcaster and participant in the realm of political communication.

Computer-Mediation Research

Over the last few decades, the topic of computer-mediated communication (CMC) has grown from literally nonexistent to voluminous. Most of the work has centered on how businesses can use computers to improve employee efficiency or improve employer-employee communications. While little of the research is specifically political, much of it is applicable to our studies. In particular, we build on past research into the effects of CMC on interpersonal behavior and support for "atypical" ideas.

The most unique aspect of computer-mediated communication is that the people involved cannot see or hear each other. While this fact is obvious, it is still easy to underestimate its importance. When people communicate face-to-face they convey much, if not most, of their message through non-verbal behaviors (Hiltz, Johnson, and Turoff, 1987; Kiesler, Siegel, and McGuire, 1984; Krauss, Apple, Morencz, Wenzel, and Winton, 1981; Siegel, Dubrovsky, Kiesler, and McGuire, 1986). Smiles, frowns, shrugs, hand gestures, and eye contact are but a few of the ways in which we communicate with our bodies. But when computers are involved, all of this is lost. And the need for it is real enough that computer users have tried inventing a written "body language" to replace the physical one.[1] The loss of visual cues is also exacerbated by the loss of auditory ones. In fact, Meherabian estimates that 93% of message content is conveyed by tone of voice and facial expression (1971). Consider the sentence that reads "That's just great." We can easily imagine how the speaker would sound or look if he or she was happy, angry, or sarcastic. But in print, the mood of the speaker is less clear and consequently the meaning of the sentence is also uncertain.

The lack of visual and auditory information has several implications for computer-mediated communication as it relates to political communication. First, the lack of body language weakens the social cues that govern interpersonal behavior (Siegel, Dubrovsky, Kiesler, and McGuire, 1986). People communicating via computers are usually anonymous and this further weakens traditional social norms of behavior (Connolly, Jessup, and Valacich, 1990; Kiesler, Siegel, and McGuire, 1984). Combined, the lack of visual and auditory cues and the protection of anonymity increase the likelihood of uninhibited, antisocial behaviors. Such behaviors are common enough in computer-mediated messaging that they have been given a label—flaming. Flames are, put simply, insulting personal attacks. The natural propensity of computer users to flame each other is probably exacerbated by the fact that political discussion is inherently confrontational as people discuss policies from vastly divergent points of view. Flaming obviously poses a potential obstacle to the thoughtful debate that is at the heart of democratic politics. Consequently, one task undertaken in the chapters ahead is to document the extent to which flaming actually occurs in computer-mediated political communication.

A second implication of computer-mediated communication is support for ideas that are outside of the mainstream. The mainstream is a difficult term to define, but it can be understood as ideas that fall within a range accepted by the bulk of a group or, in this case, society. Obviously, there is no clear-cut boundary within which an idea is mainstream and outside which it is not. The point here is not to label ideas but to note the distinctiveness of them. Past research has found that computer-mediated communications increase the likelihood of a person expressing unpopular ideas. This happens for several reasons. First, the lack of visual, auditory, and status cues makes it more difficult for the dominant point of view to exclude those who disagree (Edinger and Patterson, 1983). Moreover, those expressing ideas contrary to the dominant point of view feel more free, thanks to their anonymity (Connolly, Jessup, and Valacich, 1990). More generally, computer-mediated communications focus participants on the message and not on the person, thereby weakening the social norms that typically exclude those outside the mainstream (Diener, 1980; Forsyth, 1983). In short, as Herbst points out, people from outside the mainstream will be drawn to computer-mediated communication as a way of finding or creating a more open and congenial space (Herbst, 1994). In chapter 6, we will see that leftist and rightist fringe groups and messages are attracted to the World Wide Web at a very high rate, and that their use of this new communications medium is very impressive.

If computer-mediated communication is so bad, is there anything good about it? Many of the characteristics that pose potential problems also offer potential boons. By encouraging those outside the mainstream to participate, computer-mediated communication also encourages creativity. The result can be an increase in innovative ideas and a more successful group (Gallupe, Bastianutti, and Cooper, 1991). Also, anonymity can remove the status cues that cause groups to give preference to the ideas of high-status members (the boss) while ignoring the ideas of low-status members (the workers) (Kiesler, Siegel, and McGuire, 1984). It also removes racial and gender cues that might affect how people react to the ideas of others. In short, computer-mediated groups can be effective for many of the same reasons they can be ineffective. We seek to understand how these factors balance out on the Internet.

Summary and Conclusions: A Cautionary Note

This book is about politics on the Internet. In our zeal to produce an empirical study of this important social phenomenon, we must keep several caveats in mind. First, the Internet is a moving target, changing in content daily. Some of the Web pages we analyze here may very well be gone by the time you read this. Certainly, they will have changed in their details if not overall content. Likewise, the thousands of Usenet newsgroup messages that form the data for chapters 3 and 4 rotated off the Internet long ago. Still, we fully expect that our findings here are valid and reliable in explaining the Internet as a site for political communication and activity. After all, our aim is not to merely describe "a day in the life of the Internet."

Second, there will most certainly be millions of new Internet users by the time you read this book. In fact, in the time it has taken to read this first chapter, hundreds of new users will probably have logged on for the first time. As the Internet has grown in size since 1969, its underlying character has changed. Finally, we are definitely not suggesting that the Internet is *all* about politics. As will be clear in chapters 3 and 4, around 12% of all Usenet newsgroup messages are political, leaving a whopping 88% that are not. Further, the larger Internet itself, especially the World Wide Web, is as diverse in its content as any library in the world. Table 1.2 presents data from a search for nine keywords on the Internet in mid-1997. Here we merely went to five of the major search engines and typed in each of these nine keywords: computers, sex, movies, television, politics, religion, recipes, investing, and NASCAR. These five search engines returned a combined 18,214,754 Web page and Usenet newsgroup references. Of these, a full 38.22% were referenced by the word "computers," with a very high 23.32% referenced by the word "sex." Out of these nine keyword searches on five search engines, about 6.56% contained the word "politics." While this may be a relatively low percentage compared to the others, that is *still* over 1 million Web pages and Usenet newsgroups containing the word "politics."

TABLE 1.2
The Frequency of Nine Search Terms in Five Internet Search Engines

	Infoseek	Excite	Yahoo	Altavista	Dejanews	Total	Percentage
Computers	4,673,447	637,624	4,196	1,554,493	92,169	6,961,929	38.22%
Sex	441,175	370,549	1,830	2,704,058	729,311	4,246,923	23.32%
Movies	650,142	323,531	2,785	788,307	186,122	1,950,887	10.71%
Television	448,866	396,562	3,107	824,981	35,334	1,708,850	9.38%
Politics	327,260	282,479	1,549	553,193	29,755	1,194,236	6.56%
Religion	293,654	263,950	919	538,024	50,064	1,146,611	6.29%
Recipes	176,023	102,097	1,401	323,763	9,060	612,344	3.36%
Investing	80,104	72,726	200	135,892	8,334	297,256	1.63%
NASCAR	20,994	22,950	381	42,115	9,278	95,718	0.53%
Total	7,111,665	2,472,468	16,368	7,464,826	1,149,427	18,214,754	100.00%

Source: Five Internet search engine searches by the authors using the above keywords, July 1, 1997

In the end, this book may be about only 6.5% of the Internet, but that is a *very* large piece of virtual real estate.

Note

1. Sometimes called emoticons, CMC users have a variety of nonverbal cues they can use. For example, :(for sad, :) for happy, ;) for wink, and so forth.

Internet Activists

We have two primary goals for this chapter, each related to Hypothesis 1 as described in the Introduction. Our first task in studying cyberpolitics is understanding our "cybercitizens," so we begin our study of Internet activism by looking at the demographics of Internet users. Demographics are simply the characteristics of a particular population of people such as students at a college, people living in a state, or Internet users. The characteristics we are interested in include age, income, education, race, and gender. In addition, we want to know specifically political characteristics like partisanship, ideology, political information gathering, and voting behavior. Put simply, we wish to comprehend as much as we can about *who* is using the Internet politically and how they differ from those who are not using the Internet or are not using it for political purposes. If Internet users are politically different from non-users then we would expect cyberpolitics to differ from more traditional forms of political expression.

Our second task is to document what Internet activists do while on-line. There are four major methods of Internet communication: e-mail, Web pages, the Usenet and similar bulletin boards, and chat rooms. Of these, all but e-mail are in some way public and open to study. Each of the following four chapters focuses on one of these communication tools. For now, the second part of this chapter gives a quick overview of who uses each of these tools so that later on we might better understand how they use them.

Addressing these two major topics requires demographic and political data describing both Internet users and the general public. Such data are available from the Pew Research Center for the People and the Press (1995 and 1996). Researchers there have conducted several nationwide telephone surveys focusing specifically on the Internet and politics. In 1995, they surveyed both the general public and Internet users to facilitate comparisons of these two groups. In 1996, they conducted a follow-up study of Internet users and their on-line political activities. We use the 1995 survey in the first part of the chapter and the 1996 survey in the second part.

Internet Activists and the Public

Our first goal is to describe the demographics of Internet users and compare them to the general public. There are three primary reasons for wanting to know the demographics of Internet users. First, Internet users are a subset, or fraction, of the general public. This means they will probably not mirror the characteristics of the overall population. If that is the case, we expect Internet users and the general public to hold different attitudes and to behave differently. This would then result in political activism on the Internet being different from more traditional forms of activism. Recall from our introduction that Hypothesis 1 predicts Internet activists will be more conservative than the general public. Not only that, but the literatures reviewed earlier also suggest that whatever their ideology, Internet users will be more extreme. Second, by comparing Internet users to the general public, we may learn whether the Internet changes the way people access and use information or is just an extension of old behaviors. Third, understanding the political behaviors of Internet users will enable us to make predictions about the potential political influence of the Internet in the near future.

Before proceeding, however, we must be more specific about what we mean by Internet users. Just as some people who read the newspaper ignore the front page in favor of "more interesting" topics, some Internet users will ignore its political aspects. Since our concern is strictly political, we need to distinguish between users that are politically active on-line and those that are not. Accordingly, we divide our study into three groups of people: the general public, non-political Internet users, and "Internet activists" who engage in some political activity using the Internet.[1] This makes it possible to distinguish between those engaged in cyberpolitics and those who use the Internet for other purposes.

Internet activism is determined by two questions contained in the 1995 Pew Center survey. Each respondent was asked whether they "chat" about politics or "post" political messages. Chatting on the Internet is done by typing messages to others in real time. People enter a "room," usually with a designated topic such as politics, dating, or computers, where they can "talk" with the other participants by writing messages to each other. "Posting," by contrast, means to write out a message and leave it for others to read and perhaps respond. This creates a slow but extended dialogue. Both posting and chatting represent ways in which Internet users can engage in a form of political dialogue unique to the Internet and each is explored in later chapters—the Usenet in chapters 3 and 4 and America Online chat rooms in chapter 5. In the Pew survey, 15% of Internet users had posted a message, 10% had chatted about politics, 7% had done both, and 18% had engaged in at least one activity. For our purposes, anyone that either posts or chats about politics is deemed an Internet activist.

Table 2.1 presents the first of our comparisons between the general public, Internet users, and Internet activists. For each group, we present average (mean) age and income levels, as well as breakdowns by ethnicity, gender, and educational attainment. Looking first at age, we can see that Internet

TABLE 2.1
Demographic Characteristics of Internet Users and the Public

	General Public	Internet Users (non-political)	Internet Activists
Average Age	42.7	36.6	32.8
Gender			
Male	49.0%	59.4%	71.8%
Female	51.0%	40.6%	28.2%
Race			
White	81.8%	82.2%	77.1%
Non-White	19.2%	17.8%	22.9%
Education			
High School or Less	38.9%	17.2%	10.5%
Some College	28.4%	30.0%	33.3%
College Graduate	32.7%	52.9%	56.1%
Income Level (on a 1-8 scale)	4.35	5.21	5.12

Note: Cell frequencies are based on 1995 Pew Center survey, using the unweighted sample, and exclude the over-sample of Internet users.

users and activists are considerably younger than the general public, with Internet activists averaging a very young 32.8 years. This is probably lower in reality, since the Pew Center surveyed only people aged 18 years and older, and many Internet users are teenagers. In terms of gender, we see that the Internet is still predominantly male and that Internet activism is overwhelmingly male. Non-political Internet users are divided about 60/40 between males and females, while Internet activists are 72% male. So, there currently *is* a gender gap in cyberpolitics.

The percentage breakdowns on race, however, are quite surprising, given stereotypes about Internet users. General Internet users and the public at large have very similar percentages of white and non-white users. Quite unexpectedly, however, Internet activists actually contain a *higher* percentage of non-white users than the other three groups, though the difference is small. In the end, there is no great "ethnic gap" in Internet activism.

Moving to educational attainment, Internet users and activists have a much higher level of education than the general public with 53% and 56%, respectively, having college degrees. Again, given the young average age of these two sets of Internet users, many of them are probably still enrolled in college, so these data may actually understate their level of education in the near future. Finally, Internet users and activists have considerably higher levels of family income than the public at large.

There are, then, real demographic differences between these three groups of people. Internet users and activists are quite distinguishable from the general public. They are younger (perhaps much younger), they are more likely to be male, slightly less likely to be white, much better educated, and have considerably higher incomes.

Such demographic differences present us with a dilemma. Let's assume, just for a moment, that we find massive political differences between Internet activists and the general public. The problem is, are the *political* differences caused by the *demographic* differences? We saw in Table 2.1 that these two groups are in fact different demographically. So if they are also different politically we will not know whether it is *because* of their demographic differences or *in spite of* their demographic distinctions.

We can expect, on the basis of demographics alone, that Internet users will differ from the general public. For example, we hypothesize that Internet activists will be more conservative, more politically active, and more politically knowledgeable. But in most cases, we know this is true for people who are better educated or have higher incomes, and so demographics alone could account for the differences between Internet activists and the general public. So the question remains as to whether they are different from the general public because of, or in spite of, their demographic characteristics. This requires that we control for, or take into account, the demographic differences when looking for the political ones.

Of course, based on the findings of past surveys and research in other new media such as talk radio (Owen, 1996), we begin with some expectations as to how Internet activists and the general public will differ, regardless of demographics. Building on our earlier outline and on what we know from past experience in talk radio, we can elaborate on Hypothesis 1. Earlier, we hypothesized that the Internet would be dominated by conservatives. Now we further hypothesize that Internet activists will have:

Hypothesis 2.1: increased identification with the Republican party
Hypothesis 2.2: increased strength of support for the Republican party
Hypothesis 2.3: higher levels of conservative policy preferences
Hypothesis 2.4: higher levels of information seeking and knowledge
Hypothesis 2.5: increased rates of political participation

The process of testing these hypotheses deserves some elaboration. As we know from above, we have to "control for," or take into account, the demographic distinctiveness of Internet users and activists. This requires a multivariate (meaning many variables) analysis. We use two methods: ordinary least squares (OLS) and logistic regression. OLS is used when the dependent variable (the question that we are studying) has more than two possible values, such as ideology, which has five values—very liberal, liberal, independent, conservative, and very conservative. Logistic regression is used when the dependent variable has only two values, such as voted and did not vote. For all analyses, we include the demographic variables listed above (age, gender, race, education, income, and sometimes partisanship) as control variables. The controls allow us to consider their effect on the dependent variable so that we can isolate the effect of Internet use. In other words, by controlling age, gender, and so forth, we can determine whether Internet activists are different from the general public, while simultaneously accounting for the effect of their demographic differences.

Regardless of the method used (OLS or logistic regression), the analysis is done in the same manner. First, the Internet activism variable and all of the demographic variables are *regressed* (tested) on the various dependent variables. Second, we use the results to compute a percentage change in the dependent variable for the average (median) person in the sample.[2] This represents how much the dependent variable changes between the comparison group and Internet activists. The dependent variables cover party identification, information seeking and knowledge of current events, policy preferences, and voting behavior. In each analysis we seek to determine if using the Internet politically is significantly related to the dependent variable. If Internet activism does have a significant effect it shows that activists differ from the comparison group.

The results of our multivariate analyses are presented in two tables. Each of the tables is divided into two sections. The first column compares Internet activists with the general public. The second compares Internet activists with other Internet users. We expect other Internet users will be more similar to Internet activists than is the general public. The interpretation of each table is based on the research variable—Internet activism is coded as 0, .5, or 1 with a .5 representing someone that either posts or chats and 1 representing someone that does both. The tables present the predicted percentage increase in the dependent variable for the average (median) person if he or she is a complete Internet activist (score of 1) versus a non-activist. Put more simply, the tables show how much effect being an Internet activist has on any given dependent variable for the typical person.

The analyses of party identification and ideology (hypotheses 2.1–2.3) are presented in Table 2.2. The first column compares Internet activists with the general public. Since we hypothesize activism to be related to conservatism and strong party attachments, we coded the variables so that a positive sign represents increased conservatism or party attachment. Looking at line 1, we see that, on average, Internet activists are about 12% *less* Republican than the general public. In terms of the strength of that attachment, line 2 shows that activists are not significantly different. So, hypotheses 2.1 is re-

TABLE 2.2

Relationship between Internet Activism, Partisanship, and Ideology

Dependent Variables	Internet Activists Compared to the General Public	Internet Activists Compared to Internet Users
1. Party identification (+ = more Republican)	-11.6%*** (N = 5,645)	n.s. (N = 1,562)
2. Strength of party identification (+ = stronger partisan)	n.s. (N = 5,645)	n.s. (N = 1,562)
3. Regulate businesses? (+ = No regulation)	n.s. (N = 5,189)	n.s. (N = 1,510)
4. Government help needy? (+ = should do less)	n.s. (N = 5,292)	n.s. (N = 1,471)
5. Ban some books? (+ = yes)	-17.7%*** (N = 5,410)	n.s. (N = 1,524)
6. Homosexuality acceptable? (+ = no)	-13.2%*** (N = 5,260)	n.s. (N = 1,480)
7. Regulate pornography on the Internet? (+ = yes)	-34.8%*** (N = 5,299)	-23.6%*** (N = 1,485)
8. Can understand Oklahoma City bombing (+ = yes)	+6.3%* (N = 5,551)	+10.7%* (N = 1,547)

Notes: Cell entries represent the predicted percentage change in dependent variable based on being or not being an Internet activist as compared to the reference group. Entries represent effect of Internet Activism in the presence of the control variables. Controls are not shown, but include age, education, income, race, and gender. For policy questions, party identification is also included as a control. See endnote 2 for details on methodology.

Source: All entries are based on the weighted 1995 Pew Center study.

Legend: n.s. = non-significant; *** $p < .001$, * $p < .05$

jected and in fact contradicted, and hypothesis 2.2 is also rejected, with no differences being observed in strength of partisan attachment. In other words, Internet activists are not more partisan but they are more Democratic than the general public.

The remainder of Table 2.2 focuses on ideological or policy-oriented questions. To measure ideology, we present several policy questions regarding the role of government. Reading down the first column of data, we get a mixed picture. Internet activists are no different from the general public on questions like regulating businesses and doing more to help the needy. However, Internet activists are consistently more liberal than the general public (signs are negative) on issues like banning books, accepting homosexuality as a lifestyle, and opposing the regulation of pornography on the Internet. By contrast, Internet activists are 6% more likely to say that they can empathize with the frustrations leading to the Oklahoma City bombing.

The responses to this last question pose two difficulties. The first problem is that we are not entirely certain of the political interpretation of the question. The respondents were asked whether they felt "there is no excuse for the bombing, period," or whether they felt "there is no excuse for the bombing but one can understand the frustrations and anger that may have led people to carry it out." Two aspects of this lead us to interpret the question as measuring anti-government sentiment. First, the media generally presented the bombing as the act of anti-government individuals and so we expect the public responded to the question accordingly. Second, only about one of every eight people in the general public "understood" the feelings behind the bombing. So even if we ignore the anti-government aspects, this suggests that those who reported an understanding of the Oklahoma City bombing are somewhat extreme in their views. Therefore, this question appears to measure relatively extreme and probably anti-government feelings. This supports our discussions in the Introduction and chapter 1 that the Internet is likely to attract people whose ideas are perceived as being unrepresented in mainstream society.

This leads us to the second confusing aspect. If our interpretation is accurate, the higher level of understanding among Internet activists appears to contradict their greater identification with the Democratic party. After all, Democrats tend to be more positively disposed toward the government than are Republicans (though there will be some exceptions). Unfortunately, the Pew data do not contain a measure of trust in government and so for now our conclusions regarding this question must remain tentative. That said, our interpretation of the Oklahoma City bombing question leads us to two conclusions. First, that although Internet activists are more Democratic, they are also somewhat more understanding of anti-government sentiment. Second, that Internet activists are more understanding of views held outside the mainstream.

In short, even though the picture is far from clear, we must reject Hypothesis 2.3. On two issues, activists and the general public match up; on three issues, activists tend to be more liberal; and for one issue they differ in what is probably best seen as a conservative direction. What can we make of such differences? First, note that the biggest ideological distinctions are seen in the "social" issues of homosexuality, book banning, and pornography. So activists tend to be against government activity for personal and private issues. At the same time, they tend to be somewhat more understanding of the Oklahoma City bombing, an act that appears to have been motivated by mistrust of the government. Internet activists appear to be anti-government, at least in terms of social issues.

However, we do not want to place too much emphasis on the differences between the Internet activists and the public. After all, there is also a great deal of similarity between these groups on such measures as strength of party identification, government regulation of business, and help for the needy. As we shall see later on in our content analyses, this mix of similarities and differences creates a paradox for us to explain.

Next we compare Internet activists with other Internet users. Since users and activists are drawn from the same demographic pool—people who use the Internet—we would expect these groups to be similar to each other. Column 2 in Table 2.2 shows that, by and large, they are. In terms of partisanship, party attachment, and most ideological questions, users and activists are roughly the same. Only for regulating pornography on the Internet and the Oklahoma City bombing do we find significant differences. This is most striking for the bombing question since the difference between activists and users is actually greater than that of activists and the general public—understanding of the bombing goes up to 11%. But with these two exceptions, activists and other users are quite similar.

In summary, Internet activists are more likely to identify themselves as Democrats and are also more likely to oppose government regulations of personal activities. This could be seen as consistent with the philosophy of the Democratic party except that we are uncertain as to how to interpret the greater understanding of the feelings behind the Oklahoma City bombing. These results are somewhat muted, but not entirely eliminated, when we examine just Internet users. In short, we find no support for Hypotheses 2.1, 2.2, and 2.3. Internet activists do differ from the general public, at least in terms of issues like pornography on the Net and the Oklahoma City bombing. However, they are also quite similar on many issues. If these differences are reflected in the messages the activists post, we expect our content analyses of political discussion on the Internet to show a slight anti-government bias, especially with regard to social issues.

Next we test Hypotheses 2.4 and 2.5 which argue that Internet activists will seek more political information and be more politically knowledgeable. The relevant analyses are presented in lines 1–4 of Table 2.3. Again, reading each column from top to bottom we see that activists are about 12% more likely than the general public to read newspapers for news information and about 9% more likely to listen to news or talk radio programs. They are no more likely to watch television news. One reason for this is that most people watch TV news and there is very little variance for the question. A second possible reason is that television is less informative and thus holds no great attraction for the information junkie. Neuman, Just, and Crigler (1992) demonstrate that different news formats convey different amounts of information, with newspapers being more informative than television, which ranked last in information content. So the fact that Internet activists are more likely to seek out newspapers and radio but are no more likely to watch television suggests an interest in information-gathering. That interest pays off in terms of knowledge. Internet activists score about 10% higher (a whole letter grade!) in a series of current events questions when compared to the typical

TABLE 2.3
Relationship between Internet Activism, Information Seeking, and Participation

Dependent Variables	Internet Activists Compared to the General Public	Internet Activists Compared to Internet Users
1. Read newspaper for news? (+ = yes)	+11.9%*** (N = 5,727)	+8.8%* (N = 1,579)
2. Get news from television? (+ = yes)	n.s. (N = 5,722)	n.s. (N = 1,576)
3. Listen to news/talk radio programs? (+ = yes)	+9.4%* (N = 5,726)	n.s. (N = 1,578)
4. Current events knowledge (+ = more knowledgeable)	+10.5%*** (N = 5,735)	+8.6%*** (N = 1,578)
5. Voted in 1992? (+ = yes)	+9.1%** (N = 5,645)	+5.8%* (N = 1,562)
6. Voted in 1994? (+ = yes)	+19.8%*** (N = 5,467)	+14.4% (N = 1,544)
7. Major party vote in 1992 (+ = Republican)	n.s. (N = 3,174)	n.s. (N = 924)
8. Major party vote in 1994 (+ = Republican)	n.s. (N = 2,314)	n.s. (N = 766)
9. Voted for Perot or major party (+ = Perot)	-10.4%*** (N = 3,816)	-7.1%** (N = 1,139)

Notes: Cell entries represent the predicted percentage change in dependent variable based on being or not being an Internet activist as compared to the reference group. Entries represent effect of Internet activism in the presence of the control variables. Controls are not shown but include age (and age squared), education, income, race, gender, and either party identification or strength of attachment. See endnote 2 for details on methodology.

Source: All entries are based on the weighted 1995 Pew Center study.

Legend: n.s. = non-significant; *** $p < .001$, ** $p < .01$, * $p < .05$

person. So Hypothesis 2.4 is essentially confirmed—Internet activists are more involved in information-gathering and more knowledgeable about current political events. Consequently, we expect the Internet messages we study later on to reflect the relatively well-informed nature of the participants.

If Internet activists are more knowledgeable, are they also more politically active? Hypothesis 2.5 suggests that they should be and the corresponding analyses are presented in lines 5 and 6 of Table 2.3. When compared to the general public, Internet activists were about 9% more likely to have voted in 1992 and almost 20% more likely to have voted in 1994. The larger increase associated with the midterm election of 1994 is expected. Midterms are generally less interesting and are not covered in as great detail by the press. This means that interest and political involvement play a larger role in determining who votes and who doesn't. As a result, Internet activists become even more distinct from the general public during the midterms. These two sections confirm Hypothesis 2.5—Internet activists are more politically active than the general public.

If Internet activists are more likely to vote, are they also more likely to vote for a particular party? This takes us back to hypotheses 2.1 and 2.2, which generally posit that activists are more likely to support Republicans. We tested this in line 7 of Table 2.3 but found no differences between activists and the general public in their support of the two major parties. Line 8 of the table echoes this finding, showing that in the 1994 midterms, activists were no more likely than the general public to support Republicans or Democrats.

But there is another possibility we should explore. We have seen that CMC can encourage atypical or non-mainstream participants. If this is true, perhaps activists are more likely to support candidates from outside the two major parties. Are activists more likely to vote for third (or fourth) parties than is the general public? To answer that, we placed all Democratic and Republican voters into one category and all Perot and other third-party voters into the another. Since the other third-party voters amounted to about 1% of the sample while Perot voters equaled 18%, this latter group essentially became a Perot vote category. As we can see from line 9, activists were actually about 10% less likely to vote for Perot. So rather than being disenchanted with the two dominant parties, activists actually appear to be supportive of them.

In short, Internet activists are split between the Democrats and Republicans at a rate similar to their counterparts in the general public. They are, however, more likely to stick with the major parties when faced with a third-party candidate. Electorally speaking, Internet activists are neither more Republican nor more independent than the general public. Translated into message content, we would expect that Internet political messages will be generally supportive of the major parties.

Now we turn to our comparisons of Internet activists with other Internet users. Again, since users and activists are drawn from a common group, we expect them to share greater similarities. To a certain extent that is true. Table 2.3 shows that the differences between activists and users is not as large as those between activists and the general populace. But differences do exist. Activists are about 9% more likely to read the newspaper and they score about 9% better on current events questions, although they are not more likely to listen to talk or news radio. Activists were nearly 6% more likely than other users to vote in 1992 and over 14% more likely to do so in 1994. And, as with the general public, activists are less likely than other Internet users to have voted for Perot. In short, Internet activists are more politically active than even other Internet users.

So what have we learned in this section? Controlling for demographic differences such as age, education, income, race, and gender we found that, contrary to expectations, Internet activists tend to be more Democratic than the general public but that they are not more strongly attached to their party. In terms of political attitudes, Internet activists are generally more anti-government than the general public, at least on social issues. They are also more understanding of the sentiment behind the Oklahoma City bombing. However, they hold similar views on such issues as regulating businesses and aiding the poor. The differences are larger when information seeking and political participation are examined. Internet activists are more knowledgeable and more politically active than the general public but they are less supportive of Ross Perot. Finally, most of these findings hold true when we compare Internet activists to other Internet users. In short, Internet activists are generally more active and possibly more anti-government than the rest of society. We expect these differences to be reflected in the messages the Internet activists post and the web pages they create. This issue is addressed directly in the following chapters. But first, we examine what Internet activists do on-line.

Destinations in Cyberspace: Where the Cybercitizen Hangs Out

The second part of this chapter is devoted to exploring the on-line activities of Internet activists and others. Obviously, there are significant limits as to what we can know about where people go on-line and what they do there. But the Pew Center's 1996 election survey did ask several questions relating to political and campaign information seeking. First, they asked people whether they actually looked for political news or campaign news on-line. Then, they asked what kinds of sites they went to for this information. Naturally, there are no data for the non-Internetted general public since we are looking only at people who potentially go on-line for news. But we do divide the 1996 sample into Internet users versus Internet activists so that we can compare their information-seeking behaviors. Again, activism is defined as posting a political message (political e-mail) or chatting about politics on-line. Our expectation is that *Internet activists will engage in more information seeking and utilize a wider variety of sources.*

Table 2.4 presents a breakdown of information-seeking activity and the resources used. In the first column we present the relevant percentage for Internet users, while the second column provides the same information for Internet activists. We can see immediately that Internet activists seek more political information on-line. Only about one-third of users overall went on-line to get politics information, while nearly three-quarters of activists did so. Since we are comparing the activists to other Internet users, this is not a function of having Internet access but one of choice.

TABLE 2.4
Internet Information Seeking among Internet Users and Activists

	Internet Users	Internet Activists
1. Get *political* news on-line?	35.0%	73.9%***
2. Sources of *political* news:		
A. ABC, NBC, or CBS sites	31.4%	46.7%***
B. CNN, C-Span, or MSNBC sites	44.7%	62.5%***
C. National newspaper sites	54.8%	66.9%**
D. Specialized sites (All Politics, Politics Now, etc.)	14.1%	31.5%***
E. Candidate Web sites	24.9%	42.3%***
F. Government Web sites (White House, Thomas, etc.)	27.8%	49.2%***
1. Get *campaign* news on-line?	13.5%	50%***
2. Sources of *campaign* news:		
A. ABC, NBC, or CBS sites	20.4%	29.0%*
B. CNN, C-Span, or MSNBC sites	54.7%	60.0%
C. National newspaper sites	39.4%	50.8%*
D. Specialized sites (All Politics, Politics Now, etc.)	15.9%	36.9%***
E. Candidate Web sites	32.7%	50.8%***
F. Government Web sites (White House, Thomas, etc..)	17.8%	33.2%***

Note: Source of news is calculated only for those seeking news on-line.
Number of cases = 706 for political news and 460 for campaign news. All
significance tests based on Cramer's V.

Legend: *** p < .001, ** p < .01, * p < .05

What sources did news seekers utilize? The "Big Three" television networks did not fair particularly well as on-line destinations. Only 31% of users and 47% of activists visited the Web sites of ABC, CBS, or NBC. So while activists did make more use of the network's Web sites, the networks were not especially popular with either group. However, the more specialized TV networks were more popular with both groups—45% of on-line news seekers and 63% of activists visited the Web sites of CNN, C-Span, or MSNBC (a recent joint venture between Microsoft and NBC). Again, activists were more likely to visit these sites. The most popular sites, however, were those of national newspapers such as *USA Today*, the *Washington Post*, or the *Wall Street Journal*. Over half of the general users visited one of those sites, while 67% of activists did so. Less popular were the specialized sites such as CNN's *AllPolitics.com*, *PoliticsNow*, and the like. But again, the table shows that activists are more likely than users to visit these sites. The same holds true for candidate Web sites and for those sponsored by the government. These sites were not particularly popular but did receive about as many visits as the major television network sites. But whatever the type of site, activists are more likely than other on-line news seekers to visit.

What about campaign-specific news? The second half of Table 2.4 shows that a much smaller portion of users and activists, even during the campaign season, visited a site to obtain campaign news. Just one in eight users—but one in two activists—tried to get campaign information on-line. More interesting, however, is where they went to find that information. Like the top half of the table, we can see that activists made more use of nearly all resources than did general on-line news seekers. The sole exception are the little three networks—CNN, C-Span, and MSNBC were just as popular with activists as with other news seekers. We can see that this happened because the smaller network sites were a more popular source of campaign news than general political news (55% to 45%) for the on-line news seeker. Further, notice that the big three networks, national newspapers, and government sites are more popular as general political news sites than as campaign news sites—in each case, the percentage using that resource drops in the second half of the table. At the same time, the specialized news sites and the candidate Web sites were more popular for campaign news than general news. This makes intuitive sense but it is an important point. One of the potential advantages of the Internet as an information resource is its specialization. People have the potential to seek just the type of information they want. Here we have some evidence suggesting that they are strategic news seekers—both activists and non-activists increased their use of campaign-related sites for campaign-related information. This is an important point and we will return to it shortly. In summary, Table 2.4 demonstrates two things. First, on-line activists are disproportionately likely to seek on-line news information and they use a broader range of resources. Second, both groups show a small tendency to seek out sites that are specially suited to their informational needs.

Are on-line news seekers drawn on-line because of its specialized nature? Further, are activists more, or less, interested in this advantage of on-line news? In general, why do news seeker turn to the Internet and how do activists differ in this regard? Table 2.5 examines these and other questions. We hypothesize that *activists engage in on-line news seeking because it provides them with more detail and specialization.*

We first look at the basic motivation behind following the news. We

TABLE 2.5
Reasons for Seeking News On-line

	Internet Users	Internet Activists
1. Follow news because:		
duty to be informed	64.0%	53.2%*
enjoy following politics	36.0%	46.8%
2. Have gone on-line to follow-up story from TV or paper	58.0%	77.3%***
3. Reason for going on-line for news:		
A. To get information not available elsewhere	10.0%	23.7%***
B. On-line is more convenient	20.1%	31.8%***
C. Get more information on-line	21.3%	47.3%***
D. On-line news matches my values/interests	7.5%	19.9%***
4. Can you believe what you find on-line?	74.1%	69.0%
5. On-line information has influenced vote choice?	25.0%	38.6%**

Note: Cell entries are based on just those seeking political news on-line. All significance tests based on Cramer's V.
Legend: *** p < .001, ** p < .01, * p < .05

know from studies of political participation that many people feel a sense of civic obligation or duty (Rosenstone and Hansen, 1993). This means that they believe one of the tasks of a "good citizen" is to be well informed about and active in the electoral process. People who feel this way are obviously active but for a very different reason than someone who simply enjoys keeping up with politics. Focusing on question 1, we see that activists do indeed enjoy keeping up with current events more than typical users. Interestingly, though, a majority of both activists and general users cite duty as the primary reason for their news seeking. Another potential reason for going on-line is to follow up on a story first seen elsewhere. In this situation we envision a person being interested in a story but not getting enough detail or information so they turn to the Internet for help. In question 2, we see that activists are considerably more likely to use the Internet to follow up on a mainstream press story (77% vs. 58%). Given the popularity of newspaper sites in Table 2.4, we would suspect newspapers most often spark this kind of interest.

Now we turn to a more focused look at the motivations for Internet news seeking. Question 3 asks specifically why people choose Internet-based news. Looking at the percentages for the responses, we see that no single reason stands out. In fact, none of the reasons are cited by even a majority of users and activists. This suggests that there are other significant reasons people choose Internet news. Such a result is to be expected. But for now, we wish to focus on whether the motivations of activists and general news seekers differ. In fact, they do. Activists are more likely to cite all of the reasons given—uniqueness, convenience, depth, and shared values. The most common reason cited is depth of coverage. As we suggested above, on-line sources provide more information.

The least common response is that on-line news matches the respondent's political views or interests. This is important for two reasons. First, it suggests that perceptions of media bias do not motivate most activists though it may still motivate a significant and vocal minority (see Chapter 3). Second, given the potential for specialization of news seeking on the Internet, it suggests that Internet activists look for news topics that match their interest but do not seek ideologically unique information. In other words, activists are not particularly worried about the slant or bias of information, they simply want more of it or they want it on a particular topic such as the campaign. Together, the first three questions suggest that Internet activists enjoy political news seeking more than most others, and that they most often go on-line to get more detailed and comprehensive information.

Of course, seeing is not always believing. And besides, what effect does this information have on the readers? As we discuss in chapter 6, anyone can put up a Web page (even us—*www.fiu.edu/~khill* and *www.monmouth.edu/~jhughes*). But just because it is there does not mean anyone believes it. Or do they? Question 4 in Table 2.5 asks whether on-line activists and other news seekers believe what they read on-line. A majority of both groups do believe what they read, with no significant margin separating activists from general users. This lack of skepticism is not totally unwarranted considering that the most popular on-line destinations are the sites of "reputable" publications like the *Washington Post* and *Wall Street Journal* (see Table 2.4). However, as chapter 6 shows, much of what is available on-line is not merely biased, but quite questionable in nature. Despite this fact, for the most part seeing *is* believing when on-line.

What effect does this information have? The final question shows that 25% of on-line news seekers claimed to have been influenced in their choice of candidate as a result of what they learned on-line. That number jumps to almost 39% for Internet activists. Activists appear to be more open to new information and more open-minded about changing their positions. We would like to know if this represents a small or large shift in attitudes. Unfortunately, that is impossible to measure with the current data. However, we can make some educated guesses. We surmise this represents small, rather than large, changes. Recall from Table 2.3 that Internet activists are no more likely than the general public to support either the Democrats or the Republicans (lines 7 and 8). In fact, Internet activists were shown to be more supportive than the public when voting for the two major parties (line 9). From this we conclude that Internet-based political learning does not draw people away from the established parties and so probably does not draw them away from their established beliefs. Rather, what we see is a group of well-educated, interested, but undecided voters who seek addition information via the Internet.

What kind of effect on the election could this have? The Pew Center estimates that 10% of all voters in 1996 went on-line for news about the election. If 25% of them changed their mind as a result, we have a net shift of 2.5% in the electorate. This does not sound like much, but a 2.5% shift away from one candidate and to another could be a sizable swing. While the shift would never be all for one party or candidate, this does suggest that the Internet can be a persuasive medium. In summary, Table 2.5 shows that activists are likely to enjoy following politics, seek more detailed information, and are somewhat more open to persuasion.

Summary and Conclusions

We begin our summary with the same idea that prompted our study of Internet activists. We know that people who use the Internet are demographically distinct from those who do not. Accordingly, we would expect people who use the Internet for political purposes to be politically different from those who do not engage in cyberpolitics. But the question is, how are they different and are these differences caused by their demographics or by something else? We hypothesized that Internet activists would be more conservative and Republican, more politically active, and more knowledgeable.

We find that, even taking demographics into account, Internet activists are certainly more Democratic and, within the limits of our data, only somewhat more anti-government. In our comparison of party identification, Internet activists are clearly more Democratic than the general public. Attitudinally speaking, Internet activists are different from the general public, but the differences are smaller than we expected and, in some cases, in the opposite direction. This finding is especially surprising given the results we present in the following chapters, where we regularly find right-wing biases. Of course, we do find some anti-government sentiment. Internet activists are more likely to oppose government censorship or regulation of pornography. They are also more accepting of homosexuality and more understanding of the Oklahoma City bombing. We interpret this as partial evidence of an anti-government philosophy—Internet activists appear to want to keep the government out of our private lives as much as possible. David Shenk's (1997) law of the Internet number 13 (see Introduction) needs some revision—if anything, "Cyberspace is anti-government," and it might not even be that.

In other areas we find larger differences. Internet activists are more informed and more politically active. They keep up with and know more about current events. They vote more regularly than does the general public, especially in lower profile elections such as those occurring during midterms. But their vote choices are not that much different except that they favor the two established parties. Activists are less likely to have voted for Perot but are no more or less likely to have voted Republican compared to Democratic. The fact that Internet activists are fairly typical in their vote choice not only contradicts our expectations, but seems at odds with the results we present in the following chapters. As a result, one of the main goals in our conclusion will be to explore this seeming contradiction.

Where do Internet activists go for their information and what do they learn? We find that activists are more likely than other news seekers to use every source of political and campaign information. They, like most others interested in current events, favor the Web sites of the specialized news providers such as newspapers or the cable networks of CNN, C-Span, and MSNBC. Truly specialized sites like *AllPolitics.com* and *PoliticsNow* fared better with the activists than with general information junkies, but still poorly overall. Use of the Internet is often stimulated by newsstories on TV or in newspapers, prompting activists to look for more detailed information. In fact, aside from the sheer enjoyment of following political events, getting more information is shown to be among the top reasons for using the Internet as a source of information. Finding news that fits one's personal values or interests is more important to activists than general on-line users but is not a major factor overall.

So what does this say about politics in cyberspace? Perhaps the most important finding is that activists differ from the general public even controlling for their demographic differences. That means activists are atypical, even of those that have more education and income. There are two likely explanations for these differences.

First, activists could be changed by their experiences. Their time on the Net could alter their beliefs and worldview. Table 2.5 shows some attitudinal shift in candidate choice, but remember this shift appears to be away from Perot and other third-party candidates and to both the Democrats and Republicans. The data also show that most activists see their vote choices as being unaffected by the Internet. Moreover, the support for mainstream parties and the overwhelming use of traditional sources such as newspapers suggests two conclusions. First, most activists do not seek information radically different from others in their normal environment, they simply seek more. Thus, the attitude changes are likely to be small. Second, the Internet is really used as an extension of older, more common forms of media. It is not so much a different message they are seeking but a different method of delivery.

If Internet activists are not being changed by their on-line experiences, why are they so different? The second, and more likely answer, is self-selection. They enjoy politics, they like learning about current events, they are simply interested. Thus, they flock to a form of media that offers them *more*, not *different*, information. Four facts stand out that support this conclusion. First, the two most popular on-line destinations are outlets of the mainstream media (Table 2.4). Second, almost 80% of Internet activists have used the Internet to follow up on a story first reported in the mainstream press. And where on the Internet do they go to get this information? Primarily back to the mainstream press. Third, Internet activists do not appear to be moving away from the political mainstream in their voting. Rather they are moving toward it. Finally, when asked specifically why they use Internet news sources, the most common response is to get more information and the least common one is to find information tailored to one's own values or interests. So while we certainly want to make note of the Internet's potential to change and inform our attitudes and beliefs, we conclude the primary reason for the uniqueness of Internet activists is self-selection.

Of course, now we need to understand why the explanation matters. If the Internet itself is a force for change, then we might argue that as more people get on the Internet, society itself will be changed. This is the key idea behind both the utopian and dystopian views of the Internet. After all, the higher the percentage of users, the larger the portion of society "changed" by the medium. But that is not our conclusion (though some of that does occur). Rather, the Internet as a whole is largely an extension of the media we are already familiar with. That is, people use the Internet in the same ways and for the same reasons that they use traditional media. Moreover, political use of the Internet is primarily self-selected. People use it politically because they like it and find it useful, not because the Net somehow turns someone into a political junkie. An "off-line" person who today does not care about politics will be someone with a computer and Internet connection who still does not care about politics tomorrow. In other words, the Internet does not change people, it simply allows them to do the same things in a different way. Contrary to the utopian views of the Internet, its expansion is not likely to turn uninterested, uninformed, apathetic citizens into interested, informed, and active cybercitizens. Contrary to the dystopian fears, neither is the Internet likely to fundamentally change society for the worse.

So the following chapters will not focus on how the Internet will reshape the world. Instead, we look at what things people can and are doing using the Internet—forming communities, protesting governments, debating issues—and how they do all of this. Obviously, we do not deny that the Internet will greatly affect business, marketing, information distribution, and so forth. But politically, we need to study less how the Internet affects society and more how citizens use the Internet to achieve goals that have been around for decades if not centuries. At the same time, we will examine the extent to which on-line messages reflect the differences we found in this chapter. Does on-line political communication mirror the major-party-supporting, highly informed, and Democratic nature of those who post the messages?

Notes

1. We should make it clear that many non-political Internet users are political in other ways. They probably vote, have partisan orientations, and so forth. We use *non-political* to denote their lack of political activity *on the Internet*, regardless of other forms of political activity in which they may engage.

2. The percentage change is calculated as follows. First, the OLS or logistic regression equations are computed. Then each of the control variables is set to its respective medians, while Internet activism is set to zero. From this, a predicted value (OLS) or probability (logistic regression) for the dependent variable is computed. Then, leaving all controls at their median, the Internet activism variable is set to one. The predicted value is re-estimated and the difference is presented as a percentage change in the dependent variable.

Building Political Communities in Cyberspace

Introduction to the Usenet

In chapter 1 we pointed out that politics is dependent upon communication. Politics is, at its core, a social activity taking place between two or more people. In order to engage in politics, people must communicate with others. In chapter 2 we looked at the people who engage in particular kinds of Internet-based communication—chatting and posting. In this chapter we begin our study of Internet communication content by focusing on the posting of political messages. Later on, in chapter 5, we examine chatting. In essence, what we are doing, in this chapter and in the others, is studying what cybercitizens *say* rather than who they are. Of course we expect that the two are related. What people say is dependent upon who they are and what they believe. Conservatives and liberals tend to say opposite things, for example. So we can have certain expectations as to what people are saying on the Internet. Now, of course, we have to see if those expectations are actually met or, as sometimes happened in chapter 2, not met.

Our expectations, or hypotheses, have two parts. First, as for the content of the messages, we hypothesize posted political conversations to be primarily conservative and anti-government, to be informative, to be primarily about old or long-standing issues, and to contain a relatively small number of personal attacks. Second, focusing on the behavior of those posting, we hypothesize that the newsgroups to which people post will act as social and political communities. We explain these hypotheses in more detail below, but since they are based in part on the nature of the Usenet, we need to discuss posting and the Usenet in a bit more detail.

Our first question is, why choose the Usenet and not some other bulletin board to study? We focus on the Usenet for five reasons. First, it is widely accessible. Most on-line providers, and nearly all Internet providers, carry some portion of the Usenet. Second, because the Usenet is typically not moderated, it is well suited to broad-based and open discussions concerning any topic. Third, participants are self-selected. This means that only those interested in the group will participate and those with no interest will not be exposed to it. Because people join, or "subscribe," voluntarily, we expect them to be committed to the group and to behave in ways that demonstrate that commitment (Wald, 1988). Fourth, Usenet groups have fairly descriptive titles that make it possible to identify areas of potential political activity. Finally, the Usenet is public and it leaves a readily accessible record of the messages posted to it.

Our second question is, what is the Usenet? Simply put, the Usenet is the world's largest electronic bulletin board system, carrying several million messages per year (Hill and Hughes, 1997). Most of us are familiar with bulletin boards; we have seen them around school campuses, community centers, or even on light poles. People staple or tape flyers announcing a house for rent or giving directions to a local garage sale, which they hope someone will read. Electronic bulletin boards are very similar in concept, but in practice have two important differences. They are organized into topic areas and they allow—expect, actually—other people to respond to the posted messages. Each of these characteristics is important to our study.

The organization of the Usenet into topics makes it possible to find the political messages, which we estimate comprise 5–10% of Usenet messages (Hill and Hughes, 1997). This number is very similar to the percentage of Web pages classified as political in Table 1.2. As mentioned above, all Usenet messages are collected into "groups" (also called newsgroups) and each group carries a title that describes its general topic. Depending on how you access the Usenet, you will probably have access to between two thousand and five thousand different newsgroups.

Newsgroup titles have two parts. The first part is the domain name, which is organized into broad categories such as biology (*bionet*), computers (*comp*), Internet information (*news*), recreation (*rec*), science (*sci*), society (*soc*), and general discussion (*talk*). The biggest domain is *alt,* which represents any type of alternative topic or discussion. The second part of newsgroup titles has no real convention but is used to describe more specifically the topic of the group. For example, a group to discuss humans rights violations is titled *soc.rights.human* while a general politics group carries the title *talk.politics.misc*.[1]

We used these titles to find potentially political newsgroups. Out of a list of 2,917 national and international newsgroups, we found 95 newsgroups devoted to the discussion of American politics and 104 related to world politics. The American-oriented newsgroups averaged, during July 1995, 2,870 messages, while the international groups averaged 1,907. That calculates to more than 470,000 politically oriented messages during July 1995 alone. Together, the national and international newsgroups represented 7% of all newsgroups, but over 12% of all Usenet messages (Hill and Hughes, 1997).[2]

The second important characteristic of the Usenet is the response by others. Obviously, interaction is a prerequisite for communication. One person speaking alone is a speech, two or more talking is a conversation or debate. So we focus on the conversations or, as they are more commonly called, "threads." Every message posted to a group has a subject heading similar to what you might see in the "Re:" field of a memo describing the nature or content of the message. If someone replies, the subject line is reproduced in the reply. Messages that carry the same subject line are called a thread. For example, if a person posts a message and calls it "Knowing your right to bear arms," each of the replies will say "Re: Knowing your right to bear arms." Taken together, a thread is a running transcript of a conversation. Of course, many messages never receive a reply. This is analogous to trying to start a conversation and being ignored. By focusing on threads, including those which are ignored, we can analyze the nature of actual political conversations. It is these publicly posted messages that form the basis of our study of citizen conversation on the Usenet.

Finally, what can we learn from studying the Usenet? This answer is not so straightforward, but is obviously the most important. Recall our starting point in the Introduction—we hypothesized the Internet to be largely conservative and confrontational (Hypotheses 1 and 2). Yet in chapter 2 we found Internet activists lean Democratic and have, at best, a small tendency to be anti-government. We also found that Internet activists are knowledgeable and active. We now hope to learn if what these activists communicate on the Internet matches these characteristics. What exactly are our expectations? Despite it being contradicted in chapter 2, we must still base our expectations on Hypothesis 1—that the Internet is conservative. Accordingly, we hypothesize that:

Hypothesis 3.1: Usenet threads will be mostly right-wing and anti-government

Building on Hypothesis 2 of the Introduction—that the Internet is confrontational—we can develop three more hypotheses. By confrontation we mean that people with different opinions will clash in a battle of ideas. This means the Usenet will be debate-oriented. Given the knowledge and interest of Internet activists demonstrated in chapter 2, we expect many messages will provide verifiable information. Of course we cannot say how many will meet this criterion, but given the fact that Usenet messages can be composed slowly (as opposed to chat rooms—see chapter 5), we expect people to have the time to look up and find relevant information. We know from chapter 1 that anonymity is likely to lead to anti-social behavior. We also suspect that ideological confrontation is likely to give rise to conflicts. Both of these will result in "flaming" or personal attacks. Thus, we expect to be able to document a fairly large number of flames on the Usenet. Unfortunately, we have to be vague in our expectations regarding information and especially flaming. We have no way to say beforehand what would constitute a lot of flaming or a little. This is because we have nothing to compare it to—how many people are flamed in face-to-face conversations, and how many quote sources? Lacking those answers, our hypotheses regarding flaming and information must unfortunately be vague. In general, however, we hypothesize that the Usenet:

Hypothesis 3.2: will be primarily debate-oriented
Hypothesis 3.3: threads will contain significant source information
Hypothesis 3.4: debates will have more flaming, but overall flames will be limited

Before turning to the analyses, we have one last topic to address. We have noted that the slower nature of the Usenet may alter the messages in terms of information provision. We wish to go even further and suggest that by the Usenet's very nature, it has the potential to serve as a social network. It seems pretty reasonable to conclude that most people, putting hermits aside, readily, perhaps eagerly, form social and political groups (Truman, 1951). So what does this have to do with the Usenet? We hypothesize that Usenet newsgroups act as political networks. We know from past research that other "real-world" groups affect our political attitudes—Families (Easton and Dennis, 1969), peers and workplaces (Beck, 1974; Finifter, 1976), neighborhoods (Huckfeldt, 1979), class and demographic groups (Huckfeldt, 1984), and even churches (Wald, Owen, and Hill, 1988) all have the potential to serve as centers of political discussion. What about Usenet and other computer bulletin board systems?

To answer that, we first need to know what characteristics define a group that can potentially influence us. Wald et al. suggest that, at the very least, political groups must provide political messages or communication (Wald, Owen, and Hill, 1988). Additionally, we would expect such a group to foster common norms and a group identity while also working to maintain the group's cohesion (Huckfeldt, 1979, 1984). Since our interests are strictly political, we would expect these norms to be ideologically based. That is, groups will form around a common belief system, protect it from dissent, and seek to expand by recruiting others to it. Put in the context of a computer bulletin board we hypothesize that *Usenet newsgroups will be ideologically based, will defend the group from those that disagree with it, and will demonstrate some form of recruitment to that ideology.* These hypotheses, while not part of the three described earlier, are tested below and in some of our previous work (Hill and Hughes, 1997).

Usenet Thread Content: What Are They Saying?

The data for this chapter come from a content coding and analysis of actual Usenet messages. We used a comprehensive list of Usenet groups (at least as comprehensive as available) and identified ninety-five newsgroups with potentially political subject areas. Identification was done by reading the newsgroup titles and looking for those that might attract political messages. From those identified, we randomly selected twenty-two newsgroups, which we believe represents a good cross-section of the existing newsgroups. Within each newsgroup we randomly selected threads, which were then followed for one week. We did this for ten consecutive weeks from May to July, 1995. In all, we sampled 1,012 total threads representing 5,611 individual messages, with full details as to sampling provided in the appendix. Please note, however, that our analysis is based on the *thread* and not the *message* or the person who wrote the message.

To understand the content of these threads, we coded or scored each thread based on thirteen variables. The method was simple: we read each thread and decided its score for that variable. Each author did half of the sample and we found very little difference between the authors' coding.[3] This procedure is somewhat different from the more traditional method of counting the presence of certain keywords. Unfortunately, the huge range of political topics on the Usenet makes developing a comprehensive list of keywords impossible. After all, we read messages ranging from discussions of voting (*alt.politics.elections*) to violently overthrowing the government (*alt.society.anarchy*) to helping bring about the worker's revolution (*alt.society.revolution*). Thus we were forced to rely upon our professional judgment in coding each thread's content.

The thirteen specific variables we coded for can be divided into three groups: counts, politics, and behaviors. Count variables are just what the name implies—they are counts of the number of messages in a thread, the number of messages from the person who posted the first message (the leader), and the number posted by the most active participant. These help us measure the level of activity and give a rough measure of the commitment of the leaders that start conversations.

The political variables represent an effort to measure the political content. We coded for the ideological direction of the first (or original) message in the thread. The categories for message direction are liberal/left, non-ideological, and conservative/right. Left and right are coded to conform to the standard left-right scale commonly used to describe political ideologies. Messages that reflected standard liberal viewpoints, whether promoting government intervention or supporting progressive causes such as pro-choice beliefs about abortion, we coded as liberal. The sole exception to the normal ideological model (see Campbell, et al., 1960) were anarchists, who we coded as being left-oriented (see Lenin, 1905, for a discussion of the utility of placing anarchists on the left of the political spectrum). The same logic was used to code conservative posts. We also coded for the final direction of the overall thread. This was based on the ideological distribution of the individual messages. In essence, was the overall thread predominantly liberal, non-ideological/ideologically balanced, or conservative? It is this variable that provides us with the modal ideology of the groups listed in Table 3.1. The last political variable is whether or not the thread was predominantly anti-government. Anti-government is coded to include everything from opposition to a specific federal government policy to a challenge to the legitimacy of the government itself.[4]

In addition, we coded for a number of behaviors. These are designed to operationalize and measure activities analogous to those found in typical social groups. They include whether or not the thread was a debate. A debate is characterized by two or more individuals promoting conflicting points of view. We coded whether or not the thread was about a current event, with "current" being defined essentially as those events occurring during the summer of 1995. We determined whether or not someone provided or requested information from outside the newsgroup such as a book, magazine, or some other reference source. We coded whether or not the message attempted to recruit people to an organization, an activity, or another location on the Internet such as a Web page. Finally, we also coded whether or not the thread was a "flame-fest" (series of insulting messages). We defined flames as personal, ad hominem attacks that focus on the individual poster and not the ideas of the message. These are often easy to identify since they are usually accompanied by profanity (thanks to George Carlin, we probably could have created a comprehensive list of keywords for flaming). All of these variables we coded 0 and 1 for the presence or absence of the behavior. Again, all were coded by the authors based upon our judgments concerning the content of the messages; more details for coding each variable are provided in the appendix.

Newsgroup Sample and Characteristics: Where Are They Saying It?

The first step in examining our Usenet sample is to take a quick look at the newsgroups and their ideological dominance. This will help us to test Hypothesis 3.1. Table 3.1 provides an overview of the number of threads and messages that we sampled for each of our political groups. Recall from above that our sample is based on twenty-two randomly selected groups from a universe of ninety-five political newsgroups. For each group, we present the number and percentage of threads and the number and percentage of messages. Clearly, some groups carried very few messages or threads,

TABLE 3.1
Content Analysis of Usenet Newsgroups: 10-Week Sample Size by Group

Newsgroup Name	Number/ Percent of Threads in Sample	Number/ Percent of Messages in Sample
alt.activism.d	28 / 2.8%	120 / 2.1%
alt.conspiracy.jfk	79 / 7.8%	254 / 4.5%
alt.fan.ronald-reagan	17 / 1.7%	138 / 2.5%
alt.gorby.gone.gone.gone	0 / 0.0%	0 / 0.0%
alt.law-enforcement	78 / 7.7%	391 / 7.0%
alt.org.audubon	7 / 0.7%	17 / 0.3%
alt.politics.clinton	83 / 8.2%	697 / 12.4%
alt.politics.elections	22 / 2.2%	116 / 2.1%
alt.politics.nationalism.white	50 / 4.9%	187 / 3.3%
alt.politics.org.misc	42 / 4.1%	43 / 0.8%
alt.politics.perot	22 / 2.2%	125 / 2.2%
alt.politics.usa.constitution	49 / 4.8%	305 / 5.4%
alt.politics.usa.republican	91 / 9.0%	670 / 11.9%
alt.revolution.counter	14 / 1.4%	21 / 0.4%
alt.rush-limbagh	0 / 0.0%	0 / 0.0%
alt.society.anarchy	29 / 2.9%	116 / 2.1%
alt.society.conservatism	25 / 2.5%	122 / 2.2%
alt.society.revolution	35 / 3.5%	188 / 3.4%
alt.war.vietnam	36 / 3.6%	90 / 1.6%
soc.rights.human	55 / 5.4%	236 / 4.2%
talk.politics.guns	101 / 10.0%	768 / 13.7%
talk.politics.misc	150 / 14.8%	1,007 / 17.9%
Total	1,013 / 100.0%	5,611 / 100.0%

such as *alt.gorby.gone.gone.gone* and *alt.rush-limbagh* (*sic*), which were extinct.[5] Other newsgroups had very little activity, even if they were not extinct. For example, *alt.org.audubon* received less than 1% of the threads in our sample and an even smaller percentage of messages. Of course, others carried not only more threads, *but proportionally more messages*. For example, two groups, *talk.politics.guns* and *talk.politics.misc*, account for 25% of our threads and 32% of our messages. This indicates a high rate of response to messages posted in these groups. Overall, the average length of a thread is 5.5 messages with the modal number being 1 and the maximum exceeding 100.

Before looking at the content of the newsgroups themselves, we can get a preview of one of our major findings. Looking at the list of newsgroups in Table 3.1 shows that the left wing appears to be outnumbered. Some newsgroups such as *alt.politics.elections* and *talk.politics.misc* seem devoted to neutral topics. Other groups have titles suggesting right-wing topics. But only a few appear overtly left wing. Even before examining newsgroup content we see that the left wing is probably underrepresented in our sample. Since the randomness of our sample should ensure an unbiased collection of newsgroups, Table 3.1 provides quick evidence that the right wing is better represented than the left on the Usenet. This is, of course, at odds with the findings of chapter 2, which suggested that Democratic causes might be more numerous.

Table 3.2 provides even starker evidence of this contradiction. In this table we present our classification of the threads in each of these groups. As stated above, we coded each thread as being left wing, neutral/balanced, or right wing and as being pro-government, neutral, or anti-government. The columns in Table 3.2 show the percentage of threads falling into each of these classifications. This may seem like a lot of numbers, but reading the table is pretty straightforward. Moving down the first column (ideology), we see that 36% of the messages in the newsgroup *alt.activism.d* were left wing, 18% right wing, and the rest neutral or balanced. The dominant, or modal, direction is shown in bold to make interpretation easier.

Just scanning down the table, we can see that very few groups are predominantly left wing. In fact, only three of twenty-two are classified as left wing, and one of those—*alt.society.anarchy*—is actually evenly split between left wing and neutral. By contrast, there are eight groups dominated by right-wing messages. Further, when a group is left wing, it is just barely left wing (35%, 46%, or 57%) as compared to the right-wing groups, which are often over 60% right wing. In other words, the right wing not only dominates more groups, but controls those groups more thoroughly.

A similar outcome can be seen by taking a close look at the "neutral" groups. A plurality of groups (nine) and threads (46%) are ideologically neutral. Unfortunately, we do not know if this means they are politically neutral or evenly balanced between two opposing ideologies. We suspect that latter but either way we see that in these groups, the right wing outnumbers the left wing by at least two to one. Thus, a large portion of groups are neutral but leaning right wing (neutral with right wing second), while only *alt.activism.d* qualifies as neutral and leaning left. Ideologically, the Usenet is relatively neutral but with very heavy right-wing overtones. The left wing

TABLE 3.2
Distribution of Ideology and Attitudes toward Government in
Sampled Usenet Newsgroups

Name	Ideology of Group	Group Position on Government
alt.activism.d	36% L / **46% N** / 18% R	4% P / **68% N** / 29% A
alt.conspiracy.jfk	3% / **76% N** / 22% R	0% P / **82% N** / 18% A
alt.fan.ronald-reagan	0% L / 47% N / **53% R**	0% P / **77% N** / 24% A
alt.gorby.gone.gone.gone	-----	-----
alt.law-enforcement	13% I / **67% N** / 21% R	4% P / **83% N** / 13% A
alt.org.audubon	14% L / **86% N** / 0% R	0% P / **100% N** / 0% A
alt.politics.clinton	17% L / 37% N / **46% R**	4% P / **71% N** / 25% A
alt.politics.elections	14% L / **46% N** / 41% R	0% P / **86% N** / 14% A
alt.politics.nationalism.white	4% L / 34% N / **62% R**	0% P / **80% N** / 20% A
alt.politics.org.misc	0% L / **95% N** / 5% R	0% P / **100% N** / 0% A
alt.politics.perot	0% L / **55% N** / 45% R	0% P / **68% N** / 32% A
alt.politics.usa.constitution	25% L / 31% N / **45% R**	0% P / **55% N** / 45% A
alt.politics.usa.republican	10% L / 37% N / **53% R**	1% P / **78% N** / 21% A
alt.revolution.counter	0% L / 7% N / **93% R**	0% P / **64% N** / 36% A
alt.rush-limbagh	-----	-----
alt.society.anarchy	**35% L** / 35% N / 31% R	0% P / **59% N** / 41% A
alt.society.conservatism	8% L / 28% N / **64% R**	0% P / **72% N** / 28% A
alt.society.revolution	**57% L** / 17% N / 26% R	9% P / **89% N** / 3% A
alt.war.vietnam	8% L / **86% N** / 6% R	0% P / **92% N** / 8% A
soc.rights.human	**46% L** / 38% N / 16% R	4% P / **82% N** / 15% A
talk.politics.guns	7% L / 19% N / **74% R**	0% P / **55% N** / 46% A
talk.politics.misc	21% L / **45% N** / 34% R	2% P / **77% N** / 21% A
Total	16% L / **46% N** / 39% R	2% P/ **76% N** / 23% A

Note: Some cells do not total 100% due to rounding. Bolded figures represent the modal ideology or position for group.

Legend: L= Left-wing; N= Non-ideological; R= Right-wing; P = Pro-government, N = Neutral, A = Anti-government

is underrepresented, at least in comparison to what we would expect based on the results of chapter 2. In short, Hypothesis 3.1 is partially supported: the right wing dominates the left but a plurality of all threads are neutral.

What about positions on government? We found a minimal anti-government theme in chapter 2. Is that reflected in the threads? The answer appears to be "partially." The second column of Table 3.2 shows that most threads and all groups take positions neutral toward the government. We explore this in more detail below, but for now we can note that pro-government sentiments make up only 2% of the threads, with *alt.society.revolution* being the most pro-government group at 9%. By contrast, anti-government threads constitute 23% of all threads, with *talk.politics.guns* and *alt.politics.usa.constitution* being the most anti-government groups. Oddly enough, *alt.society.-anarchy* is only 41% anti-government. So Hypothesis 3.1 is again supported in a limited fashion: the Usenet is certainly more anti-government than pro-government, but overall is classified as neutral. The limited anti-government attitudes documented in chapter 2 are partially reflected here. Most messages are neutral, but of those threads taking a position vis-à-vis the government, most are negative.

Thread Characteristics and Content

Next we turn to Hypotheses 3.2 through 3.4. Recall from our earlier discussion that we hypothesize Usenet messages to be primarily debate-oriented, informative, and somewhat confrontational. Table 3.3 provides a summary of eight characteristics for the threads we analyzed using the whole sample and a subset of only multi-message threads. We discuss each part individually and in more detail below.

One note about the analysis, though, is in order. In our discussions below we present several results in the text itself rather than tables. We note whether the differences are significant, or statistically valid, in parenthetical form such as ($p < .05$ or $p < .01$), or whether they are non-significant (n.s.). So "n.s." means the results have no statistical significance; otherwise they are significant.

Thread Length

First, we present the mean and median numbers of messages in each thread. The mean is the numerical average, while the median represents the "middle" number (50% above, 50% below). Looking first at the total sample we see that the mean is 5.5 and the median is 2. The relatively large difference between mean and median is important. It shows that half of all threads are composed of two or fewer messages. This means that many Usenet messages receive zero or only one response (and that response is often the author asking someone to pay attention to the original post!). At the same time, some threads are much longer as indicated by the larger mean. In fact, some threads in our sample reached one hundred messages in just seven days. Thus, Usenet content can be classified into two groups: a large number of very short threads with few or no responses and a smaller number of very large threads with many responses. To get an image of this, think of a large party with many groups of people talking. Some of the groups will be louder, more boisterous. These will attract new members who come over to see what

TABLE 3.3
Characteristics of Usenet Threads

Characteristics	All Threads	Multi-message Threads
1. Mean/Median number of messages	5.5 / 2	9.8 / 4
2. Threads are debates?		
No	69.9	43.3
Yes	30.1	56.7
3. Threads provide sourced information?		
No	36.6	46.6
Yes	63.4	53.4
4. Threads are a "Flame Fest"?		
No	80.8	65.6
Yes	19.2	34.3
5. Percent of threads that are:		
Left-wing	15.9	13.7
Neutral	45.5	42.2
Right-wing	38.6	44.1
6. Percent of threads that are:		
Pro-government	1.6	1.9
Neutral	75.6	73.5
Anti-government	22.8	24.6
7. Do threads involve recruitment?		
No	76.7	86.5
Yes	23.3	13.5
8. Are threads about a current event?		
No	57.7	58.0
Yes	42.3	42.0

Notes: Multi-message threads consist of two or more messages. N = 524
All threads sample includes an additional 489 single message threads. N = 1,013

the excitement is about. Other groups, the quiet ones, will lose members and their conversations will die out. The same is true on the Usenet as interesting topics attract responses while uninteresting or poorly phrased ones are ignored. So that we can better study these larger conversations we split our sample into a column for all threads and one for multi-message threads. We will see below that this classification of threads turns out to be quite important.

Debates

Hypothesis 3.2 says that the Usenet will be dominated by debate. Question 2 of Table 3.3 casts considerable doubt on this hypothesis. Of the full 1,013 threads, only 30% qualify as a debate. This suggests that fully 70% of all threads show some form of a consensus. But there is a problem with this reasoning. As we pointed out above, many threads have only one response. Obviously it is impossible for a debate to take place between one person (no multiple personality disorder jokes, please). Returning to our party analogy, we envision some people throwing out a topic of conversation. Sometimes the topic is joined but the talk is friendly (a non-debate), but other times the topic is simply ignored. It is cases like the latter that distort our picture.

In the second column we excluded all single-message threads; 489 threads had only one message. This leaves us 524 threads that could potentially be debates. Of these, 57% *are* debates. In other words, most multi-message threads become debates.

Another way of looking at this is to return to our discussion of thread length. The typical debate thread has a mean of fourteen messages, while the typical non-debate thread averages only two messages ($p < .01$). Debates are few in number, comprising only 30% of all threads; however, they represent the majority of the content—that is, the messages being sent back and forth. If we multiply the number of debate and non-debate threads by their averages we see that debate threads make up 4,245 messages while non-debate threads total only 1,366 messages, so debates represent 30% of the threads in our sample, but 76% of the messages. Thus, Hypothesis 3.2 is partially supported: debates are not the predominant thread type but the vast majority of Usenet political content is found in debate threads.

Information

Question 3 shows that most threads on the Usenet are informational in nature. This means they provide some fact or statement from a verifiable source or sources. Based on chapter 2, we expected a relatively high level of information and it appears we have found it. However, some caution is in order. Many of the informational threads we sampled came in the form of "press release" style posts. Some organization (often in *alt.politics.org.-misc*) would post a statement of their activities or concerns. In fact, many of these were actual press statements from the White House. Naturally, these rarely received a reply. Looking at the second column, we see that the number of informational threads drops to 53% for multi-message threads. Information is lower but still remains the norm or majority of all threads. We therefore can conclude in favor of Hypothesis 3.3 as Usenet threads are largely, even predominantly, informational.

Flaming

If informed debate represents a possible utopian view of on-line political communication, flaming is the dystopian nightmare. Flames are vitriolic attacks on individuals, ignoring the merits of an argument (or even the lack of them) in favor of a personal, ad hominem attack. They may take the form of an attack on the person posting, such as, "You are an ignorant, foolish, small-minded little person with no life!" or an attack upon someone else: "KKKlinton is a pot-smoking, draft-dodging, womanizing, traitorous idiot!" Of course, most flames are not so tame, but the point is clear—they offer little in the way of substance, preferring instead to offer insults. The good news is that flaming represents only about one in five threads. Of course, our definition is pretty strict—to qualify as a flame-fest, the *majority* of messages in the thread must be flames. So there are many individual flame messages that do not manage to drag the whole thread down with them. Even so, we see that flaming is in the minority. Of course, flames, like debates, usually require two people. In fact, it is difficult to imagine a one-message flame, although we did find several. Looking at the multi-thread column, we see that about one in three qualify as flame-fests. As hypothesized (3.4), flaming is common enough to be notable, but is not entirely consuming.

Ideology and Attitudes toward Government

We now return to our discussion of ideology. Recall from Table 3.2 that neutral/balanced messages are the norm but that right-wing messages far outnumber left-wing messages. We can see that this holds true both for all threads and for the multi-message thread subset. Multi-message threads tend to be somewhat more ideological or less neutral but the differences are rather small. This makes sense, but for two very different reasons. A lot of neutral threads will be single-message threads composed of a statement such as a press release or some kind of question. So we expect many short threads to be neutral. Similarly, many neutral threads will be long, drawn-out debates with both sides equally represented. This too is expected. So while neutral threads dominate both the short and long threads, they do so for different reasons. In summary, most threads are neutral but, of threads that are ideological, 71% are right wing.

What about attitudes toward the government itself? The results are similar to what we found with regard to ideology. We see that neutral threads are more numerous but to a much greater degree—about three-quarters of all threads are neutral regarding the government. Given that about 40% of threads are right wing, we would expect there to be more anti-government sentiment, since right-wing threads will normally be anti-government. This should make right-wing and anti-government messages roughly equal in number. Why are anti-government threads so proportionately fewer than right-wing threads? The answer seems to be the nature of the conversations. Many threads focus on the actions of people and not on government itself. For example, here one person discussed his/her displeasure with the Republican-controlled Congress: "You GOPers are so proud of that contract ON America that you don't care that Newtie is a crook." In this way a thread could end up ideologically left wing or right wing but, neutral regarding the government. Though we did not code for this, it is apparent from the minimal discussion of government, pro or con, that Usenet threads typically focus on people and events rather than government itself. However, we should note that when government does become the subject of a debate, it is usually criticized on the Usenet. Of the threads taking a position on government, 94% are anti-government.

Recruitment and Current Events

Finally, we introduce two variables that are not directly related to our hypotheses but are important nonetheless. Recruitment involves asking others to join your cause, to in some way participate in an act in the "real" world. For example, there were several posts with the basic theme of "Let's all hold a rally for the right to bear arms this Monday at the court house." The most impressive recruitment post we sampled came from *alt.nationalism.white* and, when printed, was over thirty pages of white supremacy contacts (telephones, P.O. boxes, Web pages), organizations, literature, and merchandise (KKK baby booties are scary). As question 7 of Table 3.3 shows, recruitment threads slightly outnumber flaming threads. This is an encouraging sign of the organizational potential of the Internet (see also Schwartz, 1996). The percentage drops considerably when only multi-message threads are examined, but this is to be expected. Messages such as the white supremacy resource list do not receive or even need a reply. In fact, many recruitment messages fit the more traditional idea of a bulletin board— people post a message to be seen, not to start a conversation. In reality, many of the responses to recruitment messages are actually people of the opposite ideology criticizing the cause or the activist. For example, one message invited readers to attend the RKBA (Right to Keep and Bear Arms) rallies being held throughout the country (but mostly in Texas). To this, one person responded, "You gun nuts are all alike, you just want to go out and kill things." More typical, however, is for recruiting messages to receive no reply. In all, the level of recruitment on the Usenet is pretty high—nearly one in four threads are explicitly aimed at drawing others into action on behalf of some cause. We explore this activity in more detail below.

Finally, we should note that current events, contrary to what we might expect, are not the predominant topic. Regardless of thread length, over half of all threads are about long-standing issues or events well in the past and sometimes in the future. This is somewhat surprising until one recalls the profile of the Internet activist. Activists love politics and political talk. They are educated and apparently informed about a variety of topics. It is probably natural that they be drawn into discussion of perennial issues like the proper role of government, how to interpret the Constitution, or the causes of the Great Depression. While such debates may seem irrelevant to many, to the activist they are crucial issues striking at the heart of governing. Thus, we read many threads devoted to older topics even while new political issues were evolving.

Relationships between Debating, Flaming, and Information

All of this provides a good overview of Usenet content, but we want to delve just a bit deeper by looking at how selected thread characteristics relate to each other. In particular, we want to focus on the characteristics of debating, informational, and flaming threads. We do this by cross-tabulating the variable of interest (debates/non-debates) with these other variables.

Debating is the heart of political discourse. Someone supposedly said if two people share the same opinions, one of them is unnecessary. That may be an exaggeration (they still equal two votes in a democracy) but the point is that democracy progresses through the clash of opinions. Of course, we prefer that they be intelligent, well-informed opinions. We cannot test the knowledge of authors of the Usenet, but we can look at what they say. On the Usenet, information is not typically used to substantiate an argument. Debates tend to have less information than non-debates (49% versus 70%, $p < .01$). This seems paradoxical. After all, why wouldn't people in a debate prefer to quote sources rather than simply make assertions? This is even more puzzling given that the Usenet allows people to respond a day or even three days after they read the original message and that these are generally well-informed people.

There are two explanations for this. One we discuss in detail below, but for now we note that many people prefer debating normative or "preference"-oriented issues. *Normative* means talking about what "should" be, while *objective* is focusing on what "is." Usenet messages tend to be normative, as people emphasize what they believe would be the ideal state of affairs. For example, in one post a person argued, "The government's job is only to protect borders and enforce voluntary contracts. Anything more is tyranny." While this may be a well-developed and logical opinion, it is normative and as such requires little factual information. By contrast, the person who argued, "Welfare is a corrupt and wasteful program," certainly could use some kind of objective evidence to support the claim. Given a preference for normative issues, we see information use actually decline in debates.

What kind of a relationship does debating have with current events? We suspect that more recent events will spark more intense responses. Moreover, older, better-known issues (such as abortion) are not as interesting as new issues. Excluding single-message threads, we find debates are more likely to concern current events than are non-debates (47% versus 36%, p < .05). Current events still remain the minority of issues debated, however, so there are apparently plenty of people willing to discuss older, more established issues.

If current events are likely to provoke enough responses to start a debate, then ideological statements should show a similar relationship to debating. It does. Again, using the multi-thread sample only, we find that 69% of debates are ideological (right wing or left wing), while only 44% of non-debates are ideologically oriented (p < .01). Recall earlier we said that we coded for the ideological direction of the original thread. By looking at the relationship between it and debates, we can see whether ideological posts are more likely to draw debate responses. Intuitively we would think they would, and empirically we see that they do. A left-wing or right-wing thread ends up in a debate about 73% of the time (using the full sample), while neutral threads stir debates only about 48% of the time (p < .01). Another way of looking at this is to see that posts that start out ideological tend to receive more responses: ideological posts attract an average of 6 responses while neutral posts attract 2.7. In short, most Usenet debate is ideologically driven.

A final concern is that the clash of ideologies may become too heated. We want ideological conflict—that is how citizens learn and society progresses. But if conflict is too high, then it degenerates into a fight and not a discussion. Using only multi-message threads, we find that debates are significantly more likely to result in flames (39% versus 28%, p < .01). This confirms Hypothesis 3.4—confrontation does sometimes bring out the worst in a discussion. But the difference, while statistically significant, is not huge. Moreover, even for debates, over 60% of all threads are relatively friendly.

Just as discourse is at the heart of democracy, information is at the heart of discourse. We have seen that information is less common in debates. Now we take a look at other aspects of informational threads. One place we would expect information is in recruitment threads. While information may only be occasionally used to persuade others in a debate, it is still possible that information is used to recruit like-minded individuals. Looking at all 1,013 threads, we find that recruitment threads are considerably more likely to contain information than non-recruiting threads (81% versus 58%, p < .01).

This provides our second explanation to the lack of information in debates. Above we showed that recruitment threads tend to be short and we also know they do not normally turn into debates—only 11% of recruitment threads are also debates. Since information is more common in recruitment threads than in debates it seems that information is more often used to recruit others than to persuade. Information is also related to current events. Given the ready availability of information in the form of newspapers, TV shows, and the like, we expect current-events discussions to contain more verifiable information. Our expectation is met. About 76% of all current-event threads contain information, as compared to 55% of the non-current-event threads (p < .01).

Finally, we take a quick look at flaming. Flame-fests, as we discussed above, are actually atypical. Only 20–30% of threads can be considered to be primarily insult-oriented. But we did show that flaming is more common in debates and that debates are less likely to involve the presentation of verifiable information. So are flames less common when information is provided? The answer is yes. Looking at the multi-message threads, we see that only 38% of flames contain verifiable information, while over 61% of non-flames provide information (p < .01). We have no way to test whether information actually deters flaming. That could be the case or there could be alternative explanation, such as people who are willing and able to provide documented sources do not need to resort to insults. But whatever the case, we can see that flaming does represent the worst aspect of discourse— limited information, personalized, and vitriolic. But again, we can add the hopeful note that most Usenet threads do not degenerate into insult contests.

What can we conclude from all of this? Utopians hope that computer-mediated discourse will make our nation more democratic, more deliberative, and more informed, while the dystopians fear it will make us more divisive, banal, and susceptible to demagogues. What we have learned about the Usenet gives some support to both groups. For the utopian, flames are relatively few and debates do make up the bulk of the content (though not of the threads). But on the less optimistic side, we see that information is used more often to recruit like-minded individuals than to persuade others, and yet it is persuasion that is the key to deliberation. Debaters may not persuade their antagonists, but they should hope to persuade the audience. This does not appear to be the norm on the Usenet. Rather, information is used in a topical, current-event-driven manner, aimed largely at finding people who think the same way as the author, not at converting people to that point of view.

Such a finding fits nicely with our discussion of communities at the beginning of this chapter. We briefly mentioned the possibility that newsgroups could form social and political groups that behave similar to real world political organizations. Given the importance of recruitment and the apparent interest in finding like-minded citizens the recruiters show, perhaps it is now time to more fully explore the idea of Usenet communities.

Usenet Newsgroups as Political Communities

In the first part of this chapter we defined three conditions or criteria necessary for the identification of a group. First, the group needs some kind of norm, or central tenet. In this case the central aspect of a newsgroup would be its dedication to a particular political ideology. Second, it needs to maintain itself by rejecting those that do not match the group's identity. Finally, the group needs to recruit new members. Below, we test each of these statements to see if they can be successfully applied to Usenet news-groups.

We begin with a look at the development of the group's central purpose or, in this case, ideology. We presuppose that political groups meet primarily to discuss politics and we further suppose that people regularly recruit and talk with others that share not only a common interest but also a common viewpoint. Obviously some people seek conflict, but what we wish to know is whether newsgroups also act to create an agreeable place for the like-minded to converse.

To find out, we use a few new variables in our Usenet data. In addition to coding the ideology of the entire thread or conversation (as used in Tables 3.1–3.3), we also coded for the ideology of the first message in each thread. We call the person who made the first post the "leader." We also coded whether the leader was the most active poster (wrote the most messages). Finally, we combined all of this with the ideological direction of the overall group as shown in Table 3.2. This enables us to see whether leaders try to shape the ideological direction of the groups to which they post. In essence, it shows whether or not we have people who try to organize the participants into an ideologically coherent group.

Our first question is whether leaders are in fact active in shaping their threads and hence their groups. The answer to that is simple—they are. In 87% of all threads, the most active person in a conversation (the author of the most messages) is the person who started the conversation. Of course, sometimes this is because no one else responded. But even for multi-message threads we find that leaders are still the most active participant 74% of the time.

What are the leaders doing with these messages? A significant part of their activity is directed toward recruitment. Obviously, if a thread is recruit-ment-oriented, it probably is because the leader started it that way. It is possible, however, that someone else joined the thread with his or her own recruitment message, but our concern is the activity of the leaders in recruit-ing. Given the limitations of our data, a precise measure is not possible but we can construct a rough guide of leadership recruitment. As we know from above, most of the time the leader is the most active poster, which gives us a simple indication of leadership dedication. When we cross that with recruitment, we find that leaders are much more likely to be the most active poster when the message is recruitment-oriented than when it is not (85% versus 73%, p < .05). Thus, a major function of the leader is to try to recruit others.

How sophisticated are the leaders? Do they try to recruit broadly, from just about anywhere? Or do the leaders act strategically, targeting their messages to just those who are most receptive? Table 3.4 shows that many leaders are in fact strategic in their efforts to recruit and create conversations. Section 1 shows that most leaders post to groups with same ideology. By ideology, we mean the modal ideology of the threads in each group (see Table 3.2). At 57%, the number is somewhat smaller than we might have expected. However, we must remember that even these citizen leaders are

TABLE 3.4
Leadership Activities in Usenet Newsgroups

1. Do leaders invade other newsgroups?	
Ideological consonance with group	57.4%
One step off	33.4%
Ideological dissonance with group	9.3%
N = 1,013	100.0%

2. Ideology of leader by ideology of destination group

	Leader Ideology		
Group is:	Left-wing	No Dominant	Right-wing
Left-wing	31.4%	7.6%	6.5%
No dominant ideology	32.5%	64.1%	30.7%
Right-wing	36.1%	28.3%	62.8%
N = 1013	100.0%	100.0%	100.0%
		Chi-Square = 197.05***	
		Phi = .44	

3. Leader activity level by ideological "invasion" of group	Ideological Consonance	One Step Off	Ideological Dissonance
Leader most active poster	73.8%	81.5%	54.1%
Leader not most active poster	26.2%	26.5%	45.9%
N = 524	100%	100%	100%
		Chi-Square = 18.06***	
		Phi = .18	

*Legend: *** p < .001*

not counting messages for content, but instead simply estimating the group's ideology from their readings. That said, it is remarkable that only 9% of threads are begun in a group that is the direct opposite of the leader's own ideology (as measured by the leader's starting message). The remaining one-third are messages posted to a group that is "one step off"—a right-wing or left-wing person posting to a neutral group, or a neutral person posting to either a left-wing or right-wing group. Few leaders stray far from their own ideology and most stay within groups that match their own beliefs.

Of course, some leaders are more strategic than others. Part 2 of Table 3.4 is an expansion on the first question. Across the top we see the ideology of the leader, and down the side we see that of the group (as defined in Table 3.2). We expect most leaders to post their messages to groups that match their ideology. Looking at right-wing leaders, we see that 63% of their messages are posted to right-wing newsgroups and only about 7% are posted to left-wing groups. Similarly, 64% of neutral threads are begun in newsgroups with no clear ideology and only 8% are posted to left-wing groups.

However, the story is different on the left—the modal destination for left-wing messages is actually right-wing groups. Though the differences are small, left-wingers actually post more messages to either neutral and right-wing groups than to left-wing groups. Left-wing leaders are either less strategic or merely less successful at posting to ideologically consonant newsgroups. We suspect that the answer is a little of both. We know from Table 3.2 that there are very few left-wing groups and this makes posting to a consonant group much harder for a left-wing leader. If left-leaders simply post randomly, they will end up with most messages in non-left-wing groups. But they are not posting randomly, since left-wing groups represented 14% of the sample but left leaders posted 30% of their messages to them. Instead, they appear to target right-wing groups to a much greater extent than other ideological leaders. We do not know why this is more prevalent for the left but it is probably because they post where the readers are and those seem to be right-wing and neutral newsgroups. In short, leaders from the dominant positions of neutral and right wing post to ideologically consonant groups while leaders of the minority left disproportionately post to dissonant groups.

The final section of Table 3.4 looks at this same question from a slightly different angle. Given ideological differences between the leader and the group, how do the group and the leader respond? What we want to know is whether ideologically contrasting posts result in greater activity on the part of the leader, the rest of the newsgroup, or both. The answer is, primarily the group. As stated above, leaders are almost always the most active poster in a thread. But when are they most likely to be challenged? The answer is, when they post to dissonant groups.

Reading across, we see that in ideologically consonant groups and groups that are just one step off, the leader is almost always the most active participant. But when the leader's message and the group are dissonant, leaders are the most active just over half of the time. There are two potential explanations for why this occurs. First, leaders could be less active in dissonant groups. Or, the leaders could be just as active (or even more), but be overwhelmed by the partisan response. We tested these explanations and found that leaders are not more active when posting to dissonant groups. In fact, the average number of messages by the leader is virtually the same regardless of the ideological differences the leader may have with the group. Instead, we found that the number of responses from the group increased when the message disagreed with the group's norm (2.2 versus 3.5, p < .01). Other members of the group post more messages in an effort to counter the dissonant direction set by the leader. As is necessary for any group, leaders try to control the group's direction and are dedicated to threads they begin, even those in dissonant groups. But the members of the newsgroups themselves respond to those threads. It is to this group maintenance activity that we next turn our attention.

We know that leaders are dedicated to their threads, but are members dedicated to their groups? The answer is important. Starting a group is one thing but maintaining it over time is quite another. Groups face a host of potential problems including lack of funding, lack of members, and so forth. Of course, for the Usenet, funding is not an issue, but members and membership support are. Over time members join, participate, leave, and are replaced by others. This increases the risk of the group "losing sight" of their objective or reason for existing. That is, as new members join the group it is changed. To prevent membership turnover from destroying the purpose of the group, the new members (or participants) must conform, or be made to conform, to the group's norms and beliefs. This requires, on the part of the membership, some kind of "policing" activity. Older, more experienced members must watch out for people who do not agree with the group's norms and must remove them if they refuse to conform. Of course, the Usenet is open and so participants cannot be easily excluded. But they can be policed—others can respond to and criticize the posts of non-conforming participants. So our question now is whether newsgroups show such policing activities.

The evidence, presented in Table 3.5, suggests group policing is quite common. We begin by looking at the average number of messages in threads that are ideologically similar to or at odds with the group's norm. As section 1 (Ideological Invasion) shows, the average number of messages in a thread increases with the level of ideological dissonance. Original messages that match the ideology of the group average about five messages per thread. The number is slightly higher (but not statistically significant) for messages that are one step off. But if a message is posted to the ideologically opposite

Chapter 3

TABLE 3.5
Newsgroup Maintenance of Dominant Ideology

1. Ideological invasion

Thread is:	Messages per Thread	Significant Differences		
		IC	OS	ID
Ideologically consonant with group (IC)	4.73	---	n.s.	*
One step off (OS)	5.54		---	*
Ideologically dissonant with group (ID)	10.48			---
N = 1,013	F = 10.27***			

2. Number of messages in a thread by switching of thread ideology

	Messages per Thread	Significant Differences		
		NS	OS	IR
No switch from leader's ideology (NS)	8.49	---	*	*
One step switch (OS)	12.85		---	n.s.
Ideological reversal (IR)	16.07			---
N = 524	F = 7.78***			

3. Ideological invasion by switching

	Thread is Ideologically Consonant (IC)	Thread is one step off (OS)	Thread is Ideologically Dissonant (ID)
Thread is not switched (NS)	87.1%	76.1%	42.6%
Thread changes one step (OS)	8.2%	16.3%	16.4%
Thread is reversed (IR)	4.7%	7.6%	41.0%
N = 524	Chi-square = 88.0***		
	Cramer's V = .29		

Legend: *** p < .001

group, the thread length doubles to just over ten messages. This suggests, as pointed out above, that the group responds to ideological confrontation in an effort to protect its norms.

Section 2 tells a similar story. Here we are looking at the starting and ending ideology of a thread. Remember, the starting ideology is that of the leader's post, while the ending ideology is the dominant viewpoint expressed in the entire thread. We see that threads that start and end in the same ideology have about eight messages per thread. But when the thread is "switched" just one step, that number jumps to almost thirteen. Moreover, for threads that start out in one direction but end in the opposite, the number of messages is sixteen. This shows us that groups respond to ideological differences with a greater volume of messages—sometimes enough messages to actually "switch" the thread to the dominant ideology.

A more detailed view of this is provided in the final section of Table 3.5. Here we cross-tabulated the information on invasion from section 1 with that of switching found in section 2. This shows that threads are attacked far more often in ideologically dissonant groups than in consonant groups. This may seem intuitively obvious and it is, if one is thinking about traditional groups. In any such group we would expect members to attack outsiders far more often than insiders. And this is exactly what we see in section 3. When the thread is ideologically consonant with the group, it maintains that direction 87% of the time. But when the thread is dissonant, it is maintained only 43% of the time. In other words, looking down the final column, we see that most dissonant threads are either balanced out by responses from the group (16%) or actually overwhelmed (41%). Either way, we find that groups protect their own ideological space but less commonly invade that of others. The invasion aspect can be confirmed by looking at the first column and seeing that only 5% of threads are ever switched when they are in their home turf.

Finally, we can add one little piece of information about ideological conflict. Recall from earlier in the chapter that debates are associated with increased flaming. The same relationship is found with ideological invasions. Of messages posted to ideologically consonant groups, only 18% are flamed. But of messages posted to ideologically dissonant groups, 32% become flame-fests (p < .001). Thus, we see that groups vigorously and successfully defend their electronic territory. Group maintenance is very real in Usenet newsgroups.

Next we focus on recruitment on the Usenet. Recruitment messages are not focused on bringing people into a Usenet group, since the readers must be there in order to receive the messages. As mentioned earlier, what we define as recruitment is the act of encouraging others to engage in some kind of real-world activity. We know from our earlier discussions that, although it represents only about one of every four messages, recruitment does occur. Now we want to see if recruitment is ideological in nature and whether or not it is strategically linked to the ideology of the leader and the target newsgroup. Logically, recruitment is motivated by ideological purpose and so should be more common in ideological threads than in those that are politically neutral. Similarly, we would expect most people to post their recruitment threads to newsgroups that share the leader's ideological orientation.

Section 1 (Recruitment By Ideology of Thread) of Table 3.6 shows the relationship between ideology and recruitment. To create this table, we took threads that started out left or right wing and folded them together to repre-

TABLE 3.6
Recruitment Activity in Newsgroups

	Recruitment Message Thread	No Recruitment Message in Thread
1. Recruitment by ideology of thread:		
Thread is non-ideological	47.0%	35.2%
Thread is ideological (left-wing or right-wing)	53.0%	64.8%
	100.0%	100.0%
N = 1,013	Chi-square = 10.2**	
2. Recruitment by ideology of newsgroup:		
Ideologically consonant	55.9%	62.3%
Ideologically one step off	34.6%	29.2%
Ideologically dissonant	9.5%	8.5%
	100.0%	100.0%
N = 1,013	Chi-square = 3.1 (n.s.)	
3 Recruitment by ideology of newsgroup for ideological threads only:		
Ideologically consonant	48.9%	62.7%
Ideologically one step off	35.1%	24.2%
Ideologically dissonant	16.0%	13.1%
	100.0%	100.0%
N = 552	Chi-square = 8.8*	

Legend: ** p < .01, * p < .05

sent one category—ideological threads. The other category represents threads with no dominant ideology. Here, we see that recruitment threads are more ideological than non-recruitment threads (65% versus 53%). Recruitment threads tend to be ideological, though about one of every three recruitment messages is neutral.

Section 2 examines where leaders post their recruitment messages. We see a small, but non-significant difference in recruitment destination. That is, recruitment messages do not seem to be much, if any, more likely to be posted to a group with a consonant ideological orientation. This finding, however, may be skewed by the presence of non-ideological recruitment messages. Someone recruiting without a specific ideology in mind is more likely to post his or her message randomly. So, we excluded the non-ideological messages from our sample and repeated section 2.

The results, presented in section 3, show that ideological recruitment messages are in fact targeted to ideologically friendly newsgroups. Non-recruitment (but still ideological) messages are posted to friendly news-groups 49% of the time, but ideological recruitment messages are sent to friendly groups 63% of the time. Recruitment is ideologically targeted, when the purpose of recruitment is ideological. In short, we find that recruitment is generally ideological in nature and that ideological recruitment is typically strategic—it is aimed at those groups most likely to be responsive.

Summary and Conclusions

This chapter focused on the Usenet as a medium of political communica-tion. With over two hundred political newsgroups carrying over 470,000 messages per month, we know political discussion is taking place. The real question is what are they saying?

We found that Usenet threads are predominantly neutral in terms of ide-ology and overwhelmingly neutral with regard to government policies. How-ever, of those threads that are ideological or government-oriented, most are right wing and anti-government. Thus, we find mixed support for Hypothesis 3.1: most threads are neutral but with clear right-wing and anti-government overtones. Equally important, the content analysis appears to contradict the results of our study of Internet activists in chapter 2. This contradiction is discussed in more detail later.

We also hypothesized that Usenet threads would be debate-oriented, that they would be informational, and that debates would have increased flaming. We found that many threads never receive a single reply. Thus, debate threads appear to be in the minority. But when we look at just multi-message threads, most are, in fact, debates. Debates represent a minority of threads but a majority of messages and content. Whether we look at single-message or multi-message threads, most also provide verifiable information. This gives us some cause for optimism regarding the potential for networks like the Usenet to enhance political dialogue. The number of flames, however, sends an uncertain signal. As stated earlier, we have no way of knowing what constitutes a lot or a little amount of flaming. However, we can note the presence and absence of flames in certain kinds of threads. For example, when we compare flames in debates and non-debates, we find that flaming increases in the presence of ideological conflict though it still does not domi-nate most threads. We suspect that this represents more flaming than we would see in face-to-face discourse but it is still low enough to allow politi-cal dialogue to take place. That is, flames are pretty common on the Usenet but they are not the dominant type of thread. Even in debates, flames represent only 40% of threads. So the majority of discourse on the Usenet is relatively civil.

We also found that debating, flaming, and information are interrelated. Debates are less informational than non-debates. People apparently prefer normative issues in debates as opposed to objective ones. But when recruiting, information is more common. Recruiters tend to provide information while debaters tend to avoid it.

In the last section of the chapter we explored the Usenet as a place for political communities to develop. We found that Usenet newsgroups fit the three criteria necessary for describing a group. They engage in leadership activities designed to establish a group norm, they police those who violate that norm, and they recruit others to their cause and they do so strategically—they seek out those most likely to agree with them. Thus, the Usenet is not only a means of communicating, it is a place where people can connect with others, share their views, and, at least potentially, develop their political beliefs. We cannot say if or how the Usenet shapes its readers, but we can say that Internet activists use it much as they would a real-world club or organization.

What conclusions can we reach from these findings? Answering such a question tempts us to go beyond the data presented here and that is always hazardous. But we can offer some generalizations about how the Usenet may interact with society as a whole.

In chapter 2 we argued that most Internet activists are self-selected. This means they are probably not converted from typical citizens to political junkies but are more likely to be political junkies to begin with. We see the same process at work here. If Usenet participants and their subsequent discussions are different from the general populace, it is not because they communicate via the Usenet. Certainly there may be something to that (see chapter 5). Instead, they are unique in the sense that they are interested and informed, and this draws them to the Usenet. If we are correct in this conclusion, it means the Usenet is not something that will fundamentally change people and their attitudes. Rather, it is something people use to reinforce beliefs they have already developed.

The evidence of reinforcement is found in the final section of the chapter. Newsgroups serve to protect their own dominant point of view from those who may disagree. This is an important social function, especially for people who feel like society does not reflect their point of view. Finifter (1974) pointed out that social groups often protect "misfits" or those who do not fit into mainstream society. Newsgroups appear to serve a similar function—they provide a secure environment for people to express a particular point of view. Newsgroup members do this by reinforcing those with whom they agree and criticizing, or policing, those with whom they disagree. While "misfit" sounds pejorative, that is not what we mean here. We mean someone whose beliefs are unlike those around him or her. Clearly, with their greater interest and involvement, Internet activists have the potential to see themselves as having much in common with neighbors and co-workers. Most probably find that their immediate circle of friends are not as interested and involved with politics. After all, by comparison to the activist, most of society is apathetic and indifferent. Thus, the Usenet draws a disproportionate number of political activists and dissidents who are looking for ways to express their interests and beliefs.

This brings us back to the paradox of a Democratic cadre of Internet activists and a Usenet medium full of right-wing messages. Based on the survey data in chapter 2, we would not expect the predominantly right-wing nature of the Usenet newsgroups. Based on the content analysis alone, we would predict that most Usenet participants are Republican, populist, or libertarian. Given the limitations of our data, we cannot definitively resolve this conflict. However, we can hazard a guess. We suspect that Usenet content is dominated by a relatively small and heavily active subset of Internet activists. That is, the right-wing faction of Usenet readers is far more active in posting messages than is the left-wing faction. This subset may be motivated by the sense that they are not represented by the media (see chapters 2 and 5) or by some other belief. But whatever the reason, the simplest explanation for the contradictions between chapter 2 and this one is that the right wing is simply more active.

The Usenet itself does not create anti-government or conservative attitudes. Rather, those sharing these beliefs are drawn to the medium and make better use of it. As we saw, neutral messages dominate. But every time we examined ideological threads, we found that conservatives dominated more often and more thoroughly. We also saw that right-wingers are more sophisticated in their leadership behaviors than left-wingers and that right-wing groups are better at defending themselves from ideological incursions. The left is underrepresented, the right overrepresented. If we are correct that this is a function of self-selection and not conversion, then we must wonder why right-wingers are so heavily drawn to the Usenet. We do not have an answer for that question—perhaps it is a distrust of other media or perhaps it is motivated by feelings of alienation from the rest of society. But we cannot reach any definitive conclusions yet. That will require more specific data than we currently have. Nevertheless, the pattern is clear: the Usenet draws people who are right wing and anti-government and reinforces many of those beliefs. Further evidence supporting this conclusion is offered in chapters 5 and 6.

If the Usenet continues to grow and someday tens of millions of people are using it, what will happen? Will it bring about the utopian vision of democracy with regular citizens "meeting" electronically to discuss the issues of the day? Or will it bring on the dystopian nightmare of a fractionalized society with little middle ground? Predictions of technological revolutions are notoriously fickle but we offer two tentative predictions.

First, we suspect increased use of the Usenet will lead to a watering down of its unique content. By content, we mean the aggregate or average ideology of all Usenet messages. The Usenet's content is unique because its participants are unique. If Usenet participants become more typical, so will its discourse. The more people on the Usenet, the more it will reflect the general divisions of society. We believe that someday a researcher replicating our content analysis will find that the overall ideology of Usenet threads closely parallels the overall ideology of the society being discussed. In the United States this means the left-wing messages will grow in numbers while the number of neutral messages will drop. Ultimately, the Usenet will become a reflection of the societies represented on its message boards. This gives little reason for the utopians to celebrate, however, as they may hope for a transformation, but we find little evidence that will occur (but see chapter 4).

However, the Usenet does show some of the tendencies the dystopians fear. It tends to draw people into isolated groups, conversing among themselves. Consequently, we believe newsgroups are going to become even more specialized. This means that newsgroups will emphasize particular topics from particular points of view. Conservatives will have their own newsgroups, and liberals theirs. This happens now, but as the Usenet grows, the pattern will not only continue but probably become even more apparent. The Usenet is a place of political reinforcement and support as well as debate. This means liberals will tend to avoid conservative groups and conservatives will avoid liberal groups. There will always be some crossover for those seeking confrontation. Specialization, however, will likely be the more common result. Thus, over time we expect to see two things happen on the Usenet. There will be more groups dedicated to more moderate and traditional topics to accommodate some of the newer users. But at the same time there will be more specialized and well-policed groups to provide the political support and reinforcement to particular ideologies.

Where do we go from here? First, we examine how the Usenet is used in other nations. In the United States political dissent is both legal and accepted. But that is not the case worldwide. In chapter 4, we explore how dissidents use the Usenet to protest government actions in non-democracies. Then, in chapter 5, we compare the Usenet to chat rooms to get an idea of how the medium affects the message.

Notes

1. Most computer names do not use spaces. Because of this, Usenet groups use dots or dashes to separate words.

2. Political newsgroups carry significantly more messages than non-political groups, which is why they represent more of the Usenet content than would be indicated by the number of newsgroups.

3. The only statistically significant difference in coding is that one author coded significantly more "informational" threads than the other.

4. We have lumped these two forms of anti-government behavior together for purposes of simplicity in this analysis. Had we known at the outset of this project that literally dozens of messages were questioning the legitimacy of the state itself (primarily from extreme right-wing message posters), we would have been more nuanced in our coding of this variable. Alas, this must remain unfinished work until a future component of this project.

5. Evidently no one is interested in former President Gorbachev anymore, and people prefer to post to the Limbaugh group that has the man's name spelled correctly.

Is the Internet an Instrument of Global Democratization?

Now our discussion of Usenet newsgroup use turns its focus to non–United States oriented discussion groups. As in the previous chapter, our interest here is in the political use of newsgroups. However, the analysis in this chapter is not based on left-wing versus right-wing usage of these bulletin boards. Rather, we hypothesize that people with a political interest in less democratic nations will use the Usenet newsgroups devoted to those countries as a relatively "safe" form of political discussion and even protest. Further, we expect that nationals of those countries living overseas will use these newsgroups to more openly discuss politics in those nations than they could otherwise do.

This chapter examines the content of these messages using a methodology similar to that used in chapter 3 on American politics. How many messages in these groups are explicitly political? Of those, how many are messages in opposition to the current government of the nation in question? How many messages are pro-government? Do these messages primarily serve as alternative sources of news? Are they attempts to recruit people in the subject country and around the world into some sort of political action? Are richer nations more likely to have higher levels of discussion in their newsgroups than poorer ones? These questions of content in these political newsgroups are the subject of this chapter, with our full expectation that less-democratic nations' newsgroups will contain more political and specifically anti-government discussion than the newsgroups of fully democratic countries. Formally, we propose:

Hypothesis 4.1: As the level of democratization of a country increases, the probability that a Usenet message posted about that country will be anti-government decreases

We explicitly apply this research question to the link between democracy in a nation and discussion of that nation's politics in the Internet's newsgroups. We find that political and anti-government messages in the Usenet collection of newsgroups are much more likely in groups devoted to countries that are relatively low on measures of democracy. Further, this correlation remains when other traditional predictors of democratization and Internet activity are included. We assess the implications of this link between anti-government political messages and democracy on both political communication worldwide and government attempts to regulate that electronic discourse.

How does this relate to our findings about American politics, in which conservative groups and ideas are more prevalent than liberal ones? Put simply, conservatives in the United States in the period discussed (1995–97) are a group largely out of power, since the White House during that entire period (and until at least 2001) has been controlled by the Democratic party. We hypothesize that the Internet is a natural venue for political complaining of all stripes, whether those complaints be about the current head of state's policies (as in the case of the United States), or the level of democratization in a nation. In the end, we see the Internet as a major "sounding board" and relatively safe "soapbox" from which to voice anti-government opinions.

Democracy and Communications Infrastructure

The political science literature on democratization offers little guidance on the hypothesized relationship between electronic communications and the level of democracy within a nation. This is of course not surprising, given the novelty of the Internet, e-mail, and even the widespread availability of fax machines. There are, however, some proposed links between media freedom and democratization. At a basic level, however, political scientists have proposed four major correlates to democracy: level of economic development, the "modernization syndrome" of increasing educational levels, culture, and the diffusion of power through differentiated institutions in society. It is in this last group of theories in which one finds some guidance on proposing a link between electronic political communications and levels of freedom in a country.

The most widely proposed and tested hypothesis about democracy's roots comes from the economic and political development literature. This approach theorizes that levels of democracy are strongly and positively correlated with levels of economic development (Lispet, 1959; Lerner, 1968; Lispet, Seong, and Torres, 1993; Rowen, 1995; Vanhanen, 1997). Succinctly stated, rising levels of economic development, which are usually measured by gross domestic product (GDP) per capita, cause rising levels of democratization. This is essentially an organic view of politics—the type of political system a nation has is a function of its economic system and level of development. For example, feudalism was an economic system in which peasants worked for noble landowners, who in turn paid fealty to a monarch. The natural political outgrowth of a system like this, according to an organic view of the state, is a system in which nobles have some representation with the monarch, who in turn received political loyalty from these landowners. Likewise, according to this argument, liberal democracy is a natural outgrowth of relatively new economic middle classes demanding political rights and freedoms to go along with their newfound economic prosperity. Since the current global political economy is largely a capitalist one, then we should see a natural correlation between economic prosperity and liberal democracy, according to this theory. To test this hypothesis, scholars usually construct some measure of democracy and collect aggregate level data on GDP per capita for nations.

A more nuanced, though still organic, view of democratization comes from the human development literature (Boone, 1994; Diamond, 1992). These scholars hypothesize a causal link between human development and democratization. By "human development" they usually mean aggregate levels of education and literacy in a nation, and access to health care and other services necessary to make life easier and more fulfilling for citizens of a country. The argument is simple: a healthy, more literate, more educated society is more likely to demand and receive adequate civil rights and liberties, and responsive representation—the essential ingredients of democracy. Of course, these operationalizations of "human development" and economic development are usually highly correlated, leading to problems in sorting out causality issues. Still, the direction of the causal arrows in these two arguments is clear: rising levels of human and economic development lead to rising levels of democratization in a nation.

Proposals that are more controversial have been made about the links between culture and democracy. This is of course an old argument, going back at least to Max Weber's *The Protestant Ethic and the Spirit of Capitalism* (1995). Here, scholars propose that some cultures, whether they be religious, regional, linguistic, historical, or a combination of factors, are more likely to have democratic polities than others (Huntington, 1991; Schifter, 1994; see especially Putnam, 1994 for an argument about the culture of democracy being enhanced by enduring democratic experience). In the "culture of democracy" school, however, the causal links between democracy and culture sometimes become muddied. On the one hand, is there something fundamental about "Western" culture that tends to produce a certain kind of democratic polity? On the other, has the democratic experience shaped Western culture itself? Writers in this field, while presenting considerable anecdotal evidence, never quite sort out the causal arrows. In fact, some of them are outright resistant to establishing and empirically testing cause and effect (Huntington, 1984). Nevertheless, arguments about the links between culture and democracy persist, probably in no small part because they arouse high passion.

Finally, the other major approach to studying the correlates of democratization can be called, for lack of a better term, the "diffusion of power" or "demonstration effect" school. It is this approach that seems best suited for the current analysis of the links between democracy and electronic communications. Olson (1993) and Diamond, Linz, and Lipset (1988) propose that democracy will have its best chance of survival when there is a diffusion of power throughout society. One of the essential components of this diffusion of power is the existence of free communications media. Writers such as Gastil (1985), Kedzie (1995), and McColm (1992) argue that democracy is explicitly linked to the ability of citizens to communicate political ideas to each other. One could argue that the ability to communicate effectively is surely bound up in the human development school, in that aggregate levels of education allow for better communications in a nation. Free newspapers, political magazines, radios, and television are all hypothesized to be both a *result* of democracy and a *cause* of the democratization process. Thus, there is no easy cause-and-effect relationship here. Of course, this has a certain intuitive appeal. In the pre-democratic phase, the development of opposition newspapers, pamphlets, tracts, and even radio stations builds pressure upon a government to reform or even encourage revolution. Then, as representative democracy takes hold, civil rights and liberties guarantee that free communication media remain.

In an ideal world, this is what should happen. There are, however, other complications. Gastil (1985) proposes that borders can no longer isolate political communications. No amount of jamming of broadcast signals or border checks for contraband printed material can totally stop the flow of political information from one country to another. This is the "demonstration" or "CNN" effect that the media itself has trumpeted in the last few years. For example, people in Poland, using communications media and massive social protest, cause the Communist government to fall. People listening to short-wave radios or watching satellite feeds in Czechoslovakia see this, communicate the anti-Communist Polish revolution among themselves, and in turn bring down their own Communist government. Then, after democracy is established, more and more free media develop as institutions differentiate. In the world of the 1990s, these "free media" contain another component: electronic communications, primarily computer networks such as the Internet.

In some of the first theoretical work on the subject, Howard Frederick argued that the establishment of non-face-to-face political communities was one of the hallmarks of modern society (Frederick, 1992). Beginning with reliable postal services, and extending to the invention and proliferation of the telephone, sustained communication between people in widely separated locales began to fundamentally change the ways people organize themselves politically. With the recent invention of the fax machine and the establishment of worldwide computer networks such as the Internet, geographical boundaries between people now matter less in their abilities to coordinate political information and work. Of course, this spread of information technologies has not been even. The United States continues to dominate this realm, with over 80% of Internet users and networked computers residing in North America as late as May 1997 (Intertrader, 1997). Further, skeptics fear that the development of electronic communications will only serve to exacerbate the economic and informational disparities between the developing and industrialized worlds (Panos, 1995).

Nevertheless, the fact remains that people anywhere in the world with access to an Internet-connected computer can exchange political messages with each other about any topic that they desire. Even in the face of government attempts to censor content or restrict Internet access (Internet Freedom Network, 1996), political communication about widespread global events and polities is a fact of life in cyberspace. As the results of this chapter clearly indicate, someone connected to the Internet in Bolivia can just as easily post a message to the *soc.culture.bangladesh* newsgroup as they can mail a letter to someone across town. More interesting and politically serious uses of the Internet, such as posting anti-government messages about China instead of standing in the streets of Beijing shouting anti-Communist slogans, bear careful analysis and documentation.

The Worldwide Usenet Newsgroups

As of May 1, 1997, there were approximately ninety-one Usenet newsgroups devoted to single nations. The location of almost all single-country newsgroups is in the *soc.culture* section of the Usenet. Here we find groups such as *soc.culture.spain*, *soc.culture.india*, and *soc.culture.china*. There are also about sixty other newsgroups devoted either to groups of countries or to regions within nations. Examples of newsgroups like this are *soc.culture.nordic* and *soc.culture.india.keral*. It is important to remember that these groups are very similar to the United States–based groups analyzed in chapter 3. Even though a group may carry as its name *soc.culture.canada*, the unmoderated nature of these discussion forums means that literally any message can be posted to them.

Taking the Canada group as an example, there is nothing to stop someone from posting a message to that group that is about African music, *Star Trek,* or politics in Burkina Faso. Likewise, the messages in these groups do not all have to be political. Even if people stay "on topic" in the *soc.culture.canada* newsgroup, much of the discussion may still revolve around Canadian music, hiking in Alberta, favorite recipes from Quebec, or ice hockey. Still, as we will see below, much of the discussion in these newsgroups *is* explicitly political, and significant fractions of these political messages are either pro-government or anti-government.

We could not include every one of the ninety-one single country newsgroups in our analysis, so we randomly sampled half of them. Of these, four of these groups were "extinct," in that they contained no messages, leaving us with forty-one usable Usenet newsgroups. For each of these single-country newsgroups, we first took note of the number of messages in each group during the week of October 21, 1996. Then we randomly sampled a certain number of messages from each group in proportion to each newsgroup's size. In all, 2,355 distinct messages were sampled and read fully. The number of messages per group in our sample of 2,355 ranged from a low of 13 messages in the *soc.culture.cambodia* group, to a high of 190 messages in *soc.culture.british*. Overall, for the 41 Usenet single-country groups included in our sample, there was an average of 24.03 messages per group, with a standard deviation of 11.69 messages. Table 4.1 contains the name and number of sampled messages within each newsgroup.

For each of these 2,355 messages in our sample, we coded the following four variables:

1. The ultimate domain of each person posting a message. This is the last field in a person's e-mail address. For example, a person with an e-mail address of *jdoe@aol.com* has an ultimate domain of "com," indicating that the person's e-mail account is with a commercial, United States-based provider. A message from *jacques@la-ma-chine.fr* has an ultimate domain of "fr," meaning that this person is posting a message from an Internet location in France. These domain names allow us to establish where in the world messages originate. It is crucial to keep in mind that anyone with Internet access can post to any of these newsgroups, regardless of where in the world they are. For example, there is nothing to stop someone in Taiwan from posting to the *soc.culture.bangladesh* newsgroup. By taking note of a message writer's ultimate domain, we can determine where they are. The only ambiguity that exists is in the "com," "net," and "org" messages, corresponding to commercial services and businesses, Internet backbone sites, and non-profit organizations, respectively. These addresses do not carry specific geographical information. However, almost all Internet domains within *com, net,* and *org* are located in the United States. Finally, all messages originating in the "edu" domain are from American colleges, universities, and other schools.

2. Whether or not the message is a statement about politics in the nation

TABLE 4.1
Usenet Newsgroups in Sample

Newsgroup	N of Messages	Percent Political	Percent Anti-Government	Composite Democracy Index	N of Domains in Nation
Albania	25	33.3	33.3	9.57	5
Algeria	47	20.0	10.0	0.00	2
Argentina	342	9.2	2.6	44.72	1,003
Australia	261	61.4	15.8	67.08	10,557
Austria	33	16.7	0.0	73.29	2,357
Bangladesh	260	35.1	7.0	22.69	0
Belgium	184	36.6	2.8	97.52	2,450
Bolivia	94	11.1	0.0	17.39	8
Bosnia	104	91.7	18.2	25.71	0
Brazil	142	11.6	5.8	25.47	5,577
Bulgaria	90	85.7	9.5	43.98	122
Burma	115	40.0	24.0	0.00	0
Cambodia	61	38.5	7.7	7.33	6
Canada	300	41.5	16.9	58.59	11,085
Chile	208	20.8	4.2	41.82	524
China	806	54.2	23.8	0.00	792
Colombia	91	51.5	18.2	12.92	130
Costa Rica	39	12.5	6.3	44.72	111
Croatia	125	42.9	7.1	32.92	332
Cuba	360	82.8	40.2	0.00	6
Czech	108	8.3	0.0	83.44	143
Dominican	123	0.0	0.0	20.62	19
Egypt	92	0.0	0.0	0.99	28
France	318	37.1	4.3	63.98	4,234
Germany	136	40.0	3.3	77.02	15,143
Greece	140	22.6	12.9	72.46	575
Hong Kong	388	42.4	0.0	33.13	2,299
India	541	33.6	4.2	21.86	124
Indonesia	357	34.2	20.3	1.66	210
Iran	222	20.4	0.0	3.85	8
Ireland	353	40.3	7.8	62.11	977
Israel	407	35.2	7.8	56.98	1,446
Italy	538	33.9	0.0	100.0	5,550
Japan	309	13.4	0.0	52.80	12,992
Jordan	74	0.0	0.0	2.48	45
Mexico	157	51.4	0.0	13.17	1,640
Philippines	269	13.6	3.4	38.76	119
Portugal	129	25.4	8.5	42.86	798
Spain	355	33.3	6.7	75.78	2,450
U.K.	873	14.7	0.0	69.57	26,966
Venezuela	92	16.7	0.0	31.80	110
Average	370	33.6	8.5	42.48	4,631

that is the subject of the newsgroup. Here we establish whether or not a message is political. For example, if someone posts a message to the newsgroup *soc.culture.mexico* about recipes, then the message is not political. Likewise, if a message in *soc.culture.mexico* is about politics in China, then we consider the message to be non-political, since the discussion is not about the nation in question—Mexico. Finally, if a message posted to *soc.culture.mexico* is a statement about the ruling party in Mexico City, then we do code this as a distinctly political message. Out of the 2,355 messages in our sample, we coded 791, or 33.6%, as political messages.

3. Whether or not the message is opposed to either a specific governmental policy or personality in the subject nation, or opposed to the government of that nation in general. This is our operationalization of an "anti-government" message. Again using the example of *soc.-culture.mexico*, if a person merely makes a statement offering information about the Mexican presidential elections, we consider that message to be political, but *not* anti-government. However, if someone writes a Usenet message in this group attacking the Institutional Revolutionary Party (PRI) that governs Mexico, then we code that statement as an anti-government message. Out of the 2,355 messages in the entire sample, we coded 190 as anti-government. This constitutes 8.5% of all 2,355 messages, and 24.2% of all 791 explicitly political messages.

4. Whether or not the message is explicitly *supporting* the government of the subject nation or a policy of that government. This is our operationalization of a "pro-government" message. Out of the 2,355 messages in the entire sample, we coded 150 as pro-government. This amounts to 6.4% of the entire sample of 2,355 messages, and 19.1% of the 791 explicitly political messages. Table 4.1 contains this data broken down for each of the forty-one Usenet newsgroups in our sample.

For each of our 2,355 Usenet messages, we also have several independent variables of interest. Our central hypothesis in this chapter is that people discussing politics in less-democratic nations will be more likely to post messages to newsgroups about those countries than will people discussing politics about more-democratic nations. Further, we expect that anti-government messages will be far more likely in newsgroups devoted to less-democratic nations than they will be in newsgroups about more-democratic countries. Therefore, we need to establish some type of measure of democratization for each of the forty-one nations in question.

In constructing a measure of democracy for each nation, we believe that there are three important components to any suitable definition: citizen participation in the political system, meaningfully competitive elections, and the guarantee of political rights and liberties. To this end, we constructed a composite democratization index that considers all three of these concepts about democracy.

The first two of these components were defined by Vanhanen as measures of partisan competition and electoral participation (Vanhanen, 1997). Here we quantify the percentage share of the vote captured by all non-winning parties in the latest parliamentary or executive elections. Thus, this measure can range from 0 (no parties except the winning one captured any votes) to over 50 (in cases where the party with the largest vote percentage won by a plurality instead of a majority). Vanhanen also uses a simple measure of electoral participation: the percentage of eligible voters who cast ballots in the latest elections. This measure too can range from 0 (no electoral participation allowed) to, theoretically, 100 (all eligible voters cast ballots). Finally, we add a measure of political rights and freedoms to our index. Here we take the 1994 Freedom House ratings of nations for political freedom (Kaplan, 1994). These ratings range from 1 (the most democratic nations) to 7 (the least democratic nations). We reversed the coding to make this measure consistent with the two outlined above—an increasing number corresponds to a higher level of democratization.

In constructing the composite democratization index, we simply multiplied together the measures for party competition, electoral participation, and political freedom. By multiplying instead of adding, we obtain a meaningful zero point. Here, a nation that *either* does not allow electoral participation *or* has only one party receives a zero on our composite democratization index, *regardless* of its political freedom index. We normalized this scale so that it ranges from 0 (the lowest level of democracy for these forty-one nations) to 100 (the highest level of democracy). Once again, Table 4.1 contains the democratization ratings for each of the forty-one nations represented by our forty-one single-country Usenet newsgroups. Incidentally, these three individual measures of democratization correlate with each other very highly ($r = .85$).

Another variable of interest that may help predict whether or not a message is political or anti-government is the scale of Internet access in a particular country. Internet development in a country can be measured in a variety of ways, but the most direct indicator is the number of distinct Internet domains within a nation. A domain is simply a network node that has one or more computers (hosts) or users. In fact, a single domain can be host to many thousands of users. For example, the Internet address *www.fiu.edu* is from the domain *fiu,* or Florida International University. Likewise, *tblair@parliament.uk* is the e-mail address of a user named *tblair* at the domain *parliament,* which is in the United Kingdom. There may be many hundreds or even thousands of other users at the domain *parliament.uk,* or *tblair* may be the only one. Likewise, a nation may contain from zero Internet domains (indicating no Internet presence in that country) to hundreds of thousands (e.g., the United States). We hypothesize that nations with relatively few domains have an Internet infrastructure that is easier to censor by undemocratic governments than a country with thousands of domains. So, we further expect that, somewhat paradoxically, as the number of Internet domains in a nation goes *down*, the percentage of anti-government and political messages posted to the Usenet newsgroup about that nation goes *up*. It is important to remember that, even though Cuba has only six Internet domains on the entire island—with the government controlling them all—anyone anywhere in the world is free to post messages to *soc.culture.cuba*. Still, the likelihood of someone on the island posting an anti-government message is quite low, given that the Castro regime tightly controls Internet access within the country.

What other factors might predict whether or not a given Usenet message is likely to be anti-government? One that immediately comes to mind is whether or not the message actually originates in the subject nation. After all, would we expect that a posting to *soc.culture.italy* from *luigi@machina.it* (an e-mail address in Italy) is more likely to be about Italian politics, and maybe even anti-Italian government, than a message posted to the same group from *misha@russiaweb.ru*? In addition, what about a person posting messages from "edu" sites—American educational institutions? There are many thousands of foreign-born students who attend U.S. universities, and almost all of them have Internet access through their schools. Might we not expect an Indian student at the University of Michigan with the e-mail address *apun@umich.edu* to post messages to *soc.culture.india?* And is this student more likely to feel free to write anti-Indian government statements to this group than his cousin who lives in New Delhi with the e-mail address *sanjayn@delhi.in*? This is one of the most astounding features of the Internet to those trying to come to grips with new information media. Technically, it is just as easy for someone in the United States to post to the newsgroup *soc.culture.india* as it is for someone actually in India. This is because the newsgroup *soc.culture.india* exists on thousands of host computers all over the world, and copies and updates itself almost every day at those sites. And this is one of the features of the Usenet that makes it such a ripe vehicle for anti-government protest; it is a relatively safe protest medium that is absolutely impossible to globally censor.

Finally, could there be features of the subject nations under discussion in these newsgroups that could help predict the prevalence of political and anti-government messages in these forums? Would we expect newsgroups devoted to wealthy nations like *soc.culture.germany* to contain more or fewer anti-government messages than, say, *soc.culture.bolivia*? Should nations with larger populations generate more political and anti-government discussion in their namesake groups than less populous nations' groups? That is, should we expect that *soc.culture.china* will contain a higher percentage of political messages than *soc.culture.costa-rica*? Also, does region and culture matter? Perhaps Muslim countries will have fewer political messages posted to their respective subject groups than Western European nations, simply because there are some purported cultural injunctions in Muslim society against anti-government speech that are absent in the West. All these questions are very interesting from a political point of view, and beg attention.

Anti-Government Internet Messages and Democracy

There are several ways to measure whether or not there is an association between the level of democracy in a nation and the likelihood that messages posted to that country's subject newsgroup will be anti-government. Table 4.2 presents bivariate breakdowns for the average country composite democratization index scores for anti-government, pro-government, and general political messages. For each of the three types of messages, there is a simple yes/no coding: is the message political, pro-government, or anti-government, or not?

Starting with column 1 of Table 4.2, one sees that when a message is explicitly political and posted to a Usenet country-specific newsgroup, the average democratization index for the subject country is 38.00, versus an average democracy score of 44.74 for non-political messages. Further, the difference between these two means is statistically significant. This means that political messages are more likely to be posted to Usenet newsgroups devoted to nations that are lower on our democracy scale than are non-political messages. Specifically, political messages are on average posted to

TABLE 4.2
Usenet Political Activity by Democratization of Subject Nation

	Political?	Anti-Government?	Pro-Government?
No	44.74	44.13	42.89
Yes	38.00	23.59	34.95
Average	42.37	42.37	42.37
F-value	27.35***	91.04***	10.08**

Note: Table entries are mean Composite Democratization Index Scores for the subject nations in each category.
Legend: *** $p < .001$, ** $p < .01$

newsgroups whose subject nations are 6.74 points lower on our 100 point democracy scale than are non-political messages. Thus, political discussion in these country-specific newsgroups is more likely to occur in groups devoted to less-democratic nations.

Column 2 of the table shows an even more dramatic relationship between message content and democratization levels of the nations in question. While anti-government messages are posted to newsgroups whose subject countries have an average democratization score of 23.59, non-anti-government messages (i.e., all other messages) are found in groups with an average country democratization score of 44.13. This is a difference of over 20 percentage points on a 100-point scale, and this difference is also statistically significant. Further, the difference in means here between anti-government and non-anti-government messages is much more dramatic than the 6.74-point difference between political and non-political messages. Clearly, people posting Internet messages that oppose specific governments and governmental policies are doing so in those newsgroups that are, on average, devoted to countries that are low in democratization. So, maybe people *do* use the Usenet newsgroups as a relatively safe form of political expression against less-democratic, even repressive, regimes.

Finally, column 3 of Table 4.2 indicates that pro-government messages are also more likely in newsgroups devoted to less-democratic nations. Indeed, pro-government messages as defined in this chapter are posted to newsgroups whose subject nations have an average democracy score of 34.95, while messages without explicit pro-government content are posted to groups with an average score of 42.89. This difference is approximately eight percentage points. So, at least in this bivariate analysis, messages with anti-government, pro-government, and generic political content are on average found in newsgroups whose subject nations are relatively low on our score of democratization. Further, this difference is dramatic when we specifically consider anti-government messages, which are the main theoretical focus of this chapter.

Where in the World Are These Anti-Government Messages?

Are the optimistic pundits correct? Is the Internet at this very moment being used as a vehicle of relatively safe anti-government protest by people concerned with politics in less-democratic nations? Table 4.2 suggests that the answer is yes. Still, averages only hint at real-life relationships. Another effective way of answering this question is to graphically plot the percentage of messages in a group that are anti-government by the level of democracy in that group's subject nation. This is precisely what we do in Figure 4.1. Here, the horizontal (X) axis is our 0–100 composite democratization index, the vertical (Y) axis is the percentage of messages in a newsgroup that are

89

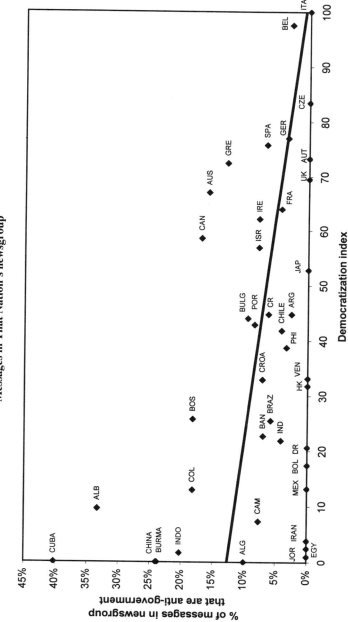

FIGURE 4.1
Democratization of a Nation by the Percentage of Anti-Government
Messages in That Nation's newsgroup

anti-government, and the data points are the corresponding values for each of our forty-one country-specific newsgroups. The downward-sloping line is the simple regression equation that fits these data, which is $Y = 12.6 - .12(X)$, where Y is the percentage of messages that are anti-government and X is the composite democratization index for each nation represented by these forty-one newsgroups. So, for every percentage point *increase* in a nation's democracy score, the percentage of messages in that newsgroup that are anti-government *decreases* by .12%. The r-square statistic for this equation, which measures how well the line fits the data, is .13, indicating that the composite democratization index explains about 13% of the variance in the percentage of messages in a newsgroup that is anti-government. So again, we have evidence that these Internet newsgroups are being used to make anti-government statements about relatively repressive governments.

An examination of the data points reveals several interesting patterns. First, we find newsgroups arrayed all along the full 0 to 100 range of our democratization measure. Therefore, our sample contains newsgroups representing a wide range of nations, from repressive to very democratic. Second, there are several interesting outliers, or newsgroups that do not fall close to the prediction line. The two most obvious of these outliers are the Cuban (*soc.culture.cuba*) and Albanian (*soc.culture.albania*) newsgroups, which both have democracy ratings of zero, but which have very high percentages of newsgroup messages devoted to anti-government discussion. Of course our regression line *does* predict that newsgroups whose subject nations score low on democratization will have relatively higher percentages of anti-government messages. Still, our model failed to predict the overwhelmingly large percentage of anti-government messages in these two repressive nations. Three other possible outliers are *soc.culture.canada, soc.culture.australia,* and *soc.culture.greece.* According to our model, these three group are "too high" in the percentage of their messages that are anti-government. Related to this finding is the fact that these newsgroups seem to cluster by the geography of their subject nations. One can easily draw a shape around the newsgroups representing the Industrialized West, the Middle East, and even Eastern Europe. With these regional clusterings of data points, we can speculate that the relationship between levels of national democracy and Usenet anti-government discussion is *region specific*, with the slope of the regression line being different for each region.

Figures 4.2 through 4.6 break out our scatterplot into six regions: the Industrialized West (the Western Europe, Canada, Australia, and Israel newsgroups), Latin America, Eastern Europe, East Asia, and the "Muslim World," which in our sample includes the Middle Eastern newsgroups along with *soc.culture.bangladesh* and *soc.culture.indonesia*. These figures are read in the same way as Figure 4.1, though the statistics for each regional regression line become somewhat unstable, given the low number of cases

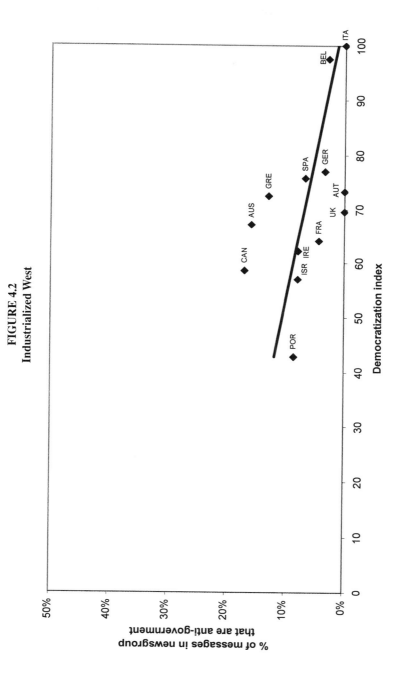

FIGURE 4.2
Industrialized West

92

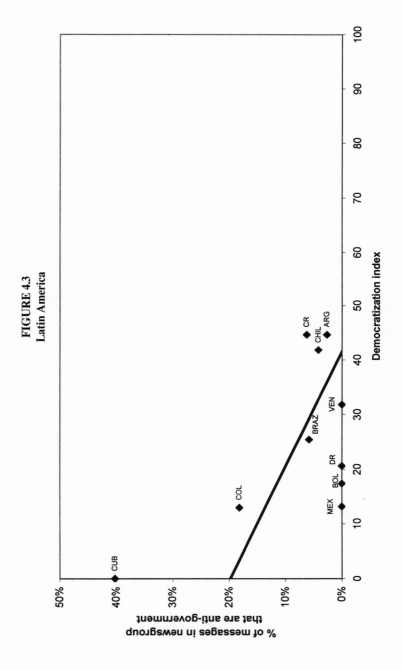

FIGURE 4.3
Latin America

in each figure. Still, we report the regression results in Table 4.3 for the sake of completeness.

Each of these five regional figures is plotted along the same scale so that valid visual comparisons are easier. The Y-axis for the percentage of messages that are anti-government ranges from 0% to 50%, while the X-axis ranges from 0 to 100 on the composite democratization index. Figure 4.2, which contains our Industrialized West newsgroups, shows a pattern similar to that of Figure 4.1, which contained all forty-one newsgroups. The level of a subject nation's democratization is still a significant predictor of a newsgroup's percentage of messages that are anti-government (the slope here is -.19, versus a slope of -.12 for all forty-one newsgroups). Looking at the graph, though, one sees that the Canadian, Australian, and Greek newsgroups still have "too many" anti-government messages, while the model also predicts that the British and Austrian newsgroups have "too few" anti-government postings (in fact, neither of these newsgroups contained *any* anti-government messages).

Figure 4.3 for the Latin American newsgroups gives us our first indication that the strength of the relationship between a country's level of democracy and the level of anti-government messages posted to that country's newsgroup is dependent on region. Here we find a much steeper regression line, with a more negative slope of -.48. This means that for the Latin American newsgroups, a one-percentage-point change in the composite democratization index corresponds to a one-half percent drop in the percentage of newsgroup messages that are anti-government. Indeed, the three Latin American nations that are generally considered to be among the most democratic in the region—Costa Rica, Chile, and Argentina—have their subject newsgroups cluster around the bottom of the regression line. Still, one must

TABLE 4.3
Anti-Government Message Frequency by Democratization of Subject Nation

	Y-Intercept (average percentage of messages anti-government in group)	Slope (relationship between anti-government message percentage and country democratization)	A ten-point increase in a country's level of democratization leads to what amount of change in the percentage of messages that are anti-government?
World	12.63	-.119	- 1.19%
Industrialized West	19.70	-.190	- 1.90%
Latin America	19.76	-.480	- 4.80%
Eastern Europe	29.20	-.400	- 4.00%
East Asia	19.40	-.440	- 4.40%
Muslim Nations	6.20	-.001	- 0.01%

94

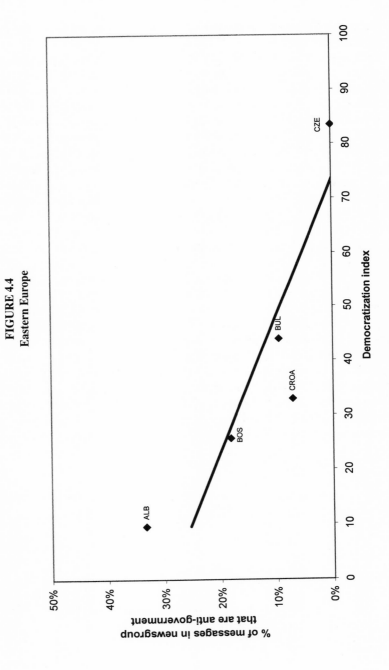

FIGURE 4.4
Eastern Europe

95

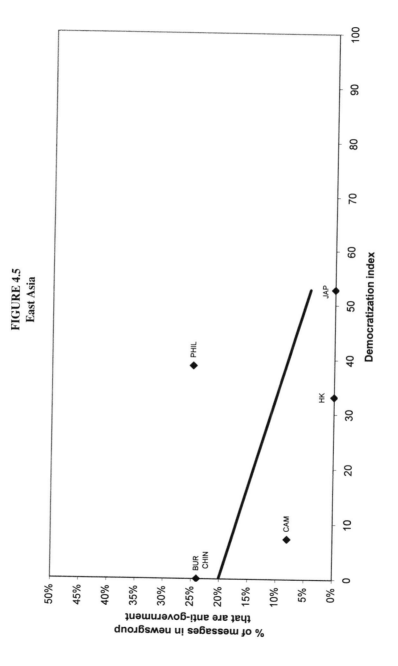

FIGURE 4.5
East Asia

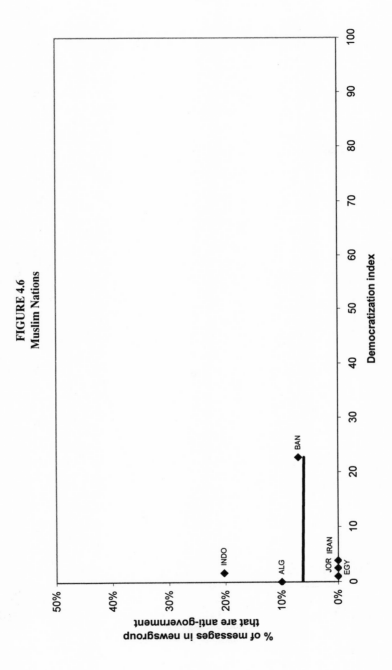

FIGURE 4.6
Muslim Nations

be careful not to read too much into this figure on its own, since *soc.culture.-cuba* is a true outlier here, and with only ten data points, its influence on the prediction line can be quite large. Then again, the same outlier status could be conveyed on *soc.culture.mexico, soc.culture.bolivia,* and *soc.culture.-dominican-republic,* neither of which contains any anti-government messages, even though their subject nations score relatively low on our measure of democracy.

The scatterplot for the Eastern European newsgroups in Figure 4.4 may be the most interesting of our regional breakdowns. With a slope of -.40, we again see a stronger regional relationship between democratization and anti-government messages posting that for the overall global scatterplot in Figure 4.1. Again using caution since we have only five data points here, these five newsgroups do fall neatly and in the predicted fashion along our regression line. The Czech Republic has the highest democratization rating of our five Eastern European newsgroups, and the lowest percentage of anti-government messages. Conversely, Albania receives a democratization score below 10 and has by far the highest percentage of anti-government messages in its subject newsgroup. Figure 4.5 for East Asia also sports a similar regression slope of -.44, but a cursory glance at the figure shows a rather poor fit. Still, the nations of East Asia that are highest in democratization have the lowest percentage of anti-government messages posted to their subject groups, a pattern that seems to endure all throughout this chapter no matter how our data are "cut and packaged."

Finally, Figure 4.6 is striking in the simple fact that it shows that in our six Muslim nations there is absolutely no relationship between a nation's level of democratization and the percentage of anti-government messages found in that country's subject newsgroup. This is more a function of almost no variance in the independent variable—levels of democratization—than any fundamental lack of relationship between anti-government messages and democracy. The fact remains that since there is so little democracy across all these Muslim nations, we can make no definitive statements about how the variance in levels of democratization affects the frequency of anti-government messages posted to newsgroups.

So, with the exception of the Muslim nations, which as we have said have precious little variance in their levels of democratization (they are all quite low), the relationship between a country's democracy level and the amount of anti-government messages in that country's subject newsgroup is significant and negative. Our original hypothesis seems true: people interested in the politics of relatively undemocratic nations are using the Internet's newsgroups to verbally blast those nations' governments. Further, they are doing so at a far higher rate than are people who complain about politics and governments in the more-democratic countries of the world. The Internet, it seems, really *is* a relatively safe tool of anti-government protest.

Who Is Posting These Anti-Government Messages?

Now we know which nations' subject newsgroups receive higher rates of anti-government messages, both in the aggregate and at the individual level of analysis. We turn now to a related and interesting question: who is posting these messages? Are these anti-government missives coming from people within the countries in question? Are they coming from students and faculty from these countries who now study in or work at American universities? Are users in certain countries more likely to post politically oriented messages? Table 4.4 presents data to answer this relatively simple, though politically important, question. Here we find a cross-tabulation of a message writer's e-mail domain by whether or not his or her message was anti-government.

TABLE 4.4
Percentage of Messages That Are Anti-Government by Sender's E-Mail Domain

	Not Anti-Government	Anti-Government	Total
Australia (.au)	82.2%	17.8%	100.0%
Brazil (.br)	96.2%	3.8%	100.0%
Canada (.ca)	85.8%	14.2%	100.0%
Commercial (.com)	90.8%	9.2%	100.0%
Germany (.de)	96.6%	3.4%	100.0%
Educational (.edu)	93.2%	6.8%	100.0%
France (.fr)	100.0%	0.0%	100.0%
Italy (.it)	100.0%	0.0%	100.0%
Network Backbone (.net)	92.6%	7.4%	100.0%
Non-Profit Organization (.org)	89.7%	10.3%	100.0%
Portugal (.pt)	86.4%	13.6%	100.0%
Sweden (.se)	97.3%	2.7%	100.0%
United Kingdom (.uk)	95.4%	4.6%	100.0%
From "Home" Nation	90.8%	9.2%	100.0%
Total (all 2,348 messages)	91.5%	8.5%	100.0%

Note: Table entries are percentages of messages from each e-mail domain with at least 25 messages that fall into each category. Other e-mail domains posting fewer than 25 messages: Anonymous, Argentina, Austria, Belgium, Bulgaria, Bolivia, Switzerland, Denmark, Dominican Republic, Spain, Finland, U.S. Government, Greece, Hong Kong, Croatia, Indonesia, Ireland, Israel, Japan, Mexico, Malaysia, the Netherlands, Norway, New Zealand, the Philippines, Singapore, Taiwan, United States, and Venezuela. Note that all "edu" messages are from colleges and universities in the United States, and that nearly all "com" messages are also from the United States.

Basically, it does not matter whether or not someone posts from an "edu," "com," "org," or "net" domain. There are no statistically or substantively significant relationships between the Internet domain of a message poster and whether or not that person's message is anti-government. This is a very interesting null finding. One may well have expected that people posting from their "home" nations—for example, a posting to *soc.culture.-belgium* from an e-mail address ending in "be"—would be more interested in the politics of that nation. One could also expect that a person would feel less safe in posting an anti-government message from a country that is less democratic, e.g., an anti-Castro message in *soc.culture.cuba* from a person in the "cu" domain. Our data show neither of these relationships. In fact, the null findings here are all the more striking when we think about the Internet as a truly international phenomenon. In the end, political and anti-government messages simply come from all over the world; the Usenet knows absolutely no boundaries.

Still, there are some interesting patterns in this data, particularly when we look at the countries of origin for some of these messages. We have included in this table all country domains from which at least twenty-five messages were received. It is important to remember that the national domains here are the e-mail domains of the senders, *and that these messages may or may not be posted to their "home" newsgroups.* For example, there are fifty-nine messages posted by people with a "de" domain, which is the German domain. Some of these messages may or may not have been posted to *soc.culture.german;* they could have just as easily been posted to *soc.culture.bangladesh.*[1] So these data give us another interesting twist: Where in the world are anti-government messages coming from? Remember that overall, 8.5% of messages are anti-government. Knowing this, several interesting facts stand out here. Notably, people posting messages from e-mail addresses in the following countries are more likely to write anti-government messages than our overall sample: Australia (17.8%), Canada (14.2%), and Portugal (13.6%). Likewise, people sending messages from the following national domains are *less* likely to post anti-government messages than our overall sample figure of 8.5%: Brazil (3.8%), Germany (3.4%), France (no anti-government messages), Italy (none), Sweden (2.7%), and the United Kingdom (4.6%). As far as measures of democratization go, there is really no pattern; all these nations except Brazil are in the industrialized West. All of them, again with the exception of Brazil, score relatively high on our composite democracy index, though Canada, Australia, and Portugal *are* three of the least democratic nations in our sample of Western nations, primarily because of the built-in moderate bias our measure of democratization contains in favor of multi-party systems.

Remember also that we only include here messages from national domains with over twenty-five messages in our sample, so that our percentage figures remain stable. If we had not placed this restriction on our data, the table would have also included messages from thrity-two additional nations. In the end, the important relationship is not between the democratization of the country where a message *originates* and the likelihood that it will be anti-government. On the contrary, the important relationship is between the democratization level of the nation *under discussion* and the chances that a Usenet posting will be anti-government. This is another significant finding that shows how utterly different the Internet is as a communications medium that does not respect national boundaries in the traditional sense. In fact, international borders are absolutely irrelevant to the discussion of world politics in the Usenet newsgroups.

Another possible predictor of whether or not someone will post an anti-government message is the size of the Internet in the subject nation. As mentioned earlier, one of the most direct ways to measure the Internet presence in a nation is to observe the number of *domains* registered in that nation. The latest domain figures available to us were from January 1997. Figure 4.7 graphs the logarithm of Internet domains in a nation by the percentage of messages in that nation's subject newsgroup that are anti-government. We use the logarithm of Internet domains for ease of visual presentation, since this figure ranges from 0 (no Internet domains in a country) to nearly 27,000 (in this case, the United Kingdom). As is apparent, there is a modest negative relationship between the development of a country's infrastructure and the percentage of messages in that nation's namesake newsgroup that are anti-government. So, as the Internet presence increases, anti-government messages as a percentage of all messages decreases, though according to the R-squared statistic, the number of domains only explains about 5% of the variance in the proportion of messages that are anti-government. Also, looking at the plotted data points one sees a similar pattern to Figure 4.1, in which democratization was plotted against anti-government messages. So, maybe the number of Internet domains in a nation is just a rough proxy for our measure of democratization; perhaps there is no "real" relationship between the two variables. This question begs to be answered in a multivariate test.

Aren't There Other Predictors of Anti-Government Postings
Besides Democracy?

What about other variables that may explain the likelihood that a message posted to the Usenet will be anti-government? How strong and direct is the relationship between electronic anti-government activity and democracy in a country under discussion? While we want to keep our analysis as simple and straightforward as possible, we really *must* include a multivariate model that considers all the major predictors of whether or not someone will make

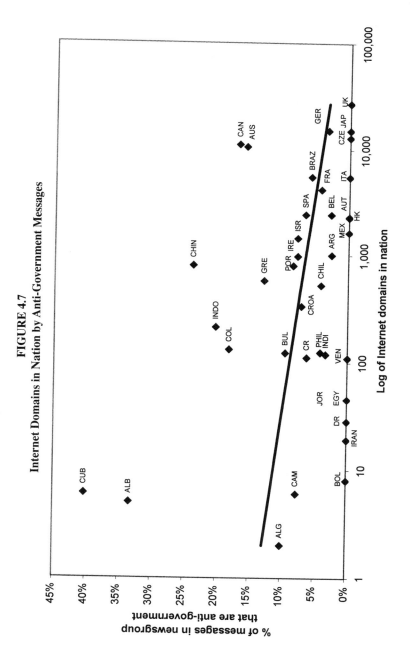

FIGURE 4.7

Internet Domains in Nation by Anti-Government Messages

104

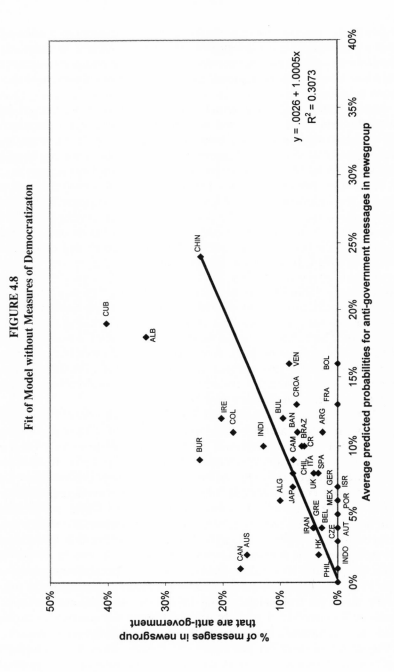

FIGURE 4.8
Fit of Model without Measures of Democratizaton

FIGURE 4.9
Fit of Model with Measure of Democratization

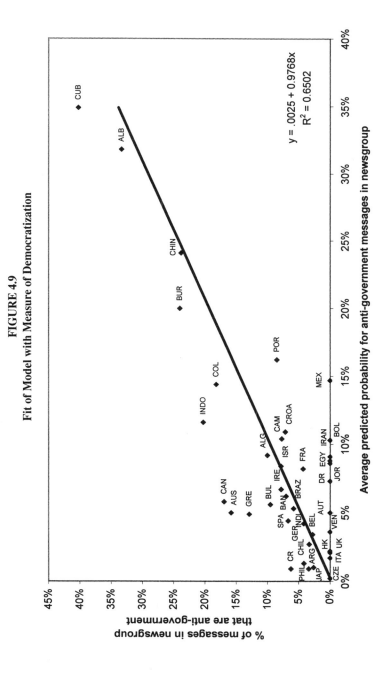

included no democracy-related information when we derived the predicted probabilities in this figure. As one can clearly see, this "control" model, which includes no information about democracy, fits our data, but in an inconsistent manner. The closer a data point falls to the line in the figure, the better the model fits for that particular newsgroup. The best possible prediction model would just have all the points falling on the line, since this would mean that the *predicted* probabilities of messages being anti-government matched the *actual* probabilities perfectly. Of course nothing in the social sciences is perfect, so we always will find some data points falling off the line. Still, a well-fitting model should have most of its points clustering near the line.

Figure 4.8, as one can plainly see, has many points that fall a considerable distance from the prediction line. In particular, this prediction model does a poor job of predicting the percentage of messages that are anti-government in the newsgroups devoted to Cuba, Albania, Burma, Canada, Australia, France, and Bolivia. In fact, the correlation between the actual percentage of anti-government messages in a group and the predicted percentage is $R = .55$; (R is a statistical measure that ranges from -1 to 1, with 0 indicating absolutely no correlation between two variables). Still, an R of .55 is a respectably large positive correlation. Remember, the independent variables used to produce these predicted probabilities of postings being anti-government only included those listed above that have nothing directly to do with our measures of democracy.

Figure 4.9 is strikingly different from Figure 4.8. Here we have the prediction results from the second model, which *did* add our measures of democratization to the mix of predictor variables used in Figure 4.8. Now the data points fall much closer to the prediction line; actual and predicted probabilities for messages being anti-government are now much closer to each other than in the previous figure. When we include measures of democratization, the newsgroups devoted to Cuba, Albania, Burma, and Bolivia fall much closer to the prediction line, while the Canadian and Australian newsgroups fall closer to the line as well. Simply stated, when we include our Composite Democratization Index to predict whether or not a message is anti-government, we obtain much more accurate predictions, this time with $R = .81$. There must be a true relationship between democratization in a nation and the likelihood that someone will post an anti-government message directed at that nation's government.

Summary and Conclusions

Politically oriented messages posted to the Usenet newsgroups are clearly not random. Chapter 3 demonstrated that conservatives are far more sophisticated in their discussions of American politics than are liberals. This, combined with the finding in chapter 2 that liberals are actually more prevalent on the Net than are conservatives is very significant. For even though there are comparatively fewer conservatives active on the Internet, their level of activity is much better organized. As we have also seen in this chapter, the behavior of individuals posting to non-American-related newsgroups is likewise predictable, though in a much different manner.

If political ideology is a significant predictor of activity in the American-related newsgroups, then the subject matter under discussion is surely the important factor in world political messages. Specifically, Internet messages about the less-democratic nations are far more likely to be anti-government than the messages about more-democratic governments. Not only is the relationship between country democracy and the probability that a message will be anti-government strong, but it is the *only* significant, consistent predictor of anti-government statements in the Usenet. The utopians that think the Internet will bring about a democratic revolution have reasons to be slightly optimistic. If the mere fact that political discourse against repressive governments is taking place is a good in itself, then the utopians have reason to celebrate. Perhaps the Internet *will* bring about a wider democratic revolution in the world. At least people *are* talking about politics and virtually protesting against less democratic governments on the Usenet.

Note

1. We would have liked to have done more analysis on this question of the origin of a message in a home domain and the likelihood that those messages would be anti-government. In the next section we do build in the origin of a message to our multivariate model, and find that messages coming from home domains are a significant predictor of whether or not a message is anti-government. But we would also have liked to have seen for *each nation* in our sample the percentage of messages in the home domains that are anti-government. Unfortunately, with forty-one nations, two categories on the anti-government variable (anti-government and not anti-government), and two categories on the "home" domain variable (yes and no), tables like this quickly become unwieldy and statistically unreliable since many table cells are empty or have only a few entries.

5

Instantaneous Political Discussion:
America Online's Chat Rooms

In chapters 3 and 4 we examined the content of Usenet political discussion. Now we turn to a study of chat rooms or Internet Relay Chats (IRCs). Our purpose is twofold. First, we replicate our chapter 3 study of the Usenet, this time focusing on chat rooms. We describe the nature and content of chat room discussions and we examine, in greater detail, the nature of debates, the ideological balance, and the amount of flaming. We follow a format similar to the analysis of Usenet messages in chapter 3. Second, we compare chat rooms and the Usenet to see whether the medium in some way affects the message.

How do chat rooms differ from the Usenet? Chat rooms and IRCs serve functions similar to that of Usenet groups in that both are forms of interactive communication.[1] On the Usenet, people post messages for someone to read and respond to at a later time. In a chat room people type messages and others read and respond to them *immediately*. It is a "chat" in the sense that the conversation happens in real time—it is instantaneous. The immediacy of feedback and reactions from others make chat rooms more interactive and faster paced than the Usenet. For example, this is an excerpt from a discussion that took place in August 1996 between three people we name Bob and Jack, and Tom:[2]

> Bob: be real the military still controls a disproportionate amount of the federal budget
> Jack: Bob: What is a proportionate amount?
> Bob: the military budget is 270 billion dollars
> Tom: 75% of the total budget is social spending . . . the rest is incidental . . . ie. military, debt

Bob, responding to an earlier comment, makes his case that military spending is too large. Immediately, Jack and Tom respond to Bob's assertion. This quick response is not possible on the Usenet. However, chat rooms suffer from a limit on the size of the messages being typed. As exemplified above, chat rooms typically limit messages to approximately 100 characters or just over a single line of type. Within this limitation it is very difficult to make detailed arguments or extended points.

Given the similarities between chat rooms and the Usenet, we expect some of the findings in chapter 3 to be replicated here. Based on our hypotheses and findings from chapter 3, but in contrast to chapter 2, we expect chat rooms to have a right-wing and anti-government tilt and to be debate-oriented. However, the limited format and quick reaction time of the chat room should cause chat room conversations to differ from the Usenet. We explore this in the last section of the chapter when we compare the Usenet and chat rooms. For now, we can make some educated guesses or hypotheses as to how conversations in the chat room will be affected. Chats are likely to be more stimulating because of their immediacy, so we will expect a great deal of debate. The immediacy should also focus chat room discussions on current events. The limited space for messages, however, will result in lower levels of sophistication, which means less verifiable information and more ad hominem or personal attacks. Finally, because chat rooms tend to be general areas, not specialized by topic as are newsgroups, we expect there to be a limited amount of recruiting. After all, given a broader audience, recruitment has less potential reward. Summarized, these hypotheses are:

> *Hypothesis 5.1: Chat rooms' threads are right wing and anti-government*
>
> *Hypothesis 5.2: Chat rooms are primarily debate-oriented*
>
> *Hypothesis 5.3: Chat rooms provide limited information*
>
> *Hypothesis 5.4: Chat rooms contain a significant amount of flaming*
>
> *Hypothesis 5.5: Chat rooms emphasize current events*
>
> *Hypothesis 5.6: Chat rooms have limited recruiting*

Data and Analyses

As stated above, our first purpose in this chapter is to describe the content of chat room dialogues. To do this, we first must find a chat room. Most commercial on-line services provide chat rooms dedicated to particular topics. Of course, most of these topics are related to dating, sex, or computers, but some are related to politics. We selected the primary political chat room on the largest commercial service—America Online (AOL). We chose to use a commercial chat room instead of an Internet Relay Chat because, in our experience, IRCs are more likely to stray away from political topics. By contrast, America Online provides several rooms dedicated to politics. The most notable of these is The Cloak Room, named for the rooms off the floor of the House and Senate where members of Congress often broker deals.

America Online's Cloak Room is open to all members and will have between twenty-five and forty participants on a given night.

To understand the discussions that take place in the chat rooms, we randomly recorded Cloak Room discussions over a 20-week period. The first 10 weeks' recordings were made from August through October of 1996 to capture discussion of the election. The second 10 weeks of logs were recorded during the relatively less political period of February through April, 1997. For each week, we randomly selected an evening.[3] For any given night, we randomly selected a time between 8:00 P.M. and 1:00 A.M. EST and recorded, or logged, approximately 30 minutes of the discussion. These twenty logs are our database of chat room discussion.

Analyzing the logs required two steps—organizing and coding. Recall from chapter 3 that Usenet messages are organized by their subject headings to create threads. This makes them easier to code, since our Usenet reader automatically organizes all the messages into threads based on the headers. Unfortunately, chat rooms are not so easily organized. In a chat room, thirty people may be carrying on ten or fifteen discussions at the same time. This is akin to a party with several small groups each discussing something different. But for someone who is trying to listen to all of the conversations, with so many messages being typed at the same time about so many topics, the "threads" of the conversations can become jumbled. For example, consider the discussion of military spending between Bob, Jack, and Tom. While they were talking, so were several others and for those "reading" along, the actual conversation looked more like this:

Bob: be real the military still controls a disproportionate amount of the federal budget
Alex: OGrady was great!
Richard: Everyone—your politicol solution is Richard Lamm
Fred: Never trust a politician who denies there bald by using the grand combover
Irene: Yea I can't wait, till the Dem's get on and tell it like it is
Steve: Nice speech by Powell the hippocrite—equal opportunity for all except if you're gay.
Carl: Summer, get a life
Jack: Bob: What is a proportionate amount?

We italicized Bob' and Jack's comments to help show how jumbled the conversation in which the two comments quoted earlier appeared actually was. Between just two lines of Bob and Jack's conversation were six other lines, each part of some other conversation. To address this problem, we read through the log and reordered it to reflect the actual conversations. When this was completed, each conversation resembled the first one quoted above.

As in chapter 3, each thread constitutes one case or unit of analysis. Over the 20-week period, we coded 295 pre-election threads and 217 post-election threads for a total of 512 chat room conversations.

The problem of coding is easier to address than that of organizing. After organizing the threads, we coded each chat room discussion in a manner very similar to the one we followed for chapters 3 and 4. Of course, given the differences between The Cloak Room and the Usenet some changes were required. In chapter 3 we coded information about the "leader" or the person that started a thread. This was not possible since we often picked up in the middle of the conversation and so could not identify the leader. For the Usenet we also examined the "group's" ideological norm. Since chat rooms are not subdivided by topic we could not code for that either. However, we did code for the ideology of the overall thread, whether it was anti-government, was a debate, provided verifiable information, was about current events, attempted to recruit others, or resulted in a flame-fest.

Having learned from our analyses of the Usenet, we also added several new variables. The first is anti-media. Basically, this is a measure of whether the thread blasts the mainstream media, lauds it, or does not discuss it. We also coded for the number of participants in each thread, whether the discussion was about the 1996 election, and what day and time it took place. Finally, we described, or coded each thread as being "easy," "hard," or neither. The easy/hard distinction is important to us because it is a rough measure of the potential for electronic democracy to enhance our deliberative process. Carmines and Stimson (1980) suggest that hard issues are closer to the democratic norm of the informed and thoughtful citizen. This is what the utopians envision as being a major contribution of computer-mediated technologies. By "easy," Carmines and Stimson mean an issue that is more symbolic than technical, deals with policy ends rather than means, and has been on the political agenda for a long time (1980). Of these, the criterion we focused on is that of policy ends versus means. Easy issues typically focus on *what* should be achieved while hard issues emphasize *how* we will achieve it. For example, an argument that taxes should be lowered would be an easy issue, while a debate concerning the merits of a capital gains tax would be considered a hard issue. In chapter 3 we suggested that the Usenet tended toward normative debates. Now, we have a more direct measure of it. Of course, a thread could be neither easy nor hard. Such threads are typically about people and events and not about actual government policies.

Chat Room Content

We begin by describing the basic nature of chat room political discussion. The information is presented in Table 5.1 using three columns: one for

TABLE 5.1
Characteristics of Chat Room Discussions

	Pre-Election	Post-Election	Total
1. Mean / Median number of chatters in thread	5 / 3	5 / 3	5 / 3
2. Mean / Median length of messages in thread	14 / 5	23 / 8***	18 / 5
3. Percent of threads that are debates	30.8	38.7	34.2
4. Percent of threads that contain verifiable information	14.6	10.1	12.7
5. Percent of threads that are: easy	20.7	29.5	24.4
neither	77.6	69.6	74.2
hard	1.7	0.9	1.4
6. Percent of threads that are a flame-fest	23.7	19.8	22.1
7. Percent of threads that are: right-wing	51.5	56.7**	53.7
neutral	35.3	39.6	37.1
left-wing	13.2	3.7	9.2
8. Percent of threads that are: pro-government	0.3	0.9	0.6
neutral	84.4	81.1	83.0
anti-government	15.3	18.0	16.4
9. Percent of threads that are: pro-media	0.7	0.0*	0.4
neutral	92.2	97.2	94.3
anti-media	7.1	2.8	5.3
10. Percent of threads involving recruitment	2.3	1.8	2.1
11. Percent of threads about current events	64.4	28.6***	49.2
12. Percent of threads about the 1996 election	46.8	5.5***	29.3
Number of cases or threads	295	217	512

Note: asterisks represent significant differences between pre- and post-election samples.
Legend: *** $p < .001$, ** $p < .01$, * $p < .05$

prior to the election, one for after, and one for all threads. We also mark the percentages that represent statistically significant differences between the pre- and post-election samples. As with Chapter 3, each section of the table is numbered and as we discuss each section we present more detailed analyses.

Thread Length

In lines 1 and 2 we present the mean and median numbers of people taking part in the thread and the number of messages contained in the thread. Line 1 shows that most threads have only a few participants—typically about three for both the pre- and post-election. Some, however, have more than twenty participants, but these are few in number.

As shown in line 2, the length of the threads is more variable. In a pattern reminiscent of the Usenet, as most threads are relatively short—a mean of eighteen lines and a median of five.[4] But a few threads are incredibly long—on the order of 150–300 messages. This skews the mean toward the long messages and accounts for the large difference between the mean and median number of messages. As with the Usenet, many threads are quite short (just one or two lines) but a few are very long. Perhaps most interesting, however, is that the length of messages is much higher in the post-election sample. We cannot say for certain why this happened, but it seems to be a combination of two trends. Current events tend to splinter off more rapidly into other conversations while older, more established, issue discussions tend to remain focused. The pre-election sample contained significantly more current events discussion. Second, before the election much of the talk centered on events and actions, and these require less debate and discussion. Thus, the number of messages increased in the post-election period. Unfortunately, many of the differences are statistically nonsignificant and so we cannot reach a firm conclusion.

Debates

Hypothesis 5.2 proposes that chat rooms will be primarily debate-oriented. It turns out in line 3 of Table 5.1 that only one in three threads is actually a debate. On its face, this would suggest that chat rooms are highly amicable places. The reality turns out to be somewhat different. We saw in chapter 3 that many non-debate threads are quite short. The same is true in chat rooms. Of the non-debate threads, many are just a single message (18%) and some are comments made by only one person (25%). This means that while there are a lot of non-debate *threads*, they constitute a much smaller portion of the *total content*. So, again we exclude the single-sentence threads and look only at those with more than one message. With single-message exclamations excluded, the percentage of debates rises to 42% (N = 422), but debate still remains in the minority.

However, if we measure debate activity as a function of total message content, we get a different picture. Non-debate threads are very short compared to debate-oriented threads (7 versus 40 messages, p < .01). Thus, on a per-thread basis, the typical debate represents about six times more message content than a non-debate thread. Put differently, the total number of messages in our sample is 9,240 in 512 threads. Of these messages, 6,944 are part of the 175 debate threads while only 2,296 messages are part of the 337 non-debate threads. So, while it appears that debate threads are in the minority, the reality is that they represent the bulk of the chat room messages and so also represent a much higher average number of chat room participants (9 versus 4, p < .01).

Information and Issue Type

In line 4 we examine the provision of verifiable information. We hypothesized above that the speed and immediate nature of chat rooms would make it more difficult for people to provide verifiable information. We find exactly that. Information can be found in about 13% of all chat room conversations. There is a slight difference between the pre- and post-election but it is not statistically significant. Even though we classified something as simple as "Hey, everyone turn on C-Span to see . . ." as informative, the amount of verifiable information is rather limited, thus confirming Hypothesis 5.3. The lack of information is probably related to a decline in the quality of the debates being held in chat rooms.

Line 5 examines the types of issues debated in our sample. Again, we classified each thread as discussing an easy issue (about policy goals), hard (about policy means), or neither (not about policy). We see that fully three-fourths of all chat room threads fall into the neither category. Moreover, only 1% of the 524 threads were classified as being "hard" discussions of policy alternatives. However, the discussion of issues rises somewhat in the post-election sample. The differences shown in Table 5.1 are marginally significant (p < .10). But if we combine easy and hard issues together and compare issue threads to non-issue threads, we see that there is slightly more issue discussion after the election (30% to 22%, p < .05). Because of the dearth of "hard" threads, from here on we will combine the easy and hard threads to create an issue versus non-issue variable.

In short, policy discussion in The Cloak Room is quite limited and what little does occur is overwhelmingly easy in nature. As we suspected but could not prove with the Usenet, chat room discussions are primarily about people and events with normative policy debates coming in a distant second. Chat rooms provide little opportunity for detailed discussion about government programs, even though chapter 2 demonstrated that Internet activists are among the most educated and informed citizens in the nation.

Flaming

If the debates largely focus on individuals and their actions, are they also personal in their criticisms? The answer appears to be no. In fact line 6 shows that flames make up only one of every five threads. Even when limited to threads with two or more participants, the percentage of flames changes very little. Whether this is high or low depends on your frame of reference. We suspect, based on the research reviewed in chapter 1, that most face-to-face discussions are not so confrontational. But, the number is about the same as what we found on the Usenet and certainly does not represent anything like a dominant type of thread. Thus, our hypothesis that flames would be more prevalent in chat rooms is unsupported.

Ideology and Attitudes Toward Government and the Media

In lines 7 through 9 of Table 5.1 we examine the ideological orientation of the threads. Chapter 2 showed that Internet activists are not necessarily more right wing, and chapter 3 found a plurality of Usenet messages are neutral but that right-wing messages outnumber left-wing ones. For the chat room, we counted the number of right, neutral, and left leaning messages in each thread and then assigned each thread an ideological value—left, neutral, and right. How does the chat room compare to our earlier findings? Line 7 shows that, of the entire sample, just over half (54%) of the threads are right wing. Remembering that the ideological direction is coded as the dominant point of view for the thread, this suggests that right-wing chatters are more "vocal" or active in the chat room even if they are not necessarily more numerous, as suggested in chapter 2. Of course, they could be both more numerous and more vocal. So yes, the right does dominate the chat room and apparently to an even greater degree than on the Usenet.

The domination of the right does vary somewhat between the pre- and post-election samples. Left-wing threads are significantly more common prior to the election, 13% compared to 4%. This can be interpreted in a couple of ways. On the one hand, right-wing chatters certainly had less to boast of during the weeks prior to President Clinton's reelection and they may have been reticent about speaking out. On the other hand, the consistent lead held by Clinton may have emboldened left-wing chatters, thereby encouraging their greater participation. Since the increase in left-wing threads is higher than the decrease in the right-wing threads, we think the latter explanation to be more likely. Of course, even at their best, left-wing threads are outnumbered by right-wing threads four to one.

Given the dominance of the right wing we can expect many of the messages to be anti-government. These could take the form of quoting, "The government that govern best governs least," or something as simple as, "Government always screws things up!" Either way, we can see that anti-government messages considerably outnumber pro-government ones, 16% to 0.6%. This pattern remains the same for both the pre- and post-election—in both cases pro-government threads are extremely rare. When they do occur, the typical pro-government thread is related to supporting the nation's defense (right wing) or regulating the environment (left wing). The most common, thread, however is neutral with regard to the government.

How can most (54%) messages be right wing but so few (16%) be anti-government? As we discussed in chapter 3, we believe the answer lies in the nature of on-line debate. Earlier we suggested the low proportion of anti-government messages was due to the relatively high percentage of threads focusing on people and events. The same is true in chat rooms. Most threads discuss what politicians are doing or have done (or supposedly did, or should have done, etc.) but do not deal with government policies. This can readily be seen by looking back at line 5 of Table 5.1—most threads are non-issue-oriented. As they have little to do with the role and scope of government, few threads can be classified pro- or anti-government even though most are ideologically right wing. For example:

Roy: Thanks to Bob Dole for a fine debate.

Alan: Dole's biggest mistake was not make more of the decline in women's wages

Alan: and disparity between Men's and Women's incomes which is now at an all time high

Tom: Dole totally skirted the questions and repeated himself continuously.

Steve: Dole did better than expected . . . but has no chance

Roy: He represented himself well and will improve the next time.

Will: His appeal to Xers was frivolous

Alan: He could have received some converts on that one

Jack: why all the fuss CLINTON is the winner has been and will always be

Matt: I don't think the constitution covers any of the "issues" "debated" tonight!!!

Tom: Dole has nothing of interest to say.

Roy: And President Clinton did?

Cindy: I must say—Dole was funny tonight.

In this excerpt, we see a clear partisan debate that has little to do with government policies, but is instead a reaction to a presidential debate. We can also see that eight of the messages are right wing (those by Roy, Alan, Matt, and Cindy), while the four messages from Tom, Will, and Jack are left wing; Steve's message falls somewhere toward the middle. In short, we see that most messages have little to do with the government and government policies, focusing instead on events and people.

Finally, what of the media? We found in chapter 2 that the feelings toward the mainstream media did not represent a significant motivational force for on-line activists. Do the AOL chats follow suit? Table 5.1 shows that they do—very few threads are about the media. In the post-election sample, however, the media became even less of an issue, so it is really the pre-election period we should examine. During the pre-election we see that the ratio of negative to positive messages is eight to one, with 7% of the threads criticizing the media. Below we examine this in more detail, but for now we can easily see that the media are not a common topic of conversation but when they do come up, the chatters are overwhelming negative.

Recruitment and Current Events

The last three lines of Table 5.1 examine recruitment and current events discussion. We hypothesized that recruitment would be difficult in chat rooms because of the fast response time and the limited space for messages. It appears, from line 10, that we are correct. Chat room participants seem quite reticent about recruiting people to join their cause—just 2% of 524 threads involved recruitment of others. The Usenet may provide fertile ground for finding like-minded people to join your cause. Chat rooms can also help people find others who share similar points of view, as witnessed by the large number of non-debate threads. But people do not typically use chat rooms to recruit others to their cause, probably because of the wide variety of opinions being expressed.

Finally, in lines 11 and 12 we examine current events and discussions of the 1996 elections. By definition, both current events and the 1996 election are topical. By that we mean that they are issues that are important for a while and then fade from our thoughts. This can be seen dramatically in line 12 by comparing the pre- and post-election percentages for current events and the election. While about one-half of the total threads dealt with a current event, that number is 64% prior to the election and only 28% afterward. Of course, this picture is even more dramatic for election-oriented chatting, which dropped from 47% to less than 6% after the election. Another way to look at it, however, is to note that during the height of a presidential campaign, 50% of the political talk had no connection to the election and 35% had nothing to do with anything happening at that time. So our hypothesis that current events would dominate the chat room appears to be inaccurate. Chat room participants are at least equally and perhaps even more likely to engage in discussions of old topics, especially if there is no major ongoing event.

Altogether, Table 5.1 gives us a good overview of the nature of chat room discussions. We can see that current events are popular but do not dominate, and that this depends on what is happening at that time. The threads have limited information, are usually not debates, and are typically friendly, in that flames are a minority of all threads. Few actual issues or government policies are debated, with the norm being discussions of events and personalities. But whatever the topic, the right wing dominates the room and to a greater degree than it dominated the Usenet. This gives us a good start toward understanding chat room dynamics.

Relationships between Debating, Flaming, Information, and Ideology

As we did in chapter 3, we now explore some of our findings in more detail. Our interest is to see what kinds of issues are debated or not debated, who dominates the debates, and how others react to all of this. We first look in more detail at debates and non-debates. Then we examine the characteristics of right- and left-wing threads. Finally, we take a second look at flaming and its place in Internet political discussion. Again, we present most of our results in parenthetical form along with the level of significance.

A debate, by definition, requires at least two people. Consequently, for our study of debates we exclude any thread that has only one person writing. Then we analyze the remaining messages to see how the debates differ from the non-debates. Our goal is to determine what a debate in a chat room is like—what kinds of issues are debated, what kinds of comments are made. We already know that debates tend to be longer than non-debates. What else can we say about them?

To begin, we see that debate threads have less information than non-debate threads (6% versus 20%, $p < .01$). The same result was found earlier for Usenet debates. In chapter 3 we offered two explanations. The first was the idea that debates are about normative issues and this in turn requires limited information. In chapter 3 this explanation was mostly guesswork. Now, using our easy/hard issue dichotomy, we can test the explanation directly. We find that debates are significantly more likely to be about easy issues (45% versus 17%, $p < .01$). Debates are not significantly related to hard issues (2% versus 1%), but this is probably because so few hard issues are debated. The much greater easy-issue content suggests that on-line debates do have the potential to be substantive. But this is still tempered by the fact that just over half of the debates are about non-issues. Non-issues, because they focus on people and events, may actually demand more information. The emphasis on easy issues, while good from the standpoint of policy deliberation, lowers informational requirements, at least compared to a discussion of a debate or speech where one might reference a current newspaper article.

Our second explanation for the lower levels of information in debates emphasized the informative role of recruitment threads. Clearly this does not apply to chat rooms, given the very low level of recruitment. Instead, the fact that about 80% of information threads are non-debates suggests that chat rooms use information differently. Rather than use information to recruit, the chat room participants seem to share it. For example, here two chatters discuss a *Wall Street Journal* article about the Whitewater scandal:

Tom: Did anyone see that great WS Journal piece on Clinton today?
Mike: No, I missed it, what did it say?
Tom: Showed how Clinton funnelled money in whitewater
Mike: I will have to look for it!
Tom: I have it on disk and will email it you.

Tom is not seeking Mike's help or support. Rather, Tom wants to support others sharing his beliefs by sharing information. Thus, we find debates have less information for two reasons. First, debates are normative rather than objective and second, information is most often shared with people holding similar beliefs.

How do people respond to debates? We would hope debates cause people to dig deeper into their issues and present more logical and well-defended ideas. But we know from chapter 3 that they may also get angry and start flaming their antagonist or his or her ideas. For example, in this conversation, the participants make known their presidential preferences:

Mark: DOLE = DEAD.
Bill: Clinton = Lier.
Sue: WISHY WASHY = CLINTON
June: Age Challenged = Dole

Unfortunately, as we found in chapter 3, flames are about twice as likely to occur in the context of a debate (32% versus 16%, p < .01). It makes sense that ideological disagreements increase the likelihood of anger coming out. It also makes sense that longer threads and threads with more participants are more likely to end up in personal attacks. But there is some good news. First, most debates are not flame-fests. Second, and perhaps most importantly, flames occur most often in non-issue oriented threads—83% of all flames occur in non-issue-oriented threads. This remains true even when we examine just debate threads (80%). A non-issue flame is typified by our example above; it is difficult to find much issue content in such a discussion. Obviously we cannot know if issues deter flaming or if flaming deters issues, but we can see that debating issues is possible and, when it does occur, the participants are generally friendly in their disagreements.

Finally, we turn to the ideological differences between debates and non-debates. Debates show a slight tendency to be more ideological, but the difference is not significant (66% versus 60%, n.s.). Unlike our findings in chapter 3, conflict is not necessarily increased when messages are ideological. Part of the reason for this may be the dominance of the right wing in our sample. With so many right-wing threads (see Table 5.1), a right-wing message is not likely to stir up much debate. In fact, any increase in the number of debates is likely to come exclusively from the left. We see that is indeed the case. Left-wing threads are over twice as likely to be a debate (4% versus 10%), while right-wing threads are found equally in debate and non-debate threads (56% versus 56%). In short, a message in dominant ideology prompts little debate while an expression of a minority viewpoint creates much more of a reaction.

There is a much clearer relationship between debate and anti-government messages. Debate threads are more likely to criticize the government (23% versus 14%, p < .01). This fits nicely with our findings regarding issue discussion. Most easy issues are about the goals or ends of policies—what we as a society should do. As such, they are often normative, focusing on what people think should be done as opposed to how we will do it. In a right-wing atmosphere such as The Cloak Room, this will result in messages like, "Government should get out of education entirely." What we find is a strong tendency for debates to be both normative and opposed to government activity. For example, 17% of ideologically neutral messages are either easy or hard issue discussion, while only 67% of anti-government and all of the pro-government messages are issue-oriented. It may seem contradictory that debates are more anti-government but not more right wing. This is at least partially due to the fact that many left-wing groups oppose government programs such as the regulation of abortion and defense build-ups. Also, we should note that there is no difference between debates and non-debates with regard to the mainstream media. Unfortunately, given the very small number of threads concerned with the media, this is not something we can readily explore.

In summary, debates tend to be much longer and involve more people. This means they are a smaller portion of all threads but a much larger portion of all content. Debates tend to have less information and more flaming, but also are somewhat more easy-issue-oriented. Specifically, debates tend to be more anti-government, but are not more anti-media or more ideological. The preponderance of easy issues over hard ones suggests a normative style of debate—arguing over the way one thinks things should be, not necessarily how we should get there. Moreover, debaters seem to think that "what should be" is far less government.

Now we can examine the right-wing nature of chat rooms in a bit more detail. We begin with what we know from above. Table 5.1 shows us that the majority of threads in The Cloak Room are right wing in nature. Remember, this does not mean the majority of the *people* are right wing. We don't know anything about the individuals chatting there, but chapter 2 does suggest that Democrats are more likely to be active in places like The Cloak Room. Our data, however, refer only to the overall nature of each thread. We know that ideology is not related to debating. So what is ideology related to? Well, we find that right-wing threads have more chatters than left-wing threads (6 versus 4, $p < .05$) as well as more messages (22 versus 9, $p < .05$). Since right-wing threads are unrelated to debating, which we also know increases chatters and messengers, we see this as evidence that right-wingers are either more numerous or more active or both. Unfortunately we cannot say for certain which of these is true, but the evidence from chapter 2 showing Internet activists to be more Democratic supports the conclusion that right-wingers are more active but not more numerous.

What about the ideological threads themselves? Are ideological debates more informative than neutral ones? We find that both right- and left-wing threads contain less information than neutral threads. Combined with the negative relationship between debate and information, we believe this further indicates a tendency for information to be offered, perhaps shared, but not discussed. Ideology is related to the type of issue being discussed. Right-wing threads are significantly more issue-oriented than left-wing or even neutral threads (31% versus 19% and 20% respectively, p < .01). This is almost certainly a result of the fact that right-wing threads are much more heavily anti-government than left-wing and neutral threads (26% versus 2% and 6% respectively, p < .01). Recall from our description of issue and non-issue threads that anti-government threads would tend to be easy-issue-oriented as opposed to non-issue-oriented ones (67% versus 33%, p < .01). Thus, right-wing threads tend to be much more anti-government and much more issue-oriented than left-wing and neutral threads. This anti-government bias of the right wing makes perfect sense—we expect people on the right to be less supportive of government.

What does not make much sense is that left-wing threads are rarely pro-government (2%) or even anti-government (2%). Instead, the left is over-whelming neutral with regard to the government. This takes us back to Table 5.1 where we saw that left-wing threads were more common in the pre-election. We suggested this was due to the supportive environment created by Clinton's easy lead in the election. This probably led to an increase in left-wing chatting about the election and this in turn accounts for the lack of issue discussion within left-wing threads.

Are right-wingers also anti-media? We see a small relationship between perceptions of the media and the ideological direction of threads, but the significance of the finding is marginal at best (p < .10), so we examined just right- versus left-wing messages and found that, while the right wing is more anti-media (7% versus 0%), the relationship is weak (p < .10). In other words, right-wing threads may be slightly more anti-media than left-wing ones, but at the most this is a small relationship.

Before moving on to our discussion of flaming, we want to touch upon one new issue. As we described above, The Cloak Room was monitored from 8:00 P.M. to 1:00 A.M. EST, or from 5:00 P.M. to 10:00 P.M. on the West Coast. Obviously from 5:00 until about 8:00, most people will be at work or eating dinner. Consequently, the West Coast would be underrepresented during these hours. So, we coded for Pacific Time and checked to see if there was a difference between threads recorded after 11:00 P.M. EST or 8:00 P.M. PST. We found that after 11:00 P.M. EST, when people on the West Coast are likely to be on-line, there are significantly more left-wing threads (12% versus 7%, p < .01). While this is unsurprising (the West Coast tends to be more liberal than the East Coast), it does point to the importance of knowing who is on-line at a given point in time. Were this an international chat, analogous to chapter 4, for example, time zone differences would be even more dramatic.

Finally, we turn to a more detailed look at flaming. Again, we are concerned with flaming because it is the antithesis of deliberative debate. If deliberation and democracy are to flourish on the Internet as utopians hope, flaming must be kept to a minimum. People's ideas should not be suppressed by the vitriol of others. Nor should the weight of one's position be based on the vehemence with which is it propounded. So what could limit flaming?

The most obvious answers are either censorship or some kind of "censureship." Flames could be eliminated from the discussion by some controlling entity such as the government or the host of the particular debate. But this kind of censorship is a large part of what the Internet is supposed to avoid in the efforts to create an electronic utopia. So what of censuring individuals who are particularly incendiary? America Online has hired "hosts" who take part in The Cloak Room's discussions and try to moderate them. They do not censor comments, which means they cannot reject and delete chat room messages. They do, however, try to maintain a friendly room through admonishments, peer pressure, and potential sanctions such as being suspended from the room. Most evenings, The Cloak Room is hosted and so our sample of chats without hosts is somewhat small (N = 121, or 24%). However, it is enough to compare rates of flaming with non-flaming. What we find will be somewhat disappointing for utopians. Flames are equally common in hosted and un-hosted chats (21% versus 25%, n.s.). This does not mean a host cannot possibly stop flaming, but it does suggest that the host would have to have a lot of power over chatters and be willing to use it, in order to be effective. As it stands now, on America Online at least, the hosts have had little success in deterring flaming.

If flaming is to be decreased, it will be necessary to understand the sources of flaming. We know from above that flaming is related to debates. We know also, from chapter 3, that flaming is less common when information is presented. Is information also inversely related to flaming in chat rooms? The answer is yes—only 6% of flame-fests were informative while 15% of non-flames supplied verifiable information ($p < .01$). Also, debating issues has a similar effect, with the percentage of flames dropping from 25% to 15% when issues were debated ($p < .05$). So while flaming does increase in debates, it is lowered when issues are discussed and verifiable information is presented. This should reinvigorate the utopian hopes for a deliberative democracy. Issues and information seem to deter flaming and they are precisely what computer-mediated democracy is supposed to encourage. Unfortunately, in our chat room sample, issues and information are quite limited.

What happens when the discussion turns ideological? Since ideological threads are also less informative and more debate-oriented, flaming should be more common when threads are ideological. This is exactly what we find. Left-wing and right-wing threads have the most flames (36% and 27%, respectively), while neutral threads have the least (11%, $p < .01$). While it appears flames are more common in left-wing threads, when we compare only right- and left-wing threads, we find no significant difference in the percentage of flames. But if we compare ideological threads (right and left) versus non-ideological, the differences are stark. Ideological threads (right or left) are nearly three times as likely to be flames as are non-ideological threads (29% versus 11%, p < .01). As with debating, ideological conflict leads to angry responses and personal attacks.

To summarize, we find that flaming is more common in debates and more common when threads are ideological. This does not bode well for electronic deliberation—after all, we need to be able to discuss our ideological differences. There is, however, some good news. We find that flaming is less common when threads provide verifiable information and when threads focus on issues, even easy ones. So the hope for limiting flaming rests with keeping the debate centered on facts and issues, not on people and events. Flaming appears to be a natural aspect in debates and ideological conversations, but fortunately it does not dominate chat room discourse and there is some evidence it can be limited.

Taken all together, what can we say about chat rooms in general? We see that the right wing dominates them, as they dominate the Usenet. We see that they respond to current events, especially major ones. We know that most threads are short and have either very few people or very little dissent. However, we also see that debates are far longer, involve far more people, and so represent a large portion of the chat room dialogue. Debates are not unique to either ideology, but are more likely to involve issues and flaming and less likely to involve information. We find that information declines in ideological discussion while flaming increases. In short, the chat room is a place of heated partisan debate as well as amicable discussion among fellow partisans. Little information is provided and a huge portion of the debate is about people and events, not about issues. The next question is how does this differ from the Usenet?

Chat Rooms and the Usenet

So far in this chapter we have made repeated references to chapter 3 and to some of the similarities and differences between the Usenet and the chat room. Now we wish to compare them more directly. To accomplish this, we merged the two data files together, and in Table 5.2 we present a side-by-side description of both media. We should note, however, that there are several variables, such as anti-media or leadership, that are unique to one of the data sets. Consequently, we must limit our comparisons to variables common to both data sets. The common variables include current events, information, debate, flaming, recruiting, ideology, and anti-government.

Our central question is how these two differ. But more specifically, we

TABLE 5.2
Differences between Chat Rooms and the Usenet

	Usenet	Chat Room
1. Is thread a debate?		
No	69.9%	65.8%
Yes	30.1%	34.2%
	Chi-square = 2.6	
	Cramer's V = .04	
2. Thread provides sourced information?		
No	36.6%	87.3%
Yes	63.4%	12.7%
	Chi-square = 351.3***	
	Cramer's V = .48	
3. Is thread about current event?		
No	57.7%	71.4%
Yes	42.3%	28.6%
(Chat Room post-election sample only)	N = 1,013	N = 217
	Chi-square = 13.9***	
	Cramer's V = .11	
4. Is thread a flame-fest?		
No	80.8%	77.9%
Yes	19.2%	22.1%
	Chi-square = 1.8	
	Cramer's V = .03	
5. Does thread attempt to recruit?		
No	76.7%	97.9%
Yes	23.3%	2.1%
	Chi-square = 112.1***	
	Cramer's V = .27	
6. Ideological direction of thread?		
Left-wing	15.9%	9.2%
Neutral	45.5%	37.1%
Right-wing	38.6%	53.7%
	Chi-square = 11.8***	
	Cramer's V = .15	
7. Is thread anti-government?		
Anti-government	22.8%	16.4%
Neutral	75.6%	83.0%
Pro-government	1.6%	0.6%
	Chi-square = 11.8***	
	Cramer's V = .09	
Number of cases: Total = 1,525	1,013	512
Legend: *** $p < .001$		

have several expectations, or hypotheses, to examine. First, we hypothesize that the Usenet, because of its organization into topics and slow response time will be used more often for recruitment. The recruitment and group maintenance functions of the Usenet will limit the amount of debate relative to chat rooms. The longer amount of time the Usenet allows for responses will increase the amount of information provided. It will, however, lower the percentage of current events discussed. We also hypothesize that chat rooms will be more vitriolic and have more flaming. Finally, we wish to examine the dominance of the right in both media forms but have no a priori expectations of the relationship between the medium and ideology. To summarize we hypothesize:

> *Hypothesis 5.7: Chat rooms will have more debate than the Usenet*
>
> *Hypothesis 5.8: Chat rooms will discuss more current events than the Usenet*
>
> *Hypothesis 5.9: Chat rooms will provide less information than the Usenet*
>
> *Hypothesis 5.10: Chat rooms will flame more than the Usenet*
>
> *Hypothesis 5.11: Chat rooms will recruit less than the Usenet*

The results of our comparison are presented in Table 5.2. In column 1, we present the percentage of Usenet threads with each characteristic. In column 2 are the comparable numbers from the chat room sample. This is basically the same information in Tables 3.3 and 5.1, simply presented together.

Question 1 shows that levels of debate are similar in both chats and posts. In both cases, about one of three messages is a debate. Of course, as we noted earlier, in both the chat room and the Usenet samples, debates are typically longer, and so represent a disproportionate amount of the message traffic. In fact, debates represent about one-third of all messages, but about three-quarters of all content in both the chat room and the Usenet. The remarkable consistency between media is interesting but contradicts Hypothesis 5.8.

Question 2 presents a more dramatic difference. The Usenet is far more informative than the chat room. Only 13% of chat room threads contain some form of verifiable information, while over 60% of Usenet threads provide such content. That the two media are different makes perfect sense. A person posting to the Usenet has hours or days to look something up before replying to a message, while a person in a chat room has only seconds or minutes. Nevertheless, the magnitude of the difference remains striking. If we are to try to establish some form of electronic deliberation, these results suggest that a Usenet-style system would be more informative.

Comparing the Usenet and chat rooms for current events discussions is somewhat problematic. Recall from chapter 3 that the Usenet data were collected during the summer of a non-election year while the chat room data were collected during an election season and afterward. Since the election stimulated a lot of discussion (see Table 5.1), we have dropped the pre-election threads from the chat room sample. Once this is done, we see that the Usenet, by a margin of 15%, is typically more current-events-oriented than the chat room. This contradicts our hypothesis, which was that the chat room's immediacy would lead to an increase in current events discussions. We believe the large difference is related to the higher information levels on the Usenet. Information is strongly related to current events and, given the high levels of information, current events are also higher on the Usenet. Of course, we do not know whether information causes current event discussion or, more likely, the reverse, but we can see that the Usenet is much more current-event- and information-oriented than chat rooms.

Question 4 compares rates of flaming. We see that both the Usenet and chat rooms have similar amounts of flaming—about 20%. We expected chat rooms to be more vitriolic, but that appears not to be the case. This is especially surprising given the much greater information content of the Usenet. We would have expected that to decrease the number of flames but apparently it did not. About one in five threads consistently turn into flame-fests.

Question 5 of Table 5.2 shows levels of recruitment. Confirming what we saw earlier, recruitment is far more common on the Usenet. Again, we suspect this is due to the greater specialization and longer time available for creating and responding to messages. But whatever the explanation, the Usenet clearly serves as a tool for activist recruitment that the chat room cannot match.

Finally, the last two questions examine ideological differences between chat rooms and the Usenet. What we find is somewhat paradoxical: the Usenet is less right wing but more anti-government than chat rooms. On the Usenet, the left wing is better represented and this in turn probably leads to more neutral threads as the left attempts to counter the right. Obviously, the left wing does not match the right, but they are much closer on the Usenet. In the chat rooms, the right wing dominates to a much greater extent. But when we look at anti-government messages, we see that they are more common on the Usenet. We see two explanations for this. First, we suspect, but cannot prove, that the Usenet has more discussion about issues and less about people and events. Discussions of people and events rarely involve taking a stance on the government, so a higher percentage of issue debates would increase the percentage of anti-government and pro-government messages. This is what we find, although the pro-government increase is small. A second explanation goes back to our coding of right and left. We placed anarchists on the left, but since they are profoundly anti-government, they would increase, by a small amount, the number of anti-government messages. Together, these two explanations increase the number of messages taking positions on the government, especially those that are likely to be anti-government.

In short, the Usenet is no more or less debate-oriented than are chat rooms. But the Usenet is more informative, is more likely to be about current events, and has a lot more recruitment. Flames are roughly equal in both formats. Chat rooms are more right wing, but are less anti-government, with most threads taking no stance on the role of government.

Summary and Conclusions

In this chapter we have examined the nature of chat room conversations. Retracing our steps, we see that most chat room threads, as with the Usenet, are short—on the order of five messages per thread. However, they were longer in the post-election period. In terms of our hypotheses, or expectations, we found support for Hypothesis 5.1—the chat room sample is heavily right wing. As with chapter 3, we suspect this is due to greater activity on the part of the right, not greater numbers. Though government is not often a direct target of the threads, when it does become the subject, the overwhelming attitude is anti-government. This is even more true for the mainstream media, which rarely become a subject but are typically criticized if the topic does come up.

Hypothesis 5.2 is partially supported. Most threads are not debates, but debates tend to be much longer and involve more people. This means they are a small portion of all threads but a much larger portion of all content. Hypothesis 5.3, though vague, appears to be accurate. Information is rarely provided in chat rooms. Flaming, however, was less than we hypothesized (Hypothesis 5.4); flame-fests make up only about 20% of the chat room sample. We expected current events to dominate chat rooms (Hypothesis 5.5) but the reality is more complex. The chat room is sensitive to current events—when something major is happening, the event takes over the chat room. But when the real world is relatively quiet, as in our post-election sample, current events discussion drops dramatically. Finally, we found that the chat room is not used to recruit others but may be used to share information and ideas with other partisans.

We also gave particular attention to debating, ideological balance, providing information, and flaming. These topics interest us because they strike at the heart of chat rooms as a potential place for democratic deliberation. We found that debates tend to be less informative and are more often concerned with easy issues, as opposed to non-issues. Further, debates tended to be anti-government. Why is information negatively related to debating? We see two reasons. First, debates are about normative issues, not objective ones, and normative statements require little in the way of evidence. For example, someone arguing that government is bad and always makes things worse is making a normative statement rather than an objective one. Thus, normative debates tend to be low in information. Second, chat room participants seem to share information with like-minded friends as opposed to using it to persuade those they debate. Finally, we also found that debates are more likely to erupt into flame-fests than non-debates, but that most debates (68%) are amicable.

What of the ideological balance in chat rooms? We found that right-wing threads not only dominate, but that the threads have more chatters and more messages. This suggests that right-wingers are more numerous, more active, or both. We cannot make a definitive conclusion but our evidence from this chapter and chapter 2 suggests that they are more active, not more numerous. When ideological positions are taken, they are often uncontroversial. We found ideology unrelated to debating, which means that an ideological statement is no more likely to be criticized than a neutral one. Again, this reaffirms our conclusion than many of the ideological discussions are for the purpose of sharing with compatriots rather than confronting others. Generally speaking, however, the use of factual information was lower when ideological positions were taken. This is attributed to the fact that ideological threads tend to be more easy-issue-oriented, thus requiring limited information in order to propound. Finally, we also found that the percentage of left-wing threads rose when the West Coast came on-line after 11:00 P.M. EST.

Our last detailed examination focused on flaming. We found that flames are unresponsive to America Online's hosting—there were no significant differences in flaming between hosted and un-hosted sessions. Flaming increased when discussions turned ideological, but flaming was lower in the presence of information and issue-based discussion. This makes us hopeful that a well-constructed discussion can be carried on in chat rooms. Moreover, flames remained fairly low even for ideological debates.

The last part of the chapter compared AOL's chat room with the Usenet. We found that chat rooms and the Usenet are very similar in their levels of debate and flaming. But they differ drastically in other ways. First, the Usenet is more focused on current events and provides far more information. Second, the Usenet is used more commonly for recruitment. Finally, the Usenet is less right wing but more anti-government.

How do chat rooms shape political discourse? Like the Usenet, chat room participants are self-selected. This is a recurring theme and an important one. Many of the unique qualities of chat rooms—their ideological balance and attitude toward government, for example—are most likely a result of self-selection. So if suddenly millions went on-line to chat politics, we would not expect the chatters to turn right wing and anti-government. Rather, what we see is a pattern of right-wing and anti-government people becoming

Internet activists in order to share their beliefs. We found that information is commonly shared in chat rooms, but we believe it is typically shared among people with similar points of view. This is analogous to the group maintenance we found with Usenet newsgroups in chapter 3. Also like the Usenet, we found the chat room to be a place that attracts people who are politically active, informed, but not necessarily part of the mainstream.

What is our prediction for the future of chat rooms? Again, predictions are risky, but we see the chat room moving in the same direction as the Usenet. In the future, chat rooms will become more specialized—there will be chat rooms devoted to individual topics and specific points of view. People will find it easier to chat with those who share their viewpoint. Chats will become more like the Usenet, more like a social group. It will be interesting to study the emerging specialized chat rooms for group behavior patterns like those documented in chapter 3. But there will always be rooms devoted to clashing ideas. These will typically be less informative, more vitriolic, and focued on easy issues or non-issues.

Will political chat rooms make our democracy better? The answer is not simple, but in general we think they will have little effect and what effect they do have will probably be negative. Chat rooms are a difficult format for thoughtful discussion. The short line space and the fast pace require people to make snap comments, not thoughtful ones. We see this in the low level of information and the small amount of issue discussion. Most chat room conversations appear to focus on the actions of people, not on the government and its role in society. All of this is close to the dystopian view of computer-mediated discourse. We, and the utopians, believe that democracy is best enhanced through a thoughtful discussion of government. This appears to be difficult to accomplish using chat rooms, even if the entire world were logged on.

Having looked at the differences between chat room and the Usenet, one might ask which is the better format? Our choice is the Usenet. It is slower and more thoughtful and so has more potential for deliberation. We saw that Usenet threads tend to be more informative and they are more ideologically balanced. Also, we believe that the issue content is higher, though this is purely impressionistic since issue type was not coded for the Usenet threads. In general, we think electronic political discussion works better in a format such as the Usenet, as opposed to a chat room style. It is not perfect, but we think it offers a better hope for deliberative democracy.

However, we must remember that the presence or absence of the Usenet itself is meaningless. Simply because the Usenet, chat room, or some future version of these exists, that does not mean citizens will take advantage of them. People must want to be informed, want to discuss, and want to learn. If they don't, having everyone connected to the Usenet via their TV will not make any difference. That is the simple result of self-selection—people must choose to use these technologies. Of course, people don't have to pick the Usenet or chat rooms. They can choose to read the newspaper and talk with friends. But if they do not do that today, they are not likely to hop onto the information superhighway and start acting like political junkies tomorrow. The Internet is not going to create a utopia simply because people can chat or post on the Usenet. They can do similar things now and many choose not to. Only if people choose to use these tools will their potential consequences be felt.

Notes

1. Internet Relay Chats and chat rooms are virtually identical. Both involve typing short messages in real time to other chatters. The primary difference between them is that IRCs use Internet hosts and are available to anyone with an Internet connection, while chat rooms are typically provided by a commercial on-line service such as America Online or Compu-Serve. For our purposes we consider them to be two versions of the same communication tool.

2. America Online users are identified by their screen names. For the purposes of anonymity, all screen names have been altered.

3. Wednesdays were excluded from this analysis because on those nights The Cloak Room is dedicated to Libertarian chat and this could potentially bias the results of the study.

4. The number of messages does not always equal the entire conversation, but is just the part that took place while we observed the room.

Web Sites, Interest Groups, and Politics

Low Transaction Costs
(Or, Why Any Group Can Afford a Web Site)

In 1994, if a political party or interest group had even a rudimentary Web site, it was a pioneer in the Information Age. In 1995, if a party or organization had a flashy series of Web pages that included graphics, audio, video, and text, it was hip. In 1996, if a candidate for president had a Web site, he would likely give out the address for it during televised appearances, as Bob Dole did in the second presidential debate against Bill Clinton. By 1997, if a party or interest group *still* did not have a Web site, it was run by a bunch of idiots. If dog years are seven human years, then one Internet technology year must be several standard decades long. The above example may be flippant, but in terms of the growth of politics on the Internet, it is fully appropriate. Any political party or interest group—no matter how marginalized on the American ideological spectrum and ignored by the mainstream media—that does not take advantage of the Internet for lobbying, member recruitment and retention, and information dissemination, is cheating itself of one of the biggest boons to organized political activity in the twentieth century. As authors, we have been skeptical all throughout this book of hyperbole concerning the Internet. The Web, however, *is* potentially the greatest thing since the postal system and the telephone for political interest groups.

Any group with just one person, even a volunteer, who has some knowledge of computer technology and access to Web publishing software, can construct an award-winning, useful Web presence. In fact, the Web may just be the cheapest publishing outlet for use by political organizations ever invented, when one considers the number of potential members and sympathizers who can be reached by the World Wide Web.

For example, the Web in 1997 was accessible by at least forty million people worldwide. An interest group could construct a "super deluxe" Web site with a powerful $5,000 computer for its server, a fast T-1 connection to the Internet for another few thousand dollars a year, server and Web authoring software for another few thousand, and one full-time "Webmaster" to write and maintain the site. By sending the Internet address of the site (say, for example, *www.anti-gun.org*) to several Internet search engines that index the Web, and getting like-minded groups and people to include a link to the new Web site in their own Web pages, our example political organization is well on its way to being viewed by several million potential Internet users.

Admittedly, such a complex Web presence may be out of the reach of some interest groups that have little in the way of constant funding. For them, a "bare bones" Web site could still be set up and maintained for literally a few *hundred* dollars per year. This cash-strapped group could buy a small amount of space on a commercial Web server for as little as $50 per month, register its unique domain name (e.g. *www.poor-interest-group.org*) for about $100, and use a volunteer and $149 Web authoring software to put together their site. They could then pay a search engine registration service about $20 to send their Internet address and a description of their new political Web site to over one hundred search engines. Now, when one of the forty million Web users goes to a search engine and types "politics," "poor," or any number of other search keywords, they receive a link to this new bare-bones site, which may in fact be as useful and professional looking as the super-deluxe sites of hundreds of other interest groups. For that matter, this low-budget way of putting together a Web site is not out of reach of a single individual posting a series of Web pages ranting about his or her favorite political topic. In fact, both authors of this book have personal Web sites at their universities, which cost us exactly nothing.[1]

No other communications technology has ever offered such widespread access to as large an audience of potential members and sympathizers. This may be the supreme irony the development of the Internet poses for politics. In the Internetted world of the late 1990s, it is actually far cheaper to get your political message to 100,000 people over the Web than it was in 1930 to get that same message to 1,000 people via long distance telephone calling. Whether using the World Wide Web for political purposes is as *effective* as using the phone, the fax, or direct mail, is another question entirely. When one considers the cost of accomplishing a certain task involving a certain number of people, one is taking into account "transaction costs." For example, a group may want to call 10,000 people on the telephone to solicit donations or sign up new members, because the group needs the money. But the people running this interest group have to consider the costs of making these calls versus the money those calls will bring in. If the transaction costs of making these calls are projected not to bring in a certain amount of money, then a wise group will simply not bother in the first place. However, a well-maintained, high-profile Web site decreases dramatically the transaction costs of contacting 10,000 people, to the point that *not* using the Web to recruit new members and solicit donations is a cost in itself. Thus the opening paragraph of this chapter: a political group without a Web site is foolish. For a more technical discussion of transaction costs and political organizations, see Moe (1980) or Bonchek (1995).

The Web as a Soapbox and as a Town Hall

Of course, it is one thing to say that a political party or group needs to have a Web site. Most people would probably agree with this statement. The usefulness and political effectiveness of such sites is another question entirely, which we will try to answer in the rest of this chapter. Before turning to our general analysis of political Web sites and our several case studies, let's take a step back and ask several questions about how a political organization might use the Web. Politically, one can view the Web and the entire Internet in at least two different ways. First, the World Wide Web is a new publication outlet, just like print and broadcast media. Second, the World Wide Web is a new "political space" in which people and groups compete for political resources: supporters, money, political allies, and prestige.

The Web As a Publication Outlet

As we saw in chapter 2, some of the most popular politically oriented Web sites (not to mention the slickest and most useful) are those that are merely extensions of the traditional media: *cnn.com, www.washingtonpost.com,* and *www.abcnews.com* are just three examples. Many of us who do not live in the Washington, D.C. area, for example, can simply log on to the *Washington Post* Web site and enjoy the daily articles that that newspaper prints and posts electronically. Likewise, if we as television viewers saw a short piece on CNN that interested us, chances are good that we can log on to the CNN Web site and get more information about the story, including Internet links to other relevant sites. For these news media giants, having a Web presence is both a form of advertising for their "main" broadcast or printed product, and a way of extending their reach into a new media venue.

On the other hand, the World Wide Web is *not at all like* the traditional broadcast and print media. Sure, the big media outfits can use the Web as a new form of print and broadcasting. On the Internet, however, the traditional media have to compete in the same space as thousands of other sources of political information, including electronic magazines, conservative, liberal, and extremist political Web sites, and even single individuals with pet political issues. The key to understanding the World Wide Web as a publishing outlet is to grasp its *unmediated* nature. CNN, ABC, and the *New York Times* are all gatekeepers of information in the print and broadcast worlds: they ultimately decide which stories to print and air, what type of spin to put on those stories, and whom to interview. They can of course adopt the same practice in their Web sites by simply regurgitating or moderately enhancing what they have said on the air or in print. However, political parties and interest groups can use their Web sites in this new publication outlet to advance their own points of view without CNN, ABC, or the local newspaper filtering that message, or even deciding that the message is not worth covering.

For example, many conservatives in the United States have complained that the media is "liberal" and biased against conservative groups and ideas. Whether or not this is actually true, conservative interest groups can now freely post their own ideas on the World Wide Web, completely bypassing the "liberal" media. In addition, they can update these news items several times a day if they wish. If the Christian Coalition believes that ABC, CBS, NBC, CNN, and the major newspapers are slanting or not covering an abortion story, then they are free to post their own news items and viewpoints at *www.cc.org,* a very large and sophisticated Web site that is one of our six case studies to follow. This may be a poor substitute for major broadcast time, but as the number of Internet users grows and search engine technology matures, Web sites may become a large source of news for many people, if not their primary news source. Thus, having a presence in the great publication outlet of the World Wide Web will become all the more important for both the traditional media and political groups wishing to get their political messages out to the public unfiltered.

Whether or not the print and broadcast media are biased against conservatives is a debatable point. What is *plainly evident,* however, is the commercial bias of the mainstream media. After all, publishers have to sell newspapers to stay in business, and broadcasters have to sell commercials. Therefore, chances are good that no news broadcast or front-page story in a major newspaper is going to cover low-profile news such as an environmental conference in Gabon; it's just not worth it for the commercial media. There may be, however, thousands of people in the world who are interested in such matters. The mainstream media can use their Web sites to deposit wire stories about such low profile events, and let people search or browse through them; CNN does just this with its Web site. On the other hand, some environmental interest group may well see this putative conference as the most important event of the year so far and devote several pages of its Web site to the conference and the issues surrounding it. Because most political interest groups are not in business to make a profit, they have the freedom to devote more time to very specific news and events that the mainstream media do not cover simply because the audience is not there for them in a cost-effective manner. The World Wide Web is an inexpensive medium for particularized news stories and editorials, and many political parties and interest groups post news and opinions every day about even the most obscure events and issues. The Web as an anarchic, unmediated press allows this.

What about "fringe" groups and attitudes? Certainly, the mainstream print and broadcast media have only limited newspaper space and air time. One consequence of this is the commercial bias against minor news stories noted above. Another consequence is a conscious or unconscious bias against non-mainstream ideas and political groups. For example, the major news networks during a presidential campaign almost never cover the Libertarian, Socialist Workers, Natural Law, or Green candidates for president. One of the reasons for this lack of coverage is that these are poorly funded candidates with ideas of limited appeal and absolutely no chance of being elected. On the other hand, it may be precisely their unorthodox political ideologies that lead the media to exclude them from their coverage of elections. After all, the media are themselves part of the mainstream political establishment, and have their own economic and political interests to protect (Parenti, 1993). Organizations calling for widespread changes in the political and economic systems, not surprisingly, get little or no coverage in the press. These fringe parties, then, are a "natural" for the World Wide Web, which allows them to get their messages out to the public without the filtering mechanism of the mainstream media. It should not be surprising, therefore, if we find in this chapter that a non-trivial portion of the Web is devoted to fringe politics.[2]

The Web as a Political Space

If the World Wide Web is an alternative medium without the filtering and agenda-setting gatekeepers of the traditional print and broadcast media, it is also a new political space. Technically, a "political space" is any venue in which politics is practiced. Usually when we talk about such political venues, we actually mean some geographical location. The United States is a political space in which we hold elections, and have a government that debates, makes, enforces, and adjudicates public policy. Likewise the state of Texas is a political space within the larger context of the United States, which duplicates these and other functions at the state level. Within Texas, of course, are other political spaces, ranging from cities and counties to neighborhoods and even homeowners associations. Within each of these units, politics is being practiced by someone; people are getting different slices of the pie.

Layered on top of geographical political spaces (and overlapping many such places) are other venues of politics. The traditional media, especially the interactive kind like talk radio and letters to the editor, are a good example themselves of a political space. A piece of pending legislation in Congress certainly will generate public and media interest. The media will broadcast or print stories about a bill in the House and/or Senate. This bill may then become the centerpiece of discussion on a call-in show like *Larry King Live* or the Rush Limbaugh radio program. There may be guests from Congress, interest groups, or the media themselves commenting on the relative merits and demerits of the bill, as well as citizens calling the programs to voice their support for or opposition to the proposed law. In this way, the media constitute a political space or venue. However, that political space is again restricted by the media's gatekeeping functions; the media decide which issues to cover, which guests to invite, how much time to give them, and which people will get on the air with Larry or Rush.

Again, the Web as a political space foils the traditional media's gatekeeper status. Any group or individual with a point of view about a political issue will simply put together a Web site within the larger political space of the Internet. This site will then be potentially accessible by all forty-million-plus people with access to the Web.

We have already covered this function of the Web being a source for unfiltered political information above. There are, of course, other actors within any political space, whether that space is geographic or not. Interest groups and political parties usually act within several political venues at once, and have several tasks to undertake at the same time. First, all political organizations provide their own viewpoints in order to educate the public to their way of thinking and they hope to gather support in the government. Second, political interest groups rely on either members or donors for financial support and "strength in numbers."

One of the most important tasks an interest group must perform is the ongoing recruitment of new members and the maintenance of existing support. A membership organization such as the National Rifle Association, the American Association of Retired Persons, or the Christian Coalition depends greatly on recruiting new dues-paying members, not only to finance its projects but also to identify and educate members who will lobby lawmakers with letters, phone calls, and faxes. After all, the more members a group can count in its annual reports and meetings, the stronger that group appears to legislators, presidents, and governors. Recruiting new members has a flip side as well: the retention of existing members. These people must be kept satisfied that the group is doing its self-declared job and that their membership is worth the cost in money and the investment of personal time. Even political organizations that do not depend on members as much as cash donations must constantly raise funds. Think tanks like the Heritage Foundation, the CATO Institute, and the Brookings Institution primarily generate research either for sale in publications or for consumption by policy makers. These non-member-based organizations need money and support just as much as membership groups do.

Recruiting and retaining members and supporters is not the end of the game. In fact, recruiting is a means to the end that all political organizations ultimately pursue: political influence through lobbying government. Testifying to Congress, making campaign contributions, writing research reports, and keeping supporters informed and persuaded to a cause are all part of the game played in any political space. The desired outcome, however, is always the same: getting the government either to do something new, stop doing something old, or change a policy. Lobbying any government takes time and effort. Traditionally, groups have offered testimony to legislative committees; exhorted their members and supporters to write, call, or telegram their elected representatives; and forged alliances with like-minded groups in pursuit of some political goal.

All of these activities—disseminating information, recruiting and retaining supporters, and lobbying government—are crucial to any interest group. They are also *possible in many political venues*. One of these venues is the World Wide Web. An interest group can certainly recruit new members through costly direct mailings and telephone solicitations. It can do the same thing much more cheaply through a well-designed, high-profile Web site. A political organization, no matter what its viewpoint or ideology, can inform and persuade current and potential members and supporters through monthly newsletters, periodic "action alert" faxes, and telephone trees. Again, the same can be accomplished much more cheaply and quickly using a Web site.

For example, a pro-life group may be strongly in favor of a ban on so-called late-term abortions. Such a ban could be coming up for an imminent vote in Congress, and the vote could be expected to be very close. This organization could of course exhort its members though a monthly newsletter to call or write their members of Congress in support of the ban. But by the time the newsletter got to all the members, the vote may well have already been taken. Long-distance calling could also be used to get the word out more quickly, but this could be very expensive and unwieldy, especially if the group's members are numerous and spread out geographically.

A Web site could accomplish the same lobbying task, albeit with a reach to only the fraction of the group's members who are Internet users. Still, even if only 10% of a membership of one million are on-line, this is still 100,000 supporters who can be reached quickly through the Web. Congress will likely not ignore 100,000 phone calls, faxes, or e-mails on any issue. A Web page could announce a pending vote on the abortion ban. Then, the group's e-mailing software could send action alerts to all 100,000 members on-line asking them to drop in on the Web site as soon as possible. There, they would read the bulletin, and click on a link to a form letter to either print out or e-mail to their members of Congress. If they did not know who their representatives were, then they could simply type in their Zip Codes, which would give them the name, postal and e-mail addresses, and political information about their members of Congress. With this kind of Web site, many thousands of letters and other communications in favor of a late-term abortion ban could be on their way to Congress in as little as a few *hours*. Such near-instantaneous communication is possible in the Information Age. Further, this is not a hypothetical example; the Christian Coalition's Web page (*www.cc.org*) engages in this kind of member communication on a regular basis.

The task before us in the rest of this chapter should be familiar by now. We have laid out a description of how the Internet (in the case, the World Wide Web) can potentially affect politics. Now we actually present evidence from empirical data gathered from Web pages to describe these political uses of the Web. In the spirit of chapter 1, here are our formal hypothetical expectations about political activity on the Web:

> *Hypothesis 6.1: there will be more conservative than liberal political sites on the World Wide Web*
>
> *Hypothesis 6.2: conservative Web sites will exhibit higher production values than liberal Web sites*
>
> *Hypothesis 6.3: Web sites on the political fringes (both left and right) will be a non-trivial percentage of all politically oriented Web sites*

Hypotheses 6.1 and 6.2 are of course derived from Hypothesis 1 in the introduction, which proposed that the Internet would be dominated politically by conservatives. As we saw in chapters 3 and 5, this is certainly the case in the Usenet newsgroups and America Online political chat rooms. It is a safe bet, we think, to propose that the Web would exhibit this same domination by people to the right of center. So, Hypothesis 6.1 is straightforward. But where did we get the idea for Hypothesis 6.2 that conservative Web sites would have "higher production values" than liberal sites? Again we base this on the experiences of chapters 3 and 5. There we saw that not only are there more conservative than liberal postings on the Usenet and in chat rooms, but also that these conservative postings are better maintained and defended than are liberal or neutral ones. So, just as conservative message threads are longer and better "policed" than liberal ones in these venues, we would expect that conservative Web sites would be "flashier" and larger than liberal or moderate ones. This is because the technical glitz of a Web site is certainly part of its maintenance.

Finally, Hypothesis 6.3 is our concession to the anarchic, free-wheeling nature of the Internet in general and the Web in particular. For reasons discussed earlier in this chapter, any group can afford a Web site, and there is no one to tell them that they cannot. Fringe groups, so often shut out of the mainstream media, are simply natural candidates for the Web, where they can present their arguments and recruit members right alongside mainstream groups and the media.

Interest Groups on the Web:
Conservatives, Liberals, Neutrals, and the Fringes

In order to test our hypotheses about politics on the Web empirically, we need a proper set of Web sites for our analyses. Randomly sampling political Web pages is not as easy as sampling Usenet messages or chat room conversations. There is no one master list of Web sites, as there is for Usenet newsgroups. Likewise, different Web keyword search engines find different pages in different ways. Just typing the words "politics" or "liberal" or "conservative" into a search engine like Infoseek or Excite or Yahoo! will not necessarily yield a random set of political Web sites. Such a search strategy would probably return several hundred thousand Web sites in no real useful order, and many of these sites would have little if anything to do with politics. Unfortunately, current search engine technology simply does not allow for the kind of targeted searching we need, and in any event without a thorough knowledge of the underlying search engine, we could never be sure the results were random. So we have turned to another aspect of the Internet search sites: their directories. Internet search services have two components: keyword searching and indexes. These indexes are arranged very much like the Yellow Pages: different subject areas contain listings of a few dozen sites or even thousands. Sometimes, these subject areas are further subdivided. We used the Infoseek "Politics" directory, under the subheading "Parties and Groups: U.S." We also used the Excite "Politics" channel, under the subheading "Miscellaneous," and also "Miscellaneous: Interest Groups."

We sampled one hundred politically oriented Web sites from these two Internet subject indexes. We did this randomly by selecting every seventh page entry in the indexes. In this way, we retrieved fifty Web sites from the Infoseek index and fifty sites from the Excite index. If one were to do the same search today, even taking every seventh site as we did, one would most likely sample a hundred entirely different Web sites, since pages are being added to the Internet and its search engines and indexes on a daily basis. In this way, we achieved a random sampling of all the political pages *that have been indexed into political subject areas* by Infoseek and Excite. Please note that, strictly speaking, we cannot claim that our one hundred Web sites are a truly random sample of the entire Internet. They are, however, a random sample of all the pages these two search services have indexed (and this number is in the tens of thousands). The names of these one hundred Web sites and their Internet addresses are reproduced in the Appendix.

Next we read through each of these hundred Web sites and assigned each to one of six ideological categories: leftist, liberal, neutral, conservative, rightist, and libertarian. Again this ideological categorization was based on the same judgment we used in chapters 3 and 5. Here, however, we added the leftist and rightist categories to differentiate fringe Web sites from mainstream liberal or conservative sites. There may be some controversy here in how to break apart liberal from leftist, and conservative from rightist. Again, we largely used our own judgment here, though we feel that in the great majority of cases, the differences between mainstream and fringe sites are self-evident. Simply stated, if a Web site is espousing a view that either the president or a significant number of the members of Congress would hold, then that Web site is not on the fringes. Here we mark the edges of the mainstream in the general ideological world of America in the 1990s.

For example, we consider the Democratic Socialists of America site (*www.dsausa.org*) to be leftist, since it openly espouses a socialist philosophy that is clearly beyond the boundaries of the American liberal mainstream. On the other hand, a group such as the League of Conservation Voters (*www.lcv.org*) is clearly in the liberal mainstream of American ideology, since they advocate no drastic changes to the political or economic system, and have dozens of supporters in Congress. Again by way of example, we consider the Empower America pages (*www.empower.org*) to be mainstream conservative, since they primarily advocate a balanced budget and less government regulation of the American economy. On the other hand, we place the Republic of Texas Web site (*www.republic-of-texas.com*) into the "rightist" category, since this group advocates the secession of Texas from the United States, a viewpoint that is clearly beyond the conservative mainstream and one which would find few if any advocates in government.

Finally, we created a new category in this chapter: libertarian. Normally, we might lump libertarian pages into either the liberal or conservative camps. However, libertarianism as a political philosophy does not fit well into either camp. A libertarian could hold the so-called liberal idea that the government should not interfere in one's sexual life, and at the same time believe that the income tax should be abolished (normally a conservative idea). We believe that Web sites espousing libertarian views are best left in their own category.

In the end, we realize that some people may quibble with our ideological categorizations, so in the Appendix we also include the ideology we assigned to each of these Web sites. Out of 100 Web sites, we found 12 leftist, 22 liberal, 22 neutral, 26 conservative, 9 rightist, and 9 libertarian sites. If one lumps the leftist and liberal sites together, as well as the conservative and rightist sites, we have 34 left sites and 35 right sites. So, if we were to make generalizations about the presence of various ideological groups on the Web, we would argue that, at least in raw numbers, there is a rough balance between left and right. However, we would also point out that a full 21% of these one hundred sites were on either the left or right ideological "fringes" of American political life. Finally, 22% of our Web sites are neutral, in that they contain ideological balance or are simply devoid of ideological content.

Major Differences between Ideological Groups

Now that we have our hundred Web sites categorized into six groups, we can begin to look for differences between them. In this section, we examine all one hundred sites for differences in their sizes, how widely they are known on the Internet, their multimedia "flashiness," and the linkages they provide to other sites on the Internet. Later on in the chapter, we will go beyond these generalizations to examine in detail one site from each our six ideological groups. There we will be more interested in *how* these sites are used in the context of the Web as a publication outlet and as a political space. The analyses to follow are based on these one hundred Web sites as of August 14, 1997. One of the major advantages of the Web as a publication outlet is that information contained in these pages can be updated often, even several times per day. By the time you read this, some of these sites may have disappeared, grown in size, or had complete multimedia makeovers.

Site Size and Presence

As anyone who surfs the Internet knows, Web sites can vary widely in size. Here, we measure "size" as the number of distinct pages in a Web site.[3] For all 100 sites, this number ranges from a low of 1 page to a maximum of 652 pages, with a mean of 82 pages. We make no assertions in this section about the usefulness of the information contained in these pages, the logic of their layout, or whether all the pages in a site are truly needed. It is possible to convey much political information in a single Web page, since such pages are theoretically unlimited in size. However, most people do tend to take advantage of the hyperlinked nature of the World Wide Web, presenting information in relatively short pages, while placing hyperlinks in the text to other pages of interest. Still, large sites are more complex and harder to manage than small sites, so the number of pages is a rough indication of the complexity of the site.

Figure 6.1 presents the average number of pages per site for each of our six ideological groupings. Immediately one notices that, on average, the conservative Web sites are two times larger than their liberal counterparts. Further, both the libertarian and neutral sites closely match these conservative sites in size. It is also interesting that the conservative Web sites are much larger than their right-wing fringe counterparts. However, mainstream

144

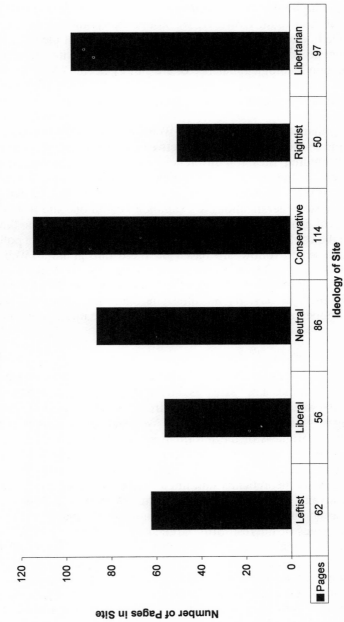

FIGURE 6.1
Number of Pages for 100 Web Sites by Ideology

	Leftist	Liberal	Neutral	Conservative	Rightist	Libertarian
■ Pages	62	56	86	114	50	97

Ideology of Site

Number of Pages in Site

liberal sites are actually slightly *smaller* than the left-wing fringe sites. Are we seeing even more hints of conservative dominance on the Internet, at least in the relative size of their Web sites?

These average figures for the number of pages in a site are intriguing, but become even more pronounced when we consider how well known these sites are to the larger Internet community. Figure 6.2 can help us understand this important concept. Here, instead of plotting the number of pages in each ideological type on the vertical axis, we plot the number of links to these sites from other Web sites. We gathered this data on the number of links to a site from Infoseek's search engine, which allows one to not only search for keywords on the Internet, but also to search for the number of links to a site.[4] The vertical positions of the bubbles in Figure 6.2 indicate the average number of links to these sites. The *size* of the bubbles, however, indicates the "Net presence" of these sites. Here, we measure Net presence by multiplying the number of pages in a site by the number of links *to* those pages. This way, the size of a site (the number of pages) is considered to be enhanced by the number of external links to that site. The assumption is that, even though a relatively small site may have many links to it from other sites, the physical size of a Web site also is an important component of its Net presence.

Remember that, on average, conservative sites are larger than all others, especially right-wing, left-wing, and liberal sites. In Figure 6.2 we see by the vertical positions of the bubbles that there are two groups of sites, as far as links to them from the rest of the Internet are concerned: conservative and libertarian sites on the one hand, versus all the other sites. On average there are 398 links from other Internet locations to each libertarian Web site, and 303 links to each conservative site. None of the other categories has even a substantial fraction of this number of links to its pages; the liberal sites come closest, with an average of 139 links to them from other pages. Clearly, then, not only are the libertarian and especially conservative sites larger, as seen in Figure 6.1, but they are also more frequently linked to by other sites, as seen in the vertical positions of these bubbles. What is even more striking is the Net presence of these six ideological categories of Web sites. Not only do the conservative and libertarian sites have the most links to them, but also this number of links is greatly exaggerated by the sheer size of these sites. Remember that the size of these bubbles is the number of pages per site *multiplied* by the number of links to the sites. In these two figures we find even more evidence that liberals and leftists are disadvantaged on the Internet vis-à-vis conservatives and, in this case, libertarians.

Site "Flashiness"

The size of a Web site, along with the number of external hyperlinks to that site from other Web pages, is not the end of the road. These figures say

146

FIGURE 6.2
Site Visibility for 100 Web Sites by Ideology

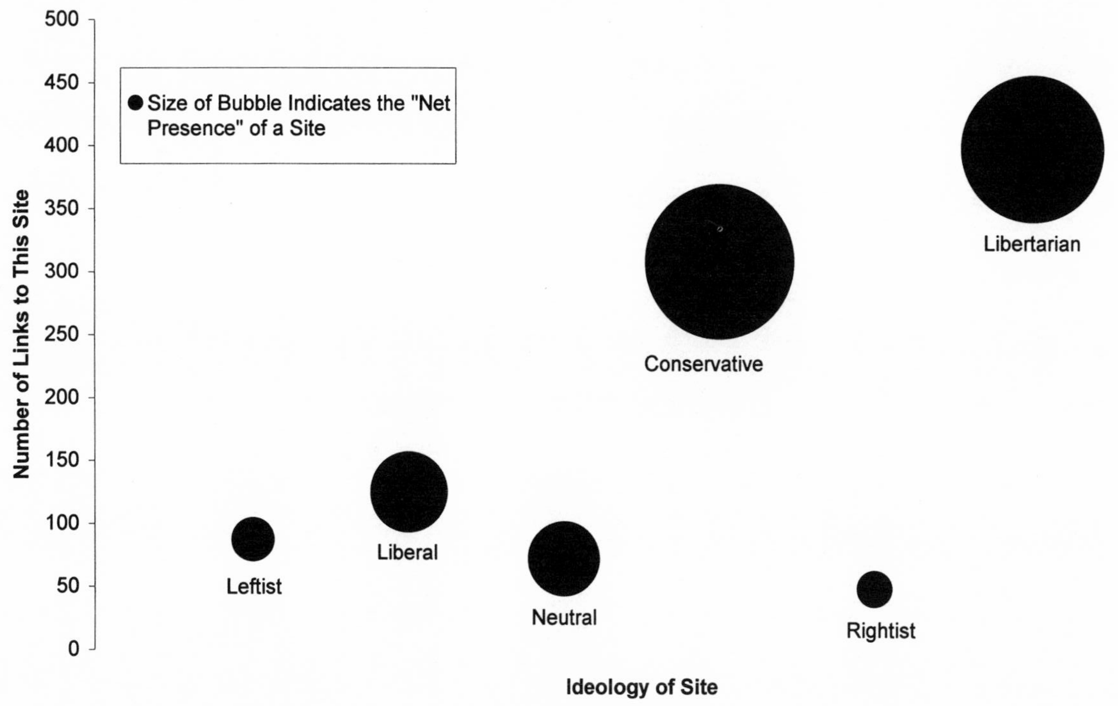

nothing about the actual layout or content of these Web pages. One of the most compelling qualities of the World Wide Web from a user's standpoint is the ability to incorporate visually appealing graphics. Web sites can be easily packed with maps, colored buttons, graphical toolbars, photographs, and video. A site that uses graphic elements intelligently is much more appealing and easy to use than a site that simply contains text and hyperlinks. Of course one could also argue that Web sites can use *too many* graphics, which tends to either crowd out the textual information in the site, or slow its download speed because of the larger size of graphics vis-à-vis text. In any event, the number of graphical elements in a site is, we believe, another rough indicator of that site's complexity. And as Figure 6.3 shows, the graphical "flashiness" of Web sites differs markedly between our ideological groupings.

Figure 6.3 is another bubble chart. Here, the vertical axis represents the average number of graphic elements per page, so the vertical positions of the bubbles correspond to this figure for each of the six ideological groups. The *size* of the bubbles indicates the actual raw number of graphic elements in a Web site. We use the measure of graphics per page to get a rate of graphical "flashiness" for Web sites regardless of their size, while the size of the bubbles preserves the information about the actual number of graphics in a site, which is largely a function of the site's overall size in pages (see Figure 6.1). Looking first at the rate of graphics per page, we see that conservative and neutral Web sites tend to have the most graphical "flashiness" per page, with .72 and .64 graphics per page, respectively. On the other hand, leftist Internet sites have on average only .20 graphics per page, with the other three groups falling about midway between. Again, especially when we compare conservative sites to liberal or leftist ones, conservative Web sites tend to be more complex, if only in the number of graphical elements they use.

Turning to the actual size of these bubbles, again we see that the conservative sites have more chrome, polish, and glitz than the other five types of sites. While conservative Web sites contain on average nearly 40 graphical elements, liberal sites contain only half that number (20), while left-wing Web sites contain even fewer (11), and rightist sites only 14. When we turn to our six case studies later in the chapter, we will pay close attention to how sites actually *use* these graphical elements to enhance their messages. Suffice it to say here that conservative sites are larger and flashier than all other sites, especially their liberal and leftist counterparts. This is more evidence that conservatives are using the Internet politically much more effectively than other ideological groups, at least in the design and packaging of their sites. We should again point out that creating custom graphics is not prohibitively expensive, since any commercial graphics editing package or even shareware can be used to create 3-D text, scrolling marquees, interactive

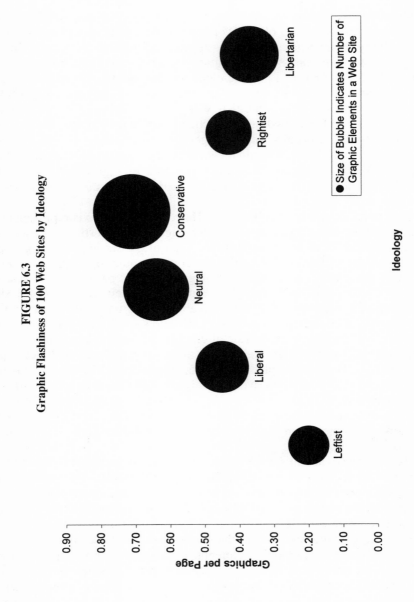

FIGURE 6.3
Graphic Flashiness of 100 Web Sites by Ideology

toolbars, and textured backgrounds. Some might argue that conservative sites are flashier simply because conservatives have more money at their disposal than do liberals. While the latter may be the case, there is no logical reason that money is a cause and site flashiness is an effect. Therefore, we do not argue that conservative Web sites are flashier because these groups have more money.

Site Linkages to the Rest of the Internet

Graphic images and text are not the only components of Web pages. In fact, they are not what make the World Wide Web a truly unique publishing outlet. What sets the Web apart from newspapers, television, books, and magazines are *hypertext links*. Embedded within either the text or graphics of a Web page, hypertext links (or hyperlinks, or simply links) when clicked on send the user to another page, either at the current site or anywhere else on the Internet. This way, pages can link to each other, to other sites of interest, to e-mail addresses, and so forth. The phrase "surfing the Web" comes from this practice of following links from one page to another. Indeed, the "Web" gets its name from this ability to hyperlink to and from pages all across the world.

For political groups, this ability to link to other sites on the Internet is very important. One of the major tasks that any interest group or party must accomplish is alliances with like-minded groups and lawmakers. The hyperlinking facility of the Web easily allows this. For example, the National Rifle Association (*www.nra.org*) could provide in its Web site links to all its local chapters, other anti-gun-control groups, and the home pages of sympathetic members of Congress. Likewise, a group could provide links to the e-mail addresses of undecided legislators on the eve of a crucial vote.

Figure 6.4 presents our findings about the linkages to the outside Internet world contained in the one hundred Web sites under examination. Again, we use a bubble graph to present data about three variables at once. This time the vertical axis measures the average number of links per page contained in each of our six ideological groups of sites,[5] while the size of the bubbles indicates the average raw number of links in an entire site. So the interpretation of this figure is just like Figure 6.3, which dealt with graphics per page and the raw number of graphics. Here we find that liberal Web sites contain far more links per page than all other sites—1.34 links per page, compared to an overall average of .65 links per page for all 100 sites. Conservative, right-wing, and libertarian sites contain a comparative low rate of links per page, with .38, .09, and .29, respectively.

The size of the bubbles—the raw number of links per site—tells a different story. Recall from Figure 6.1 that liberal and left-wing sites are quite small, especially when compared to neutral, conservative, and libertarian

150

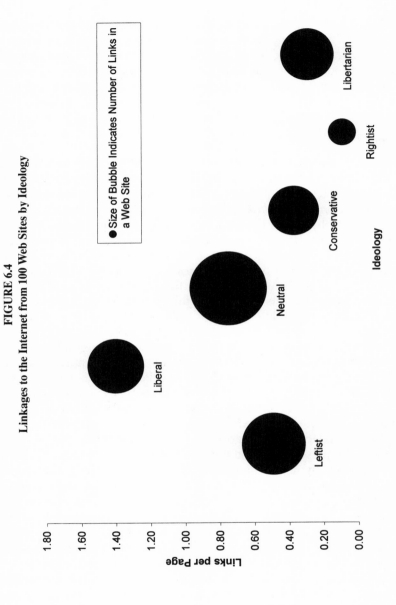

FIGURE 6.4
Linkages to the Internet from 100 Web Sites by Ideology

Web sites. It is not surprising, then, that neutral sites contain the highest average number of links overall (49), while liberal sites contain about 25 total external links on average, quite close to the conservative sites' 22. Thus, even though liberal sites have a higher "rate" of links in them, in terms of raw numbers they place close to the overall average of 28. Right-wing sites appear to be the most "self-contained" of all six ideological types, with only .09 links per page and an average of six external links in an entire site.

Political Priorities in Web Site Design

Is this politically meaningful? Do the number of links per site and per page really translate into some political advantage or disadvantage for an organization's effectiveness on the Web? Again, we leave the discussion of actual site content for our case study analyses below. At this point, however, a comparison of links to graphics is in order. Technically, when a "Webmaster" puts together an Internet site, he or she does not face an insurmountable tradeoff between graphics and external links. It is just as easy to design a site with lots of graphics *and* external links as it is to write a site with a graphic bias or a links bias. However, the ratio of links to graphics is, we believe, a rough indicator of political and organization priorities. A site with lots of "flash" is an exercise in self-promotion: "Look at my site; it's cool!" Just as broadcast advertising is essentially visual, so is the Web. A dull, colorless Web site simply does not convey the same message as a flashy multimedia extravaganza. Therefore, we would propose that sites heavy on graphics and relatively low on links are primarily engaging in advertising, which for political groups means recruitment and lobbying. Recruiting is a form of advertising for new members, while lobbying (i.e., getting members and supporters to contact an elected official) is also a form of second-hand advertising. On the other hand, sites that are heavy on links to other resources and groups but relatively low on glitz are primarily engaging in information provision and the maintenance of ties to like-minded groups. In this way, we see the balance of graphics and links in the same light as broadcast-versus-print news. Television news shows are more immersive and visceral than print stories, but inevitably cannot offer the same depth as a newspaper article. A graphically intense, link-deprived political site is, in our mind, the Internet's equivalent of the television. On the other hand, a link-heavy, low-glitz site is a newspaper. We hasten to point out, though, that there is nothing technical stopping a Web site from being essentially balanced between links and graphics.

Figure 6.5 depicts this putative tradeoff for our six ideological groups of Web sites. On the vertical axis, we have plotted the average difference between the number of graphic elements and the number of links in our one

FIGURE 6.5
Graphic Elements Minus Links for 100 Web Sites by Ideology

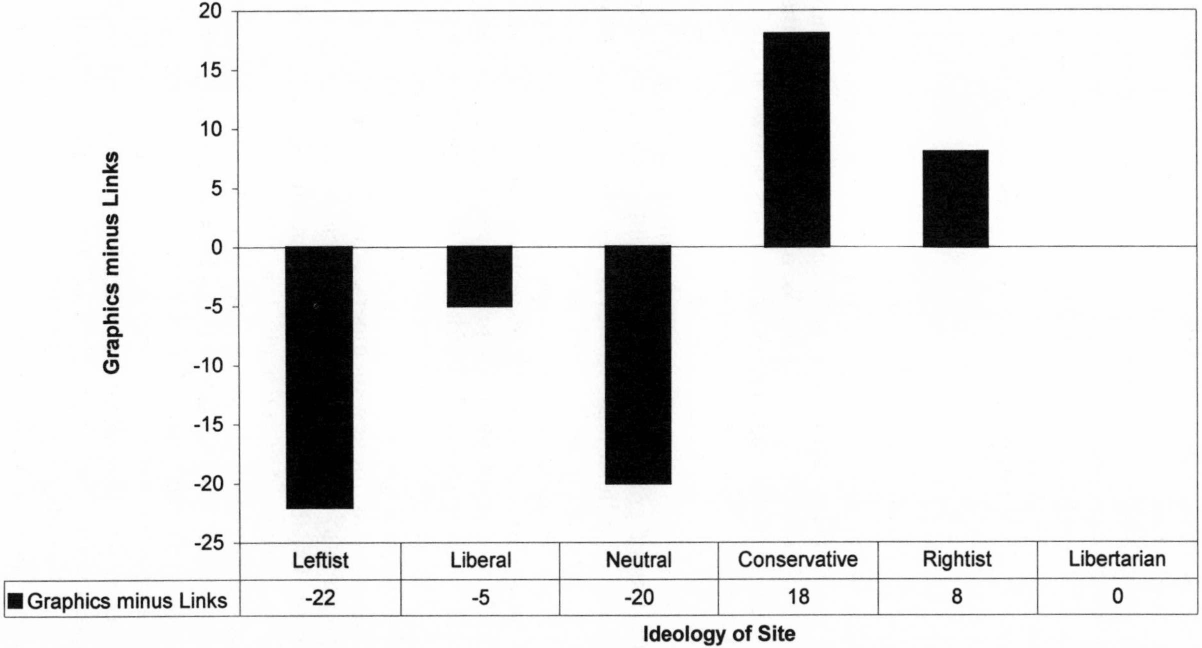

	Leftist	Liberal	Neutral	Conservative	Rightist	Libertarian
■ Graphics minus Links	-22	-5	-20	18	8	0

hundred Web sites. A positive number indicates that a site has more graphics than external links, while a negative value indicates the opposite; a score of zero would be a perfect numerical balance between links and graphical elements. There is a clear ideological pattern in this data. Leftist groups on average have Web sites with twenty-two more links than graphic elements; neutral groups favor more links over graphics as well. Conversely, right-wing Web sites slightly favor graphics over external links to other parts of the Internet, while mainstream conservative groups have quite a large bias toward flash over links. Our nine libertarian sites strike a balance here between links and graphics.[6] Interestingly, liberal sites slightly favor links over graphics, but the balance is very close—on average, these sites contain only five more links than graphic elements. In the terms we discussed above, then, right-of-center sites are primarily advertising, leftist sites are providing information, and libertarian sites are balanced between these two functional uses of the Web. Whether these generalizations are actually supported by deeper evidence is one of the primary questions we ask with our six case studies below.

In summary, conservative Web sites are larger, flashier, and more visible on the World Wide Web than are either liberal or left-wing sites. On the other hand, liberal sites contain many more hyperlinks to other Internet sites, and strike a balance between graphic flashiness and the number of these links. Finally, extremist right- and left-wing sites are smaller, less visible, and in the case of left-wing sites, far less flashy than their mainstream counterparts.

Table 6.1 presents the top five sites out of our sample of one hundred in each analytic category discussed above. As one can see, there is a good mix of mainstream sites; none of the fringe sites shows up in this list of the five largest sites. On the other hand, all of the top five sites by number of graphic elements are either conservative or libertarian. When one counts the raw number of links per site, three of the top five in this category are neutral, one is left wing, and one is conservative. In fact, this is the only category in which a fringe group (in this case, the Democratic Socialists of America) shows up in a top-five list. The top five sites in graphics minus links are again mixed ideologically, with two conservative, two neutral, and one liberal. Note, however, the relative size of this graphics minus links figure for the top two sites: the Christian Coalition and the Ethics and Public Policy Research Center. These two sites, especially the Christian Coalition site, have a far greater excess of graphics over links than the other three sites in this list. Since the Christian Coalition site is one of our six case studies, we will discuss the flashiness of this site in some depth. Finally, out of the top five sites by links to them from other Internet sites, two are conservative, two are libertarian, and one is liberal. The reader is urged to explore all these sites with his or her own Web browser (site addresses are in the Appendix).

154

TABLE 6.1
Top Five Sites in the Sample

By Number of Pages:		
1. Christian Coalition	Conservative	652
2. Vox Pop	Neutral	534
3. Conservative Generation X	Conservative	362
4. Golden Key Campaign	Libertarian	346
5. Federation of American Scientists	Liberal	267
By Graphic Elements:		
1. Christian Coalition	Conservative	241
2. Ethics and Public Policy Center	Conservative	111
3. American Coalition for Fathers and Children	Conservative	89
4. Golden Key Campaign	Libertarian	85
5. Conservative Generation X	Conservative	74
By Links in the Site:		
1. Presidents of the United States	Neutral	358
2. Public Access Project	Neutral	217
3. Democratic Socialists of America	Leftist	200
4. Vox Pop	Neutral	190
5. Conservative Generation X	Conservative	187
By Graphics Minus Links:		
1. Christian Coalition	Conservative	225
2. Ethics and Public Policy Center	Conservative	97
3. Political Chat!	Neutral	65
3. Common Cause	Liberal	65
5. Journal X	Neutral	57
By Links to the Site:		
1. RAND Corporation	Conservative	2,921
2. Libertarian Party	Libertarian	2,067
3. Town Hall	Conservative	1,855
4. Federation of American Scientists	Liberal	1,249
5. Golden Key Campaign	Libertarian	1,186

Note: These statistics were based on these Web Sites as of August 1997

Using the Web for Politics: Six Case Studies

Now we have at least an impression of how the Web looks ideologically. We know that conservative Web sites are on average bigger and glitzier than their liberal, leftist, and rightist counterparts. On the other hand, liberal sites contain many more external linkages to the rest of the Internet. We have speculated that there may be some political significance in this graphics-versus-links tradeoff. The best way to answer such a question is through analytic case study descriptions of Web sites within each of our six ideological groups. Further, case studies will allow us to better measure (or at least describe) the basic interest group functions taking place on the Web: member recruitment and retention, lobbying, and information provision. There are, of course, methodological problems with a case study analysis. The most glaring problem with case studies is in one's ability to generalize about a social phenomenon from such a small sample. All throughout this book, we have used aggregate and individual level statistical analyses to make general statements about political behavior on the Internet. Here we shift gears just a bit by eschewing the general for the specific. We do, however, believe that studying these specific cases within the broader context of our general large sample analyses in this chapter and the rest of the book is a fruitful research strategy.

Another thorny methodological problem case study research faces is in the choice of case study subjects. If I am examining economic development, which handful of countries do I choose? Likewise, if we have a sample of a hundred political Web sites, how do we choose which sites to study? Do we do this randomly? Do we base the choice on our "favorite" sites? In this chapter, we opted to do neither. Instead, we selected the Web site within each ideological category that had the highest Net presence. Recall that this is the number of pages in a site multiplied by the linkages to these pages from other Internet locations. In this way, we chose the highest-profile sites within each category. This saves us from conscious or unconscious selection bias in choosing personally favorite sites. It also gives us six sites that share at least one trait: they are the largest and most well-known sites in their ideological categories within our sample of one hundred Web sites. Therefore, we are in this chapter comparing case studies that share at least one variable in common.

Our six case study sites are, in order of their Net presence: the Christian Coalition (conservative, net presence = 730),[7] the Golden Key Campaign for Private Communications Online (libertarian, 410), the Federation of American Scientists (liberal, 333), Vox Pop (neutral, 317), the Democratic Socialists of America (leftist, 32), and the John Birch Society (rightist, 20). Even though these are the sites with the highest net presence scores from their respective ideological categories, they do not all have the same high profile on the Internet. The Christian Coalition page has a presence twice as high as its liberal counterpart, and is almost that much larger than the libertarian site. Further, the liberal, conservative, libertarian, and neutral case study sites are *at least* ten times larger in their net presence than the two fringe groups' Web sites.

Before moving on to a comparison of these highest-profile sites to each other and their ideological groups, we want to offer a short description of each case study site's sponsoring group. The Christian Coalition is a very large membership organization that lobbies federal, state, and local governments on behalf of "pro-family" issues. They are strongly anti-abortion, oppose any preferential treatment for homosexuals, and are opposed to government financing of family planning.

The Golden Key Campaign for Private Communications Online is an advocacy coalition sponsored primarily by the Electronic Frontier Foundation, the American Civil Liberties Union, and the Center for Technology and Democracy. This libertarian site is actually hosted and maintained by the Electronic Frontier Foundation. The Golden Key Campaign is an attempt to protect the cryptography rights of private U.S. citizens and corporations from government interference. The campaign opposes any government attempt to curtail the rights of people to encrypt their e-mail communications or documents. As such, the Golden Key Campaign Web site is a natural for a large net presence, since its primary constituency is Web users.

Our liberal case study site is that of the Federation of American Scientists. This is an advocacy and membership organization that was originally founded by several Manhattan Project nuclear scientists. It primarily engages in peace advocacy, and its membership is open to any natural or social scientist.

Vox Pop, our neutral site, is different from all the others. Our other five sites are either the official Web sites of real-world organizations or, in the case of the Golden Key site, a project-specific page sponsored by several real-world groups. Vox Pop is actually a collection of links to all types of political Web sites, as well as an e-mail directory of politicians and a gigantic political bulletin board. It takes no open political stances nor does it favor one ideological view over the other. Rather, Vox Pop is a free commercial service that is supported by advertising. As such, Vox Pop is one of the early commercial attempts to "cash in" on the Web's popularity as a venue for both electronic publication and political discussion.

Finally, our two case study fringe sites are near-polar opposites ideologically, as one would expect. The Democratic Socialists of America are a soft-left (i.e., non-Stalinist) membership organization primarily confined to American academia. They sponsor conferences, have strategic ties with other political groups in the United States, and are part of the larger international socialist community. The John Birch Society is a fiercely isolationist, anticommunist membership group that opposes United Nations membership for the United States, supports gun ownership rights, and has a soft spot for right-wing conspiracy theories. Remember that even though these are the fringe sites with the largest net presences in their ideological categories, their actual net presence scores are at least ten times lower than those for the mainstream organizations.

Case Study Sites Compared to Overall Averages

In this section, we will briefly replicate Figures 6.1 through 6.5, this time using the actual data for the six individual case studies rather than for all one hundred groups. In this way, we can see not only how the case study sites differ from each other in size, flash, links, and so forth, but also how they are unique within their own ideological groups. Please remember that the earlier figures dealt with *averages* for each of our six ideological groups, while the case study sites are each in their own way *unique*, being the sites within each political category with the highest net presence.

Figure 6.6 presents the data on size for these six Web sites. Of course, all these pages are larger than the average for their categories. This size differential ranges from Vox Pop and the Christian Coalition sites—over six times larger than the average neutral and liberal site, respectively—to the two fringe sites, only twice as large as normal for their categories. Still, the overall pattern is the same: the conservative site (in this case, the Christian Coalition) and the neutral site (Vox Pop) are the largest. The one real break in the pattern is the size of the Federation of American Scientists site, which is much larger than the two fringe sites. Recall from Figure 6.1 that the average liberal site was slightly *smaller* than the fringe sites.

Site visibility is the subject for Figure 6.7, which again contains the number of external links per site on the vertical axis, and the net presence figure in the size of each data bubble. Again we observe basically the same pattern as in Figure 6.2; our conservative and libertarian sites have the most Internet links to them, and the highest net presence. On the other hand, our two fringe sites—the Democratic Socialists of America and the John Birch Society—have far fewer Web links to them, and have miniscule net presence when compared with the mainstream and libertarian sites. As with Figure 6.6, the one major break from the average pattern is in the Federation of American Scientists (FAS) site, which has a much higher profile than the average liberal site in Figure 6.2, where we saw that liberal sites were seriously disadvantaged vis-à-vis conservative sites in the number of links to them. Here, the FAS site actually has slightly *more* Internet links to it than does its conservative counterpart.

Another way to explain site visibility and Web presence that we have not discussed yet is to examine how well each page is constructed for keyword

FIGURE 6.6
Number of Pages for Six Case Study Web Sites

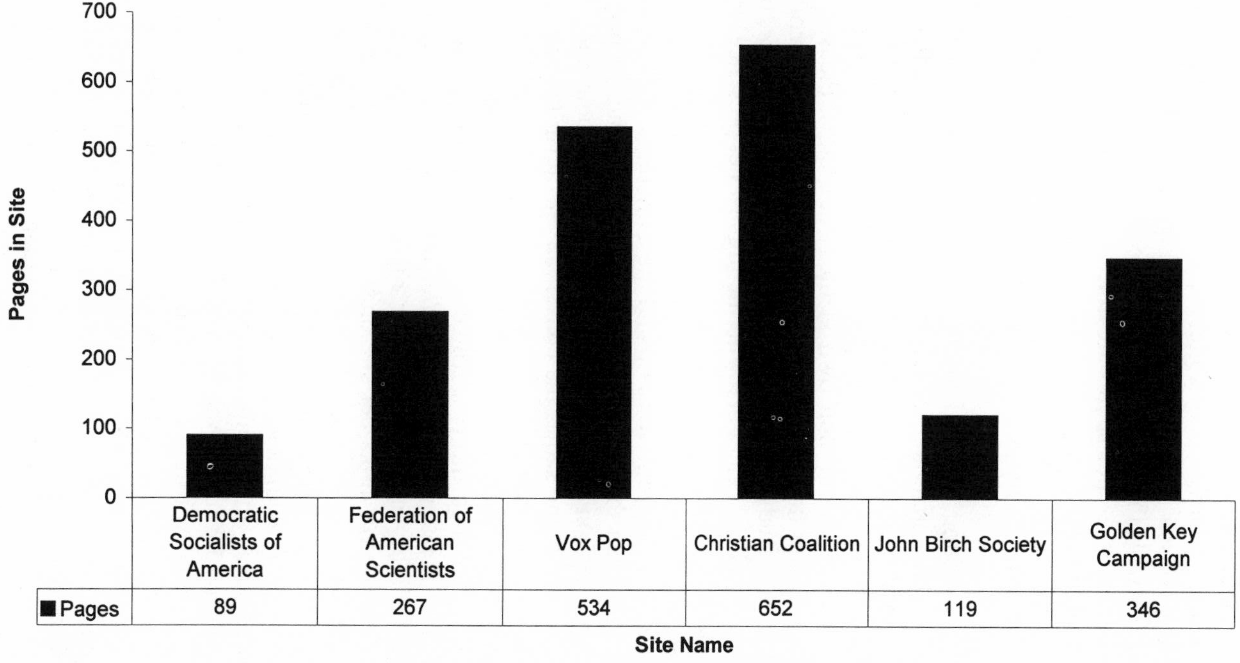

Site Name	Pages
Democratic Socialists of America	89
Federation of American Scientists	267
Vox Pop	534
Christian Coalition	652
John Birch Society	119
Golden Key Campaign	346

159

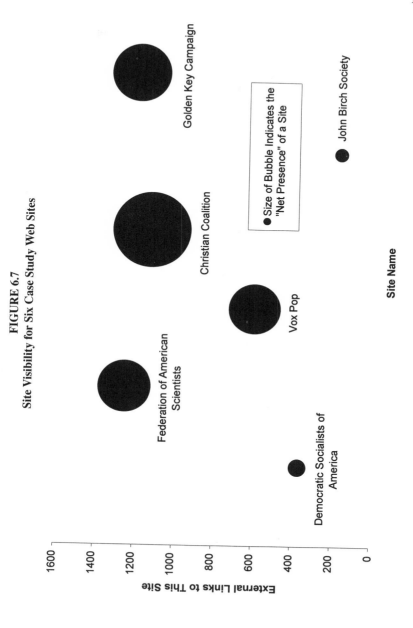

FIGURE 6.7
Site Visibility for Six Case Study Web Sites

indexing. Many of the keyword search engines on the Internet, including Infoseek and AltaVista (*www.altavista.digital.com*), make use of a special HTML programming language convention called the <META> tag when indexing sites on the World Wide Web. People who construct Web sites are usually well aware of this practice, which involves intentionally embedding keywords into one's site. These keywords are not actually visible to the person viewing the page, but are part of the Web page's programming. Theoretically, a Webmaster is supposed to put keywords that accurately describe his or her site between two <META> tags so that people keyword searching one of these search engines will get a reference to their site. For example, a site may deal with politics, so it will use the keyword "politics" in its <META> tags. Then a person searching Infoseek or some other engine that makes use of these tags will get a reference to this page when they keyword-search for "politics."

Table 6.2 lists the keywords that appear in the <META> tags of these six sites. Notice that the Democratic Socialists of America, the Christian Coalition, and the Golden Key Campaign home pages contain no keywords. Therefore, these sites are not taking advantage of one of the ways to increase one's presence on the Internet. This is interesting particularly for our conservative and libertarian case study sites, which have by far the highest net presence scores even though they do not use <META> keyword tags. Maybe they do not need them, since these sites are so large and have links from other Web sites at such a high level. The John Birch Society has merely embedded its name as a keyword. The Federation of American Scientists site makes liberal use of <META> tag keywords, with illustrative keywords that relate to its major political goals and agendas. Finally, the Vox Pop site is humorous, in that it not only contains "relevant" embedded keywords like "politics" and "voting," but also words irrelevant to its site content, such as "sex," "nude," and "picture." Apparently, this is an attempt to cash in on the Web's somewhat deserved reputation as being an incredibly large source of pornography. One can only imagine what the poor soul who types in the keywords "nude sex picture" thinks when he or she gets a reference to a political index like this!

Figure 6.8 reprises our analysis of Web site "flashiness." Again, the vertical axis measures the number of graphics per page for each of the six sites, while the size of the data bubbles corresponds to the raw number of graphics in a site. Here we see a fairly large break from the average pattern of Figure 6.3. Whereas on average neutral and conservative sites contain the most graphical elements and leftist sites the fewest, here we observe that Vox Pop, our neutral site, contains practically no graphics. This is probably a function of Vox Pop being a site that contains links almost exclusively. Also, the Democratic Socialists of America site actually is much closer to its liberal counterpart here in flashiness than the average leftist site is to the

TABLE 6.2
Search Engine ⟨META⟩ Tags in Six Case Study Web Sites

Democratic Socialists of America	None
Federation of American Scientists	science, military, arms, arms control, secrecy, government satellites, rockets, security, classification, intelligence, missiles, ships, tanks, aircraft, weapons, virology, medicine, nuclear, non-proliferation, biological weapons, chemical weapons, defense spending
Vox Pop	politics, government, sex, voting, jefferson, project, ZIP codes, dog, democrat, nude, republican, libertarian, election, picture, internet, voice, exon, shareware
Christian Coalition	None
John Birch Society	John Birch Society
Golden Key Campaign	None

Note: These keywords were embedded in the <META> tags of these six Web sites as of August 14, 1997.

average liberal site. Still, the conservative Christian Coalition site remains king of overall glitz in our case studies, with a slightly higher rate of graphics per page and a far higher raw number of graphical elements than any of its five counterparts.

Similar data for links per page and the raw number of external links in a site appears in Figure 6.9. Here we get a pattern very unlike that for all one hundred Web sites found in Figure 6.4. Clearly the Democratic Socialists of America (DSA) site dwarfs the other five sites in the rate of links per page. Further, the raw number of external links found in the DSA, Vox Pop, and Golden Key Campaign sites is much higher than that found in the two mainstream liberal and conservative sites. The Federation of American Scientists and Christian Coalition Web pages are rather self-contained, with comparatively few linkages to the rest of the Internet. Notice that the John Birch Society site does not even show up on this graph, since it contains *not one link* to the rest of the Internet.

162

FIGURE 6.8
Graphic Flashiness of Six Case Study Web Sites

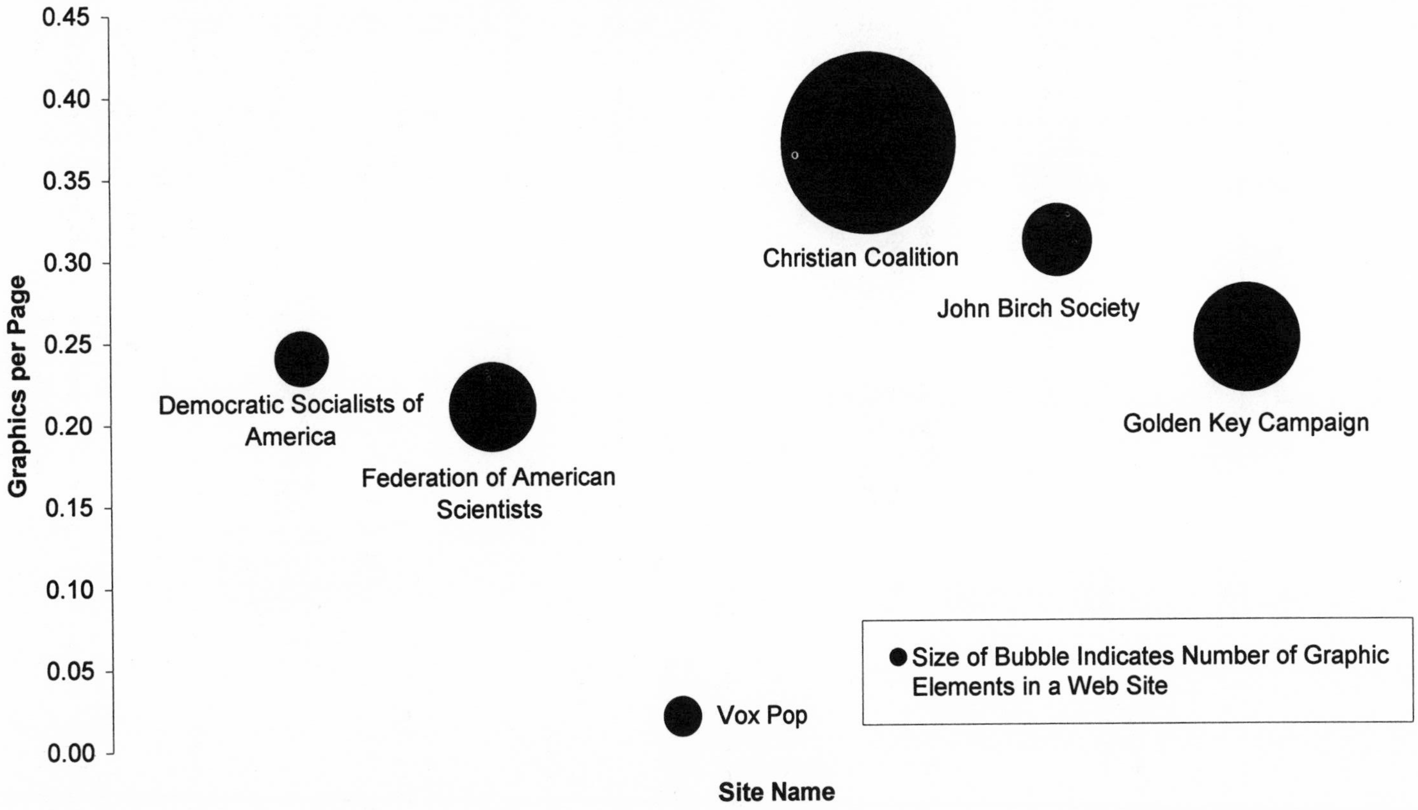

● Size of Bubble Indicates Number of Graphic Elements in a Web Site

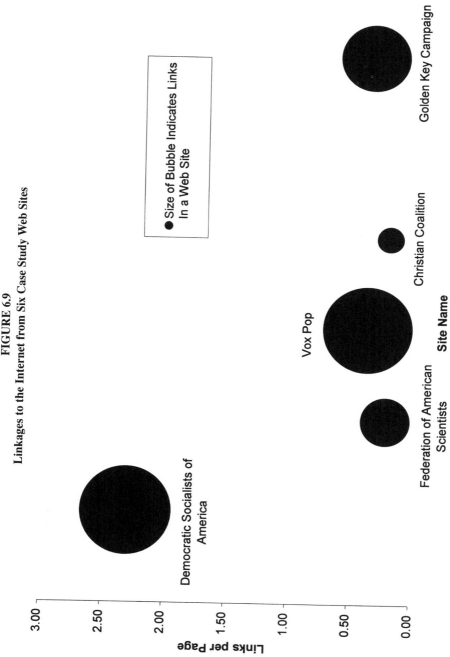

FIGURE 6.9
Linkages to the Internet from Six Case Study Web Sites

Finally, Figure 6.10 presents data on the graphics-versus-links phenomenon. Here we see a pattern very similar to that found in Figure 6.5. The conservative and right-wing sites contain many more graphic elements than links, while the leftist site is overwhelmingly devoted to links at the expense of flash. Notice also that the Federation of American Scientists site is absolutely balanced between the two forms of Web communication, while Vox Pop is also heavily slanted toward links, this being primarily an index to other political sites on the Internet.

In the end, although these six case study sites are larger and more widely known on the Internet than the averages for their respective ideological categories, they basically follow the same patterns in their size, flashiness, and Web interconnectivity, with the notable exceptions detailed above. The reader, then, can be fairly confident that the case studies to follow are not merely an exercise in the idiosyncratic, but will yield some generalizable data about the political uses of the World Wide Web by people of differing ideological stripes. What follows is our analysis of the actual content of these six Web sites. We present them in no particular order, and we strive to maintain a common structure of discussion for each of the six case studies.

The Christian Coalition (www.cc.org)

Simply stated, the Christian Coalition Web site is a multimedia powerhouse, which is also very well suited to political life on the Web. Stylistically and substantively, this is a site to be emulated by other groups, regardless of political motivation. The largest and most graphically intense of our one hundred Web sites, the Christian Coalition pages are primarily geared toward legislative action alerts and news of pending state and federal laws of interest to members. This site is not heavily engaged in new-member recruiting, although it does provide a page where potential members can request more information on joining the Christian Coalition.

The site contains textured backgrounds with the Christian Coalition's logo throughout the massive site. It sports flashing banners, animated buttons and icons, and clickable 3-D text that provides logical links to all parts of the site from any other part. At the bottom of the opening page, the site also presents graphical banners of all the design and content awards it has won recently. There is a keyword search function available on almost every page, which allows users to search the site for news and information. This is obviously very important, since the site is so large that it is easy to become lost. There are even tips on the search page for making one's search more successful.

The opening page is presented in a newspaper format, with headlines about current legislation that change on almost a daily basis. Each news item is hyperlinked to another page providing more information, and if the news

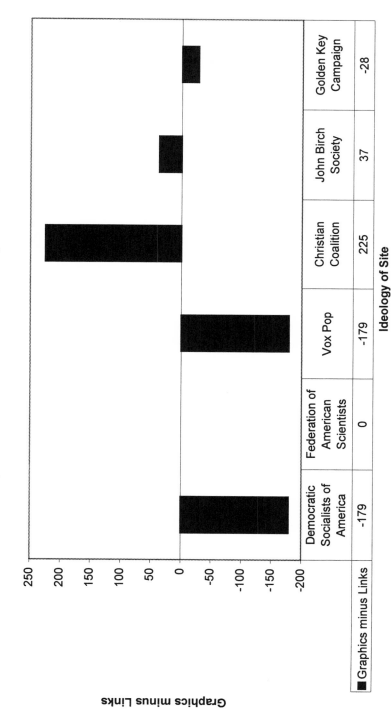

FIGURE 6.10
Graphic Elements Minus Links for Six Case Study Web Sites

item at hand is about pending legislation, links to send e-mail to members of Congress and the president are offered. There is even a section of this site that allows a user to enter his or her Zip Code to find his or her representative and senators. Here the Christian Coalition offers e-mail addresses, fax and telephone numbers, and postal addresses, as well as information on how the legislators have voted on bills of interest to the coalition in the past. The site also contains an archive of previous action alerts and news bulletins. For example, on August 14, 1997, the opening page of the Web site contained a large article on the partial-birth abortion ban. Below this article was a link to a form letter the user could send to President Clinton electronically, asking him not to veto the partial-birth abortion ban that had passed the Senate. In this way, the Christian Coalition is using the multimedia and hypertext-linking capabilities of the Web in a very skillful way to both provide political information and lobbying functions simultaneously. Interestingly, none of the five other case study sites presented nearly this level of political and technological sophistication. Further, this site contains very few links to outside sources of information on the Web, instead being content to provide its own political content and keep readers within its confines. This is not surprising, given that conservative sites contain comparatively few external links, especially when compared to liberal sites.

When combined with the multimedia and other technological aspects of the site, the Christian Coalition's lobbying and information provision functions on the Web show just how effectively a Web site can be used politically. If other conservative sites even come close to this level of combined political and technological sophistication, they will then absolutely dominate the political parts of the Web, especially in their ability to connect Web technologies to real-world political lobbying. Recall that, on average, conservative sites *are* larger and flashier than their ideological counterparts. A large membership-based organization like the Christian Coalition takes this size and glitz comparative advantage and adds political muscle.

The Federation of American Scientists (www.fas.org)

Inevitably, one of the natural comparisons we make here in our case studies is between the conservative Christian Coalition site and the liberal Federation of American Scientists site. Even though these two series of pages are devoted to totally different issues, the comparison is valid, since they are our "representatives" of the two mainstream ideological positions in American politics. They are both the largest sites within their categories, and they are tops in their categories in external Internet links to them. While the Christian Coalition site is primarily devoted to abortion politics, the series of Web pages from the Federation of American Scientists concerns itself with a wider variety of issues, including arms control, nuclear and chemical weapons proliferation, science funding, and open dialogue with the Castro regime in Cuba. It is not surprising, therefore, that the FAS site is a bit less organized that the Christian Coalition site, although this is still a very effective and well-designed Web site.

The Federation of American Scientists uses its Web site a bit differently than the Christian Coalition. Instead of being devoted primarily to lobbying and information supporting lobbying, the FAS site is first devoted to news of its deeds, and also to recruiting potential members. Regarding multimedia glitz, the FAS home page sports a textured background, albeit without a stylized logo like the Christian Coalition uses. The colors of the home page are a muted green with a beige background. However, the use of these colors and texture schemes is inconsistent throughout parts of the site, primarily because the Web site is broken up into a series of project-specific pages, unlike the Christian Coalition site and its current (as of August 1997) devotion to a single issue—abortion. Similar to the conservative site, the FAS Web site contains a search function that is accessible from almost any page. Again, with the diversity of material offered on topics ranging from food additives to chemical warfare, the FAS site greatly benefits from this well-implemented search function.

Information provision—both news of interest to members and updates on FAS actions—is the major focus of this Web site. The Federation's major projects are logically listed on the top of the home page, where the user can follow hyperlinks to their "subsites." Indeed, the Federation of American Scientists page is arranged somewhat differently from many other sites. Alongside separate series of pages devoted to news, updates, recruiting, and feedback, the FAS site also splits itself into project-specific pages. For example, if one is interested in nuclear proliferation, one merely clicks on the appropriate project hyperlink and is taken to a whole new series of pages devoted to news, current and past legislation, and the FAS's opinion on the issue. This sort of Web strategy turns out to be very useful, especially for an organization like this which has a diverse range of legislative and professional interests. There is a price: since these project-specific subsites are maintained by various departments and people in the FAS, their layout and multimedia content is inconsistent, giving the site as a whole a less professional feel than the Christian Coalition's pages.

Besides the project-specific subsites, the federation also includes sections where one can view and download current and past press releases, interact with others in subject-specific bulletin boards, and read the various "physical" publications the federation offers. A person browsing the site is given full access to several publications, including the *Public Interest Report*, the *Secrecy and Government Bulletin,* and the *Arms Sales Monitor.* Further, there are hyperlinks to many outside sources of news on the Internet, a stark contrast to the Christian Coalition's practice of keeping all news and information sources in-house. One must wonder whether putting all these publications on-line makes long-term sense from a member-recruiting standpoint, since the *Public Interest Report* is one of the perks one receives upon joining the Federation of American Scientists. By making it available on-line, the FAS may be undercutting its recruitment and member retention efforts, since this incentive to join is now "non-selective" (Olson, 1968), meaning that anyone can have access to the *Report,* regardless of member status.

There is a limited amount of lobbying at this Web site. Again, this lobbying is rather inconsistent across the various projects the FAS maintains on its site. There are action alerts about pending legislation and in some cases the names of committee members in Congress, along with contact information. Other than this, the site is not at all geared toward lobbying in the real world. Organizational maintenance and member recruiting are other major focuses of this liberal site, along with the information provision discussed above. The site contains links to a "Join" page on almost every other page, thus reminding the reader of the site that the federation is, after all, a membership-supported organization.

The "Join" page contains details about joining, including the various levels of membership. Since this is an elite rather than a mass interest group, the site explains how only natural and social scientists can obtain full memberships. Still, this section of the Web site does include solicitations for money, and explains that such funds can be earmarked for specific projects. One can fill out a Web-based membership application, send it to the federation electronically, and get invoiced for the membership fee via regular mail. There are also on-line opinion surveys and feedback for suggestions about the various projects the federation sponsors. The only material incentives offered for becoming a dues-paying member are a pocket calendar and the *Public Interest Report,* the latter of which is available to anyone on-line regardless of their membership status. In short, the Federation of American Scientists site is a well-designed series of pages primarily providing information about current projects, with an eye toward member recruitment rather than lobbying. As such, this liberal site is quite different from our conservative Christian Coalition case study, which focused its efforts squarely on lobbying.

The Golden Key Campaign for Private Communications Online (www.eff.org/goldkey.html)

Libertarianism has never fit very well into our American concept of left-versus-right ideology. After all, libertarians share with liberals a common desire to see government interference in one's private life kept to a minimum. On the other hand, libertarians share with conservatives the suspicion of government interference into one's economic rights as well. The one over-arching theme in libertarian thought and practice, then, is a deep suspicion of government intrusion into anything. Our nine libertarian sites all share these traits in common, even though they may at first glance appear either liberal or conservative. Our set of libertarian sites includes groups advocating the abolition of motorcycle helmet laws, extremely low taxes, the legalization of hemp for smoking, and the present case study site. The Golden Key Campaign is a cooperative venture of several civil liberties and privacy groups, and the Web site under study here is sponsored by the Electronic Frontier Foundation (EFF), a computer and communication rights group. The Golden Key Campaign surely has the most specific agenda of any of our case study Web sites. The campaign is to support the rights of on-line users, software developers, and corporations to encrypt their private communications. Currently, the United States government does not allow the export of certain types of commonly available encryption technology. Indeed, sending an e-mail message that has been encrypted with 128-bit technology to a colleague overseas is technically arms smuggling in the eyes of the federal government. The Golden Key Campaign lobbies for the repeal of these types of laws that it sees as infringement on people's electronic privacy rights.

The Golden Key site, therefore, has a very specific agenda, especially when compared with the diverse interests of the Federation of American Scientists site. Being sponsored by a group with a narrow agenda, the Golden Key site is narrowly tailored to providing highly specialized information. Indeed, this case study is politically different from all the others here. Instead of a real-world group hosting a Web site to cash in on electronic media technology, here we have a group that would not even exist without the technology of the Internet. Since privacy concerns are of non-trivial interest to on-line users, it is not surprising that the EFF site, which hosts the Golden Key Campaign pages, is one of the four most linked-to sites on the World Wide Web. What *is* surprising, however, is the fact that this Web site has a far less sleek and professional look than do our liberal and conservative case study sites. One would expect a site maintained by computer and communications industry professionals would be glitzier than this site. Still, maybe this points to the fact that much of the multimedia chrome and finish used by so many commercial and political organizations on the Web is largely superfluous to the task of providing information. In addition, the lack of a working search function is a fairly serious oversight for a site that presents so much information.

Even though this site does not score very highly on the "flashiness scale," is does manage to accomplish its goals of providing news and legal information, and in recruiting viewers of the site to support the campaign. Remember that the Golden Key Campaign is not in itself a membership organization, but rather a cooperative venture of several other organizations.

Therefore, the Golden Key Campaign Web site does not actively solicit donations or offer people membership applications. Having said that, this site ironically may be the most effective recruiting device we see in these case studies. The site contains dozens of graphics, mostly depicting golden keys, which users are encouraged to download and incorporate into their own pages. In this way, the golden key graphics become the Web version of bumper stickers. People put the golden key graphics on their Web sites, use the graphics as a hypertext link to the Golden Key site, and thereby expose even more people to the electronic privacy initiative. This is probably one of the reasons that the Electronic Frontier Foundation site that hosts these Web pages is one of the most linked-to sites on the entire Internet.

The Golden Key site is in these ways unique, but it also shares some similarities with our other case study sites. Information provision as a vehicle for recruitment (in this case, to spread the word about electronic privacy) is the main focus for this site, making it similar in motivation to the Federation of American Scientists pages. The opening page of the site includes links to not only the sponsoring organizations for the campaign, but also to various legal and legislative update pages and reports of a more technical nature. Also on that first page are all the graphics that the campaign offers for download. Again, one is impressed by the focused nature of this site, especially when compared to the FAS and even Christian Coalition sites, which devoted themselves to a far broader range of interests. This Golden Key Campaign site is a good example of how to politically organize a series of Web pages around a very specific (even esoteric) political issue. Even if this page lacks the flash and pizzazz of the Christian Coalition's site, it does serve its purpose.

Vox Pop (www.voxpop.org)

Vox Pop is the only Web site in our case studies that is neither the official home page of a political organization nor a project sponsored by real-world interest groups. This site is really more of a service than anything else. It is a series of pages devoted to cataloguing political links on the Web, providing e-mail addresses and other contact information for legislators, and being a Web-based political bulletin board system. Since the site takes no overt political stance, we classify it as neutral. Vox Pop is maintained by Star Dot, a private company. This begs the question of why someone would go to the expense of constructing such a first-class site and not charging for access to it. Simply stated, Star Dot *does* charge advertisers to put their banners and links in the site. As such, Vox Pop is one of the growing number of Web sites that follows the model set by free weekly newspapers: give away your product to the public for free, but pack it with ads. At this point, there are very few ads in the Vox Pop site, and the ones that are there do not get in the way of a viewer using this site. In fact, regardless of political stripe, readers of the book will surely find the Vox Pop site a very useful one.

Visually, the site is very appealing. Although it uses no textured backgrounds, the site has a consistent white background color throughout, uses soft, muted 3-D graphics and text that enhance the professional feel of the pages, and includes text links to its various pages so that the person with a slow Web connection can still enjoy the site. Vox Pop is further divided into three major sections. The Jefferson Project is a series of categorized political links and is keyword-searchable and updated often. The Zipper is another search function which allows a person to input his or her Zip Code to look up contact information on U.S. representatives and senators. Finally, the Voice Box is a Web-based bulletin board system where users can engage in arguments and debates about political issues.

Since Vox Pop is a service rather than an instrument of political persuasion, there really is not anything like the lobbying and recruiting here that goes on with our other five case study sites. Still, since the service offers the Zipper service, which includes e-mail addresses for elected officials, one could see this section of Vox Pop as "roll your own" lobbying. For a small fee, a user can even send a fax or telegram to any senator or representative. As for recruiting, the site is free for anyone's use, so member recruitment is not an issue at all. Of course, Vox Pop does court advertisers, which in some ways could be considered recruiting, but this is not a membership-based organization. In short, Vox Pop probably tells us more about the future of advertiser-sponsored reference sites on the Web than it does about interest group activity. Nevertheless, Web sites like this are an important subset of politics on the Internet, since they do provide pathways to partisan political Web sites.

The Democratic Socialists of America (www.dsausa.org)

Our left-wing fringe case study site will certainly win no Web multimedia design awards. Further, the Democratic Socialists of America site will never be anyone's alternative source for updated news, since the page's contents had not been changed in over eight months as of August 1997. This site is mainly not engaged in information provision, recruiting, or lobbying, although it does a bit of the latter two. Like so many leftist organizations, the Democratic Socialists of America seem to be using their site more to provide their context within the myriad American left. The DSA provides an interesting history of itself and the rest of the American left, a massive number of links to other left-wing sites all across the globe, and even its bylaws and constitution, written in a bewildering combination of legalese and obscure Marxist jargon. If anything, this site focuses itself on organizational maintenance and justifying its place in the American political spectrum.

None of the pages employs a textured background image, although the site does consistently use a white background throughout. There are very few graphics, which is not in itself bad, since too many graphics can bog down a site, especially for users with slower Internet connections. The one graphic element that is present on most pages is the DSA's red-rose-in-a-fist logo, which is rather striking. No part of the site is keyword-searchable, an unfortunate omission for such a relatively large site that is so text-intensive. Other design problems include the absence of toolbars and other navigational aids at the tops and bottoms of pages, which would help the user to negotiate this large series of pages. The one "table of contents" that does provide such linkages is to be found in the middle of the first page, which is not where a long-time Web surfer would expect to find such a navigational aid. In our opinion, the Democratic Socialists of America site is the least professional-looking site of our six case studies.

Having said that, the site is still very impressive in the amount (if not the kind) of data it presents. There are hundreds of links to other left-wing sources: leftist organizations worldwide, a few leftist members of the U.S. Congress, commentaries and periodicals, and many academic sites. The Democratic Socialists of America also offer everything the interested reader could ask for about the way the internal politics of the group works. There is very little in the way of current news, and absolutely no attempt to get members and sympathizers to lobby any legislature. That should not be too surprising, since many American leftists believe that traditional lobbying of the government is futile, since the political system is a gigantic sham in the first place. As for recruitment activities, the DSA page does have a form which a viewer can fill in to request more information about the group and to join.

The John Birch Society (www.jbs.org)

The Democratic Socialists of America site would be much more impressive were it not for how it compares to its "natural rival" in our case studies—the right-wing John Birch Society. This site has a very professional look, with consistent toolbars, graphics, and backgrounds throughout. The John Birch Society uses its Web site almost exclusively as a recruitment vehicle, although there is limited lobbying and some news and information.

It is very interesting to compare these two fringe sites. Please remember that these Web sites on the right and left have a comparatively tiny net presence vis-à-vis the mainstream sites in our case studies. Therefore, with such a limited presence on the Web, it is very important that these sites take advantage of the relatively cheap and effective Internet as a venue for publishing, lobbying, and getting their respective messages out. On these scores, the right-wing John Birch Society (JBS) is light-years ahead of its left-wing Democratic Socialists of America counterpart. In fact, regardless of political content, the JBS site is one of the most visually appealing and easy to use of the one hundred Web sites in our sample.

Upon entering the John Birch Society site at its home page, one sees a clickable image map that leads to all the major parts of the site—publications, information on what the John Birch Society is, current activities, and of course information on joining. For people with slow Internet connections, the site also offers text-based links to these subsections. A miniature version of this image map is duplicated at the top of each subsequent page, making site navigation quite easy. Also on the front page are flashing "What's Hot" buttons that do capture one's attention. There is a search function available from every page, which indexes the site—something the DSA site lacked.

Most of the news and information in the site, as well as limited lobbying of public officials, is geared toward getting people to join the John Birch Society. The current issue of the *John Birch Society Bulletin* is available online, as are back issues. There is an on-line bookstore from which one can electronically order various right-wing publications, as well as a directory of congressional e-mail addresses. There is very little in the way of current news posted on the site, though as of August 1997 there was an entire section devoted to various rightist speculations on the Oklahoma City bombing. There are several pages of John Birch Society history, including sections about the leaders and founders of the group, and a "who we are and what we believe in" section. As for lobbying, there is one section that provides a link to Representative Ron Paul's (R-Texas) office. Paul is an ally of the John Birch Society, sponsoring a bill to remove the United States from United Nations membership. This, however, is the end of the line as far as news and current political lobbying are concerned.

In the end, the John Birch Society Web site is more of a huge billboard or advertisement than any other site in our case studies. Under the "Join" section, the site lists twelve reasons why a person should become a member. There is an on-line survey one can fill out to see how close one's views are to those held by the JBS. The society advertises its various publications and even its summer youth camp to encourage people to join. Indeed, the JBS is the only organization in our case studies to use purposive, selective, and solidary incentives in its Web site to solicit new members (Wilson, 1961; Olsen, 1968). Purposive incentives are political reasons to join a group; if one agrees with the political goals of a group, one is tempted to join. All the membership-based sites in our case studies tried to appeal to the political ideology of their readers. Selective incentives are goods and services available only to group members; the Federation of American Scientists' pocket calendars are an example. Solidary incentives are socially based reasons to join an interest group. One may choose to join a group to be around like-minded people with common interests. The John Birch Society Web site heavily pushes the solidary benefits of membership, especially through its summer youth camps. Therefore, the JBS site tries to appeal at three different levels to recruit new members. Indeed, their whole Web presence revolves around this member recruiting.

Summary and Conclusions:
Is the Web Yet Another Conservative Playground?

Table 6.3 summarizes our case study findings, presenting a score card for each Web site in the information, lobbying, and member recruitment activities that take place in their respective sites. The Democratic Socialists of America use the Web primarily to provide hypertext links to other leftist sites, advertise their local chapters, and give people purposive political reasons to join. The liberal Federation of American Scientists employs its Web site to perform a much wider variety of tasks, heavily concentrated on information and member recruitment. Vox Pop, being more of a service than an interest group, does not fit very well into this functional scheme, though of course people can use their resources for do-it-yourself lobbying. The conservative Christian Coalition uses the Web in a wide variety of ways, similar to its liberal FAS counterpart; however, the Christian Coalition couples information with lobbying, rather than information with recruitment. The John Birch Society engages in a much wider range of Web activities than its left fringe counterpart, making it look more like the mainstream sites in its use of the Internet. Finally, the Golden Key Campaign uses its site to lobby and recruit people to its very specific political issues.

We saw in chapter 2 that demographically conservatives are in a minority among Internet users. Then in chapters 3 and 5 we started to get a different picture. In those previous sections of the book, we found that even though conservatives are the minority of Internet users, they dominate the Usenet political newsgroups and America Online's political chat rooms. Now we are faced with the same question in chapter 6: Do conservatives likewise dominate the political portions of the World Wide Web? Here we focused more on the ways in which people use the Web politically as well as the sheer numbers of left versus right Web sites.

Hypothesis 6.1 proposed that there would be more conservative than liberal sites on the World Wide Web. Our findings do not support this conclusion. If one lumps liberal and leftist sites into one group, and conservative and rightist sites into another, there is rough ideological parity on the Web between the two groups. We simply do not find the wide gap in sheer num-

TABLE 6.3
Interest Group Functions Present in Six Case Study Web Sites

	Democratic Socialists of America	Federation of American Scientists	Vox Pop	Christian Coalition	John Birch Society	Golden Key Campaign
1. Information						
Testimony	*	*				*
Public meetings						
In-house news		*		*	*	*
Outsource news		*		*	*	*
2. Lobbying						
Legal action						*
Communication to politicians		*	*	*	*	*
Mutual support for sympathetic politicians	*			*	*	*
3. Recruitment and Maintenance						
Selective incentives	*	*		*	*	
Purposive incentives		*	*		*	
Solidary incentives					*	
Identification of potential members		*	*	*	*	*
Fundraising		*	*	*		
Feedback from Web site users				*	*	
Alliances to other groups (links)	*	*				*

bers between left and right that we saw in chapters 3 and 5, though of course conservative sites *are* larger than liberal sites on average. Further, the net presence (the number of pages multiplied by links to the site) was overwhelmingly higher for conservative than liberal sites.

What we *did* find, however, was support for Hypothesis 6.2's proposition that conservative Web sites would have higher production values than their left and liberal counterparts. As measured by the number of graphics and graphics per page, this was supported in our overall and case study analyses. Our conservative case study site—the Christian Coalition site—was clearly the most professional looking of the six we reviewed, though the liberal FAS site was well designed also.

Hypothesis 6.3 offered the notion that there would be a non-trivial number of fringe political sites on the World Wide Web. A full 21% of the one hundred sites in our sample were classified as either right-wing or left-wing fringe sites. This is surely a non-trivial number. A person turning on a television would certainly not find that one out of five news programs were coming from the left or right fringes of the American ideological spectrum. Likewise, a shopper at the local bookstore would surely not find that 21% of all the current events and politics titles were from the political fringes. We earlier proposed that because of the open, non-mediated, and inexpensive nature of hosting a Web site, fringe political groups would naturally make use of this new electronic medium. It appears we were correct, since a large chunk of our political sites are on the fringes. Our case studies also showed that, at least in the case of the right-wing John Birch Society, the production values of a political fringe Web site can rival those of any mainstream Internet presence. Still, these right- and left-wing fringe Web sites have by far the lowest profiles on the World Wide Web, when compared to mainstream political sites. Nevertheless, the fringes of politics absolutely cannot be ignored on the World Wide Web.

What are we to make of all this? When the Oklahoma City federal building was blown up in a right-wing terrorist bombing in April 1995, people immediately began to point fingers at the Web as being a depository for bomb recipes. In 1996, Congress passed and the president signed the Communications Decency Act. One of the underlying assumptions of this bill was that the Web was a vast breeding ground of filth and sexual perversion. Also in 1996, all the presidential candidates established Web sites, and more than one news story touted the ability of the Web to change politics for the better by giving citizens more access to candidates. All of these statements, when stripped of hyperbole, are of course correct in some measure. There *are* places on the Web where one can find instructions for making bombs. One can also go to the local library to find this information. In addition, there *are* many thousands of World Wide Web pages dedicated to pornographic pictures. Then again, the local convenience store has these, too. Yes, the candidates major and minor had Web pages in 1996, but they also ran television ads.

Those utopians who think that any expansion of political communication is a good thing would surely point to the findings in this chapter with some glee. After all, there is rough ideological balance in political Web sites, and even the smallest, most obscure political group can create an effective Web presence. Then again, the dystopians who fear uninformed mob rule and uncivil political discourse may also point to this chapter and shudder. One in five Web sites in our sample is outside the mainstream of American public life. Some of these sites are highly specialized, and some may fear that this specialization is another step toward the tribalization of American society. The Web is a political reflection of "real life," though the reflection sends some light into the rarely seen fringes of the American spectrum.

Notes

1. If you are interested, Kevin Hill's personal Web site is at *www.fiu.edu/~khill.* John Hughes' site is at *www.monmouth.edu/~jhughes.*

2. Of course, the term "fringe group" may change over time and certainly across national boundaries. Certainly, a socialist group would be on the left fringes of the American ideological spectrum in the 1990s, while that same group would be squarely in the political mainstream in Sweden. Likewise, the Christian Coalition is a mainstream conservative group in the American context, but such a group in Sweden would probably constitute the fringes of the right.

3. For all the quantitative results in this chapter, we only examine the top three levels of each Web site. That is, when counting the number of pages, graphics, or links, we include only the first (index) pages in a site, all the pages linked to that page, and all the pages linked to those pages. The result looks somewhat like a family tree. We limit ourselves to the top three levels since some sites contain tens of thousands of pages, some of which are very small and contain little if any useful data. In the end, though, nearly all the Web sites we examined here contained no more than three levels anyway.

4. This is accomplished on Infoseek by typing the following in to the search box: + *link:*[site address] -*url:*[site address]. For example, to find the number of Web sites linking to the Libertarian party's page, one would type: + *link:www.lp.org -url:www.lp.org.* The first part of the search looks for all links on Web pages to *www.lp.org,* while the second excludes all links to *www.lp.org* from other pages at *www.lp.org.* In this way, we get only the number of links to the Libertarian Party Web site that are contained in pages *other than* the Libertarian Party's own pages.

5. Only links to outside resources—links to pages not part of the Web site they are contained in—are included. We call these "external links."

6. In the figure, we have indicated that the value for graphic minus links for libertarian sites is zero. Actually, the value is .11, but this is so close to perfect balance that we rounded to the nearest integer.

7. Actually, these net presence figures are divided by 1,000 for presentation purposes. The true net presence value for the Christian Coalition is 730,240.

The Internet and the Future of Political Communication

It has been our position all throughout the book that the Internet is a great thing. At the same time, we maintain that the Internet is merely an extension of the fax machine, the telephone, the postal system, the picket fence, and cable television in being a medium of political communications. Surely the Web is a publication medium and political space that has an immediacy and uncontrollability unparalleled in human communications. Having said that, political groups are *not* suddenly transformed in their thinking and practices when someone says in a staff meeting, "Hey! Let's put together a Web site!" Rather, the printed brochures, the handbills, the television commercials, and the other documents all get transformed into Web pages. These Web sites then join the stable of lobbying, information, and recruitment devices that interest groups rely upon in everyday life. The Internet is a supplement to political discourse, not a gigantic paradigm shift. As we have seen here, conservatives, libertarians, and to a lesser extent right-wing extremists have caught on to this idea quicker than others. Further, the Usenet discussion groups and various political chat rooms are venues in which people can talk to each other, exchange ideas and information, and hurl some choice insults.

We started with the research question, How does the Internet affect politics? We then proposed three hypothetical answers to this question. First, we thought that the Internet would be dominated by Republicans, conservatives, and libertarians. As shown in chapter 2, Internet activists as a group are actually more *Democratic* and *liberal* than the public at large. If we had stopped with this analysis of the demographic and political profiles of Net users in general, we may well have abandoned the hypothesis that the Internet is conservative, Republican, and libertarian. But chapters 3, 5, and 6 all demonstrated that the actual *content* of the Usenet newsgroups, chat rooms, and the World Wide Web's political areas is in fact dominated by conservative ideas. We have an apparent contradiction here: if the bulk of Internet activists are Democrats and liberals, how in the world can the Net's major venues be dominated by conservatives? After all, aren't these liberal, libertarian, and Democratic activists the very people posting messages, engaging in chats, and creating Web sites? Yes and no. While it is always a tricky proposition to compare aggregate and individual results in any analysis, we strongly believe that based on our empirical evidence, politics on the Internet is dominated by a relatively small, though vociferous and technologically savvy, conservative minority. While Internet activists as a group may not be overwhelmingly conservative, a conservative subset of those people is very active posting messages, engaging in political chats, and creating Web pages.

Second, we hypothesized that the Internet would encourage more confrontation of a personal nature than would a face-to-face meeting in "real life." On this score we did find that there was a substantial amount of "flaming" taking place in the Usenet discussion groups and in America Online's political chat rooms. However, in the presence of discussions about issues and the provision of political information, the majority of these written discussions were in fact civil. Therefore, those dystopians who fear that computer-mediated political communication will lead to a decline in civility need not lose sleep.

Third, we proposed in the introduction that the Internet would be more open to non-mainstream groups and points of view than would be the traditional media or other venues of political discussion in real life. Certainly the results from all five substantive chapters bear out this hypothesis. A large portion of the postings written in Usenet newsgroups about American politics were explicitly anti-government, as were the chats on America Online. Chapter 6 also showed that a full 21% percent of our sample of Web pages were posted by groups and individuals whose views are clearly on the left or right fringes of the American ideological spectrum. As for the rest of the world, Chapter 4 clearly showed that as the level of democratization in a country decreases, the number of anti-government postings about that country on the Usenet increases. Left-wing and right-wing fringe discussion of American politics is absolutely more prevalent on the Internet than it would be in the mainstream print or broadcast media. Likewise, people seem to be more willing to express anti-government feelings against repressive governments on the Usenet than they could comfortably do in the streets of many capital cities worldwide.

In the end, we strongly believe that our three major hypotheses have stood the test of empirical scrutiny in this book. While we cannot take credit for being the first people to think of these propositions about the Internet, this book *is* the first major step in empirically testing these propositions. After all, theoretical and off-the-cuff statements about any social phenomenon are great fodder for debate and speculation. Nevertheless, the job of the social scientist is to test these propositions in the harsh light of empirical data. We hope that *Cyberpolitics* has accomplished this goal, and that future research tests more propositions that may arise out of the findings in these pages.

Will the Internet Transform Politics?
Or Will Politics Transform the Internet?

The utopians propose that as more and more people connect to the Internet and engage in political conversation, governments will become more accountable to the people, direct citizen input into the political process will become ubiquitous, and viable on-line political communities will form. Conversely, the dystopians fear that such direct democracy will amount to nothing more than mob rule and rash decision making, and that the flood of information provided by the Internet will wash up a large share of outright misinformation that does nothing but obscure sensible political dialogue. Some people fervently hope that computer-mediated political communication will make the world a smaller place, serving to break down ethnic, geographical, age, and gender barriers. Of course, there are also people who fear that, as the Internet grows in size and takes on more users, people will flock to specialized sites and newsgroups, thus furthering the tribalization of the world. The one idea that utopians and dystopians share is that, for better or worse, the Internet will fundamentally alter the political landscape of the United States if not the entire world. The bulk of analysts agree that political and societal change are the *effect,* and the Internet is and will be the *cause.*

This logic of cause and effect at first blush is unassailable. Any new technology often generates hopes and fears, and the twentieth century in particular is full of examples of how technology has changed society. The invention of the atomic bomb and the intercontinental ballistic missile fundamentally changed the logic of global warfare. Television and radio changed the ways in which people communicate with each other, and how government reaches its citizens. The Hubble Space Telescope has served to alter our understanding of the far reaches of the cosmos. Even farther back in modern history, Galileo's tiny refractor served to change our view of Earth's place in the universe and solar system. It is logical, then, that so many pundits and scholars have proposed that the Internet will be another technology that will alter politics, society, and interpersonal relationships. There are always people who fear the changes that new technologies bring in daily life and even in our worldviews. These dystopians were behind the censuring of Galileo, and the same logic probably applies to the United States government's rash attempts to control data encryption and the putative spread of pornography on the Internet.

Someone using that logic after reading this book may arrive at different conclusions than we ultimately provide here. For example, the utopian may read our chapters on the Usenet, chat rooms, and the World Wide Web and be encouraged that direct democracy may indeed develop out of the Internet in the near future. Conservative and libertarian utopians and partisans would be even more encouraged; at this point, their sides seem to hold sway over the bulk of the Net's political content. Likewise, the dystopians who fear mob rule, a flood of misinformation, and the decline of civility in interpersonal communications may come away from this book even more disheartened. Based on our reading of the data presented here and how it fits into our hypotheses about human behavior in cyberspace, we believe that almost all the utopians and dystopians misunderstand the *real* dynamics of cause and effect here.

Our parting shot in this book, and indeed our major finding, is that the Internet is not going to radically change politics. Rather, we see cause and effect in a different way. As more and more people log on and participate in the Net's political forums, politics and society will *change the Internet*. This belief is not only grounded in our data here, but also offers us an opportunity to join the utopians and dystopians in some rank speculation. Right now, politics in cyberspace is undoubtedly the playground of conservatives, libertarians, and those with some kind of anti-government sentiment. However, it is not our contention that the Internet itself has made these people conservative, libertarian, or anti-government. On the contrary, these early days of the mass Internet have merely attracted these groups of people because they feel that the government and the traditional media are not listening to them. The open, anarchic nature of the Internet naturally attracts the disaffected, who can play on a level field with everyone else. After all, anyone with Net access can post Usenet messages, engage in political chats, and create a Web site. Conservatives, libertarians, and those on the fringes of the spectrum feel shut out by traditional politics and the media. As such, they have been the first to flock to the Internet's political areas. Our strong suspicion is that as more and more people get Internet access, the differences between real life populations and the Internet's population will diminish. Simply put, the Net's uniqueness will become diluted, particularly in the United States.

In the early days of public opinion polling, the *Literary Digest* confidently predicted that the Republican Alf Landon would trounce President Franklin D. Roosevelt in the election of 1936. This bold prediction was based on a mail questionnaire the magazine sent to millions of telephone subscribers and automobile owners. Of course the poll was woefully wrong because only a relative handful of people owned telephones or cars at the height of the Great Depression. The telephone subscribers were a biased sample of the American population: they were substantially richer, and thus far more Republican, than society at large. Does this mean that public opinion analysts no longer rely on the telephone to conduct random sample surveys? Absolutely not; anyone who has sat down to dinner only to be interrupted by a marketing or political survey knows this. The telephone has revolutionized public opinion polling, primarily because over 98% of the American population can be reached this way relatively cheaply and quickly. Telephone owners are no longer a small, biased sample of the American population; almost everyone now owns a telephone.

We believe that in the next few years, enough people will have access to the Internet to essentially dilute the political and demographic differences between the connected and the unconnected. As the demographic and ideological uniqueness of Net users decreases, the current conservative, anti-government, and libertarian bouquet of the Internet will merge into one shared by society at large. Of course as we saw in chapter 2, generic users of the Internet are already somewhat more *liberal* than society at large. But the rest of this book has shown that these people apparently are not taking advantage of their larger numbers in the same way as is the conservative minority. Of course, liberals could catch on soon. When will this day come? Currently, forty million people have access to the Internet. Many of these people live in the United States. The number of people who bother to vote in presidential elections is about eighty million. Although many people fret about this number being appallingly low, the fact remains that there are few major ideological and partisan differences between voters and non-voters. As the number of Internet users expands, so will the percentage of liberals and moderates. Of course, this proposition can be tested empirically over time, and we anxiously await the day that time series data become available to accomplish this important research task.

We found very little data to support the supposition that the Internet changes people's minds politically. Rather, reading Web pages seems to be an act of self-selection; people go on-line to find out more information about a subject, not to be transformed. Likewise, debate and information-based discussion in the Usenet newsgroups and political chat rooms serves to reinforce pre-existing ideological positions, not to change them. Currently a large chunk of the on-line population engaging in these activities are conservative, libertarian, and anti-government. There is nothing inherent about the Internet that dictates this will always be the case.

Many Internet old-timers will probably agree with our arguments here that the Internet will not change people as much as people will change the Internet politically. Back in the "old days" when the Internet was the warren of tech-heads and academics (circa 1990), the Net was in essence a tekkie and egghead playground. But with the advent of widespread Net access, particularly through the commercial services like America Online, the Internet has become increasingly diversified and commercialized. Anyone reading Usenet newsgroup titles in 1992 or 1993 would have seen some new groups like *alt.flame.aol* or *alt.newbies.die.die.die*. These were (and are) places where the old-timers could complain about the newfangled Internet, and how it was being ruined by "newbies." Many people rued the flood of new Internet users as an unwelcome dilution of the "true" character of cyberspace as a place where only computer programmers came to exchange ideas. Of course a large proportion of the Internet's newsgroups, Web sites, and FTP servers are *still* devoted to more tech-minded pursuits. Just because newcomers created millions of new Web pages and tens of thousands of newsgroups, the older parts of the Net did not disappear. In the near future, we believe that more and more liberals and moderates will log on to the Internet, and create another wave of Web sites, newsgroups, and chat rooms. That day is not here yet, and politically the Internet is *still* the domain of conservatives, libertarians, and to a lesser extent right-wingers. But it will not remain so for long, although of course the conservatives, libertarians, and right-wingers are not going to leave the Net. Rather, the Internet will grow to accommodate new users.[1]

Globalization or Tribalization?

The utopians believe that computer-mediated political communication will serve to not only facilitate grassroots democracy, but will also bring people all across the world closer together. Functionally, the Internet cannot help but to do the latter. A link in a Web page can just as easily point to a Web site in Australia or Brazil as it can to a page hosted on a site down the street. A Usenet newsgroup devoted to the politics of Singapore can be read and posted to by people in Singapore, of course, but an Internet user in Zimbabwe or the United States or Canada can also read this group and write messages for it. Real-time chat on the Internet can involve a live text-based conversation between people with Net-connected computers anywhere on the planet (or in orbit when the space shuttle is there, since it also has the capability to hook into the Internet). Globalization of communications via the Internet is a reality.

But does the technological potential for such communication necessarily mean that people flung over the four corners of the globe will be more understanding of each other? The same potential for uncivil flaming in newsgroups and scandalous Web pages that impugn someone's integrity also are part and parcel of this globalization. The authors have seen Web pages in Norway devoted to extremely offensive jokes aimed at blacks. Likewise, a hot topic of conversation in the newsgroup *alt.politics.french* is insults hurled back and forth across the English Channel between people in Britain and France. Just as the Web allows (even makes inevitable) fringe right- and left-wing American groups a worldwide forum, it can encourage "virtual" ethnic and nationalist conflict. Simply because people can talk to each other regardless of distance does not mean they will cooperate. Indeed, the studies of computer-mediated political communication mentioned in chapter 1 predict that such disembodied communication will almost always be less civil than face-to-face conversation.

On the other hand, the dystopians should not garner too much fear of a world gone mad solely because of the Internet. This communications medium does allow right-wing Cuban-American organizations in Miami to hurl insults at the Cuban government, while the latter does the same to the former with its official web page.[2] Such an exchange, while sometimes heated and unseemly, does serve an educational function for anyone interested in Cuban politics or the mechanisms of propaganda. Further, this exchange is a classic illustration of free speech on the part of Cuban exiles, and government advertising by the Castro regime. We believe that the Internet per se is benign in regard to globalization. It is simply another communications technology that serves to not only bring people "closer together," but also to allow insulting each other. We opened the book with the observation that the Internet is sacred *and* profane. A medium as truly gigantic as the Internet is inevitably going to contain a little bit of everything. While we are not confident that any natural force is going to serve to balance out each point with an equal counterpoint in cyberspace, we do not see any reason that malignant communications will hold sway over beneficial political missives on the Net.

Pundits worry publicly that the Internet will destroy society as we know it, obliterating the concept of common public spaces and fundamentally changing human interaction for the worse. These people are essentially in fear of increasing tribalization and a societal disconnectedness. The Internet will turn us all into geeks cowering in some dark corner of the basement, basking in the soft glow of a computer monitor rather than chatting with our neighbors over picket fences. Further, the argument goes, the Internet leads to dangers such as the posting of bomb recipes or the proliferation of pornography. The same arguments have been used in the past about cable television. Who has not heard the phrase "500 channels and nothing is on"?

In fact, we believe that if one must have a metaphor for politics on the Internet, it is cable TV. Cable channels allow a degree of specialization and a targeting of audiences not possible when there were only four or five channels. There are networks devoted solely to golf, food, sports, country music, and classic movies. On the other hand, the general interest networks and news channels have not faded away. We believe this is what the Internet does at a much larger scale. There are general interest political Web sites such as those maintained by the major news networks and newspapers. There are also very specific Web sites and newsgroups devoted to esoteric political ideas, events, and personalities. People can tune into any "channel" they desire, and can choose their level of interactivity: merely reading a Web page or deciding to start a conversation in a newsgroup. Technologically, the day may not be too far into the future when cable television and the Internet physically merge.

We are not denying that the Internet has a huge potential to change our political interactions with each other and established political institutions. Rather, our final belief after analyzing all this empirical data is that people will mold the Internet to fit traditional politics. The Net itself will not be a historical light switch that turns on some fundamentally new age of political participation and grassroots democracy. On the other hand, computer-mediated political communication is not going to destroy society as we know it and lead to mob rule.

During the heyday of the Pax Britannica in the late nineteenth century, British culture and symbols appeared in many parts of the world. As British colonization expanded to cover a large portion of the globe, so did British symbolism and ideas. To this day, statues of Queen Victoria stand in parks and plazas in Africa, lakes and waterfalls still bear her name, and countless streets hold some permutation of the names "Victoria" and "Albert." On the other hand, local names still persist. For better or worse, British foods like kidney pies and blood pudding can be bought on the streets of Calcutta, but so can samoosas and curries. Turning around the equation, London itself probably has more curry restaurants per capita than any city in Europe, one can buy African music CDs at Virgin Records, and the West Indian cricket team routinely trounces England in test matches.

Wherever the British went, they brought their culture with them. After independence for their colonies, the diverse cultures of those places flowed back up the colonial pipeline to London, Manchester, and Glasgow. Whenever people open new frontiers and confront new experiences, they bring their ideas, methodologies, and histories with them. This is happening on the Internet.

Political parties in the late nineteenth and early twentieth centuries went door to door canvassing for candidates. When the telephone spread into wider use, they started calling people at home, *but did not stop personal canvassing*. When people got fax machines and electronic mail, they started communicating politically with each other, *but did not abandon the telephone*. Now that people can use the Internet for political communications, they are not going to stop engaging in all these other tasks. Rather, just as British colonialists in southern Africa brought a little slice of England with them, people bring "real life" experiences and techniques to the Internet. The Net is not going to radically change us; we are molding it to our own ways of thinking and action. It is neither a monstrosity nor a savior; it is a new venue for the same old human compunction: politics.

Notes

1. We are not saying that the Internet can continue to grow ad infinitum. Theoretically, since the Internet is decentralized, adding new Web pages, newsgroups, and chat rooms will

not be a problem in and of itself. Still, the physical backbone of the Internet itself may become jammed as more and more people try to use the same number of resources, so slowdowns in connection speeds may plague the Internet. However, this is a technological problem far beyond the scope of this book.

2. Anyone interested in this topic should point their Web browser to the Cuban American National Foundation's Web site at *www.canf.org* and the Cuban government's CubaWeb at *www.cubaweb.cu.*

Appendix

2: Internet Activists

1995 Research Variables

Internet Activist: This is scaled variable composed of two questions: "Do you ever engage in on-line discussion about politics or engage in political activity on-line?" and "Have you ever expressed an opinion about a political or social issue to a bulletin board, on-line newsgroup, or e-mail list?" Both are coded 0 = no, 1 = yes. The two are added together and divided by two to yield 0 = no activity, .5 = posted or chatted, 1 = did both. The reliability for this measure is a = .68 for Internet sub-sample and = .72 for the general sample.

1995 Control Variables

Age: Coded as actual age in years
Gender: 1 = female, 2 = male
Race: 1 = nonwhite, 2 = white
Education: 1 = less than high school, 2 = high school graduate, 3 = some college, 4 = college graduate, 5 = post-graduate
Income: 1 = < $10,000; 2 = $10,000 to < $20,000; 3 = $20,000 to < $30,000; 4 = $30,000 to < $40,000; 5 = $40,000 to < $50,000; 6 = $50,000 to < $75,000; 7 = $75,000 to < $100,000; and 8 = $100,000 and up

1995 Dependent Variables

Party Identification: A branched question. First, "Do you consider yourself a Democrat, a Republican, or what?" If other, then "Do you lean more to the Republican party or more to the Democratic party?" Coded 1 = Democrat, 2 = leaning Democrat, 3 = independent or other, 4 = leaning Republican, 5 = Republican.
Strength of Party Identification: Based upon party identification. Coded 1 = nonpartisan, 2 = leaner, 3 = partisan.
Regulate Businesses: 1 = government regulation of business is necessary to protect the public interest, 2 = government regulation of business usually does more harm than good

Government Do More for Needy: 1 = government should do more to help needy Americans, even if it means going deeper into debt, 2 = the government today cannot afford to do much more to help the needy

Ban Books: 1 = public school libraries should be allowed to carry any books they want, 2 = books that contain dangerous ideas should be banned from public school libraries

Homosexuality Acceptable: 1 = homosexuality is a way of life that should be accepted by society, 2 = homosexuality is a way of life that should be discouraged by society

Regulate Pornography on the Internet: "Would you favor or oppose a law that would make it illegal for a computer network to carry pornographic or adult material?" 1 = oppose, 2 = favor.

Understand Oklahoma Bombing: 1 = there is simply no excuse for the Oklahoma City bombing, period, 2 = there is no excuse for the bombing but one can understand the frustrations and anger that may have led people to carry it out

Read Newspaper: "Do you happen to read any daily newspaper or newspapers regularly, or not?" 1 = no, 2 = yes.

Watch Television News: "Do you happen to watch any TV news programs regularly or not?" 1 = no, 2 = yes.

Listen to News Radio: "Do you listen to news on the radio regularly or not?" 1 = no, 2 = yes.

Overall Knowledge: A scale composed of four current event questions. 1—"Who is the Speaker of the House?" 2—"Do you happen to know which political party has a majority in the U.S. House of Representatives?" 3—Do you happen to know the name of the country where the currency was collapsing and the United States made loan guarantees to help stabilize the situation?" and 4—"What is the name of the president of Russia?" All questions are coded 1 = wrong, 2 = right. The responses were added together and divided by four. Reliability is = .73.

Turnout 1992: "In the 1992 presidential election, when Clinton ran against Bush and Perot, did things come up which kept you from voting, or did you happen to vote?" Coded 1 = did not vote, 2 = voted.

Turnout 1994: "In the 1994 elections for Congress last November, did things come up which kept you from voting or did you happen to vote?" Coded 1 = did not vote, 2 = voted.

Vote Choice 1992—Democrat vs. Republican: If respondent voted, who did respondent vote for? Coded 1 = Democrat, 2 = Republican.

Vote Choice 1992—Mainstream vs. Out-party: If respondent voted, who did respondent vote for? Coded 1 = Democrat or Republican, 2 = Perot or other independent.

Vote Choice 1994: If respondent voted, who did respondent vote for? Coded 1 = Democrat, 2 = Republican.

1996 Research Variables

Internet Activist: This is scaled variable composed of two questions: "Do you ever engage in on-line discussion about politics or engage in political activity on-line?" and "Do you ever contact or e-mail groups, organizations, or public officials about political issues or public policy questions?" Both are coded 0 = no, 1 = yes. The two are added together and divided by two to yield 0 = no activity, .5 = posted or chatted, 1 = did both. The reliability for this measure is = .45.

Politics/Campaign News On-line: Does respondent ever go on-line to get political or campaign news?

Sources of News: If respondent does seek politics/campaign news, respondent was asked if he or she ever visited a list of seventeen sites. These were combined into A) ABC, CBS, NBC; B) CNN, C-Span MSNBC; C) national newspapers; D) specialized news sites such as All Politics, Rock the Vote, Citizen 96, or Politics Now; E) candidate Web pages; and F) government Web pages.

Reasons for Following News: Some people go on-line for campaign news because they are very interested in politics and enjoy following it. Others get no enjoyment out of following politics but they keep up with it because they feel it's their duty to be well-informed. Which comes closer to your view? 1 = Enjoy politics, 2 = duty.

Reasons for Going On-line: Which comes closest to describing why you go on-line to get news and information about the 1996 elections (multiple responses allowed). 1 = because you can get information not available elsewhere, 2 = because getting information on-line is more convenient, 3 = because the web offers news sources that reflect your own interests or values, 4 = because you don't get all the information you want from traditional news sources such as the daily newspaper and the network TV news, 5 = other.

Follow-up Media Stories: Have you ever gone on-line to follow-up or get more information on a news story you saw or heard in a newspaper or on TV? 1 = Yes, 2 = No.

Believe What You See On-line: Which of the following statements comes closer to your opinion of the Internet: 1 = these days you are more likely to find accurate information about what's going on in the world on the Internet than in daily newspapers or on network news; 2—a lot of what you find on the Internet cannot be believed.

Did On-line Information Affect Choice: Has any of the information you have received on-line about the 1996 elections influenced your choice of candidates? 1 = yes, 2 = no.

3: Building Political Communities in Cyberspace

Content Analysis Methodology

1. Samples:
   a. A random sample of twenty-two out of ninety-five explicitly political groups. This is an intentional oversampling of political groups.
   b. Article threads within each of the twenty-two groups were randomly selected as follows:
      i. On Monday of each week, each researcher downloaded all new headers in all the groups. Before doing this we set up our newsreader to purge all headers older than 7 days.
      ii. Each researcher then *independently* rolled one six-sided die to determine the starting header for all groups (e.g., a roll of 4 means the researcher started with the fourth header in each of the twenty-two groups; if a group had less than six new headers, one was picked at random).
      iii. Each researcher then *independently* rolled three six-sided dice to determine which Kth headers to watch (e.g., I roll a 4 as above; then a 9, so start with the fourth header in each group and then watch every ninth thread for that week).
      iv. We then each used the "watch thread" feature of our newsreader to follow our selected weekly threads. Then, we download the text of our threads and actually make an archive for safekeeping.
      v. This way we were watching threads only for a 7-day window, but it was possible that when we started again the next week, we would pick up some of the same threads again.
2. Coding and Operationalization.
   a. Usenet dot domain.
   b. Group name.
   c. Ideology of leader's original post (Left, No Dominant, Right).
   d. Thread length in messages.
   e. Overall ideological direction of entire thread (Left, No Dominant/Balanced, Right).
   f. Number of messages from the thread originator (leader).
   g. Number of messages from the most active poster.
   h. Is the thread a debate?
   i. Is the thread a reaction to a current event?

j. Is the thread predominantly providing "information" from an external source?

k. Is the thread predominantly anti-government and/or anti-government on a specific government action?

l. Is the thread a "piling-on-flame-fest" of a person with an opinion that runs contrary to either the thread or the group in general (e.g., maybe the thread is one person calling people in alt.supremacy.white "a bunch of Nazis," then sixty-seven replies against that person).

m. Is the thread a recruiting strategy (giving out URLs for Web pages, announcing meetings, trying to persuade someone to the cause, etc.)?

4: Is the Internet an Instrument of Global Democratization?

See Table A.1.

5: Instantaneous Political Discussion

1. Sample:
    a. 20 chat room logs from America Online's Cloak Room, collected as follows:
        i. Two 10-week periods were chosen. The first lasted from August until October of 1996. The second lasted from February until April of 1997.
        ii. Once per week, a day was randomly selected by rolling a six-sided die. Wednesday, which is devoted to libertarian chat, was excluded. For each day, an hour between 8:00 P.M. EST and 1:00 A.M. EST was selected by rolling a six-sided die. Each logged session lasted approximately 30 minutes.
        iii. Chat logs were recorded. Since messages are typed in real time and become jumbled, they were reorganized to re-create the conversation or thread. The judgment of the coder was used to determine the intended target of each message.
        iv. Certain messages were excluded from the log. These include salutations (e.g., "Nite everyone"), greetings from the hosts, and host admonishments (e.g., "Please don't use profanity").
        v. Once reorganized, each individual conversation was coded for content. Coding was double-checked by the other author and any discrepancies were discussed and resolved.
2. Coding and Operationalization.
    a. Pre- or post-election.
    b. Date and time.
    c. Whether a host was present.

TABLE A.1
Anti-Government Messages in 41 Usenet Newsgroups

	Without Measures of Democratization	With Measures of Democratization
Constant	-.910 (.994)	-.559 (1.25)
Posting of .com, .org, or .net Origin	-.011 (.356)	-.209 (.336)
Posting of .edu Origin	-.231 (.466)	-.326 (.496)
Posting of Origin in "Home" Nation	.722* (.370)	.744 (.409)
Number of Internet Domains	-.00007 (.00005)	-.00006 (.00004)
N of Messages in Newsgroup	.001 (.002)	.00007 (.0016)
GDP per Capita in Subject Newsgroup's Nation	-.0001 (.0001)	.00001 (.00009)
Population in Millions in Subject Newsgroup's Nation	.0004 (.001)	.0002 (.0009)
Percent Population Urban in Subject Newsgroup's Nation	-.006 (.012)	.002 (.012)
Composite Democratization Index	____	-.036* (.018)
East Asia	-1.22 (.904)	-.737 (1.16)
Eastern Europe	-.305 (.905)	.379 (1.19)
Latin America	-.312 (.908)	-.033 (1.08)
Muslim Nations	-1.20 (.958)	-1.66 (1.18)
India	-2.85*** (.889)	-1.81 (1.06)
Democracy Index*East Asia	____	-.052 (.044)
Democracy Index*Eastern Europe	____	.379 (1.19)

(Continued on next page)

(Table A.1, continued)

Democracy Index*Latin America	———	-.056*
		(.027)
Democracy Index*Muslim Nations	———	.020
		(.040)
N	2326	2326
Model Chi-Square	399.48***	375.74***
Log Likelihood	-610	-574
Pseudo R-Squared	.091	.145

Note: Table entries are logistic regression coefficients for the likelihood that a message is anti-government (vis-à-vis the government of the Usenet national group in question). Robust (Huber-White) standard errors are in parentheses.

Legend: *** p <.001, * p <.05

d. Thread number (for identification).
e. Number of message lines.
f. Number of people contributing to thread.
g. Overall ideology of thread calculated by counting the number of right, left, and neutral messages and selected modal category.
h. Is the thread predominantly anti-government and/or anti-government on a specific government action?
i. Is thread predominately anti-media?
j. Is the thread predominantly providing "information" from an external source?
k. Is thread predominately about current events?
l. Is thread about the 1996 elections?
m. Is thread predominately a debate?
n. Do participants in thread provide verifiable information?
o. Is the thread concerned with an "easy" or "hard" issue or neither?
p. Is the thread a "piling-on-flame-fest" of a person with an opinion that runs contrary to the thread?
q. Is the thread a recruiting strategy (giving out URLs for Web pages, announcing meetings, trying to persuade someone to the cause, etc.)?

6: Web Sites, Interest Groups, and Politics

See Table A.2.

TABLE A.2
Web Sites Used in Chapter 6

Site Name	Site Address	Ideology
A WEPIN (Weapon) for Freedom and Sovereignty	colossus.net/wepinsto/wshome.html	Rightist
Adopt-a-Convict	www.webserve.com/phrantic/adoptcon.htm	Neutral
Alliance to Expose Government Corruption and Corporate Crime	www.well.com/user/pfrankli	Leftist
American Coalition for Fathers and Children	www.acfc.org/	Conservative
American Intelligence	www.amintel.com	Neutral
Americans for Hope, Growth, and Opportunity	www.ahgo.org	Conservative
Americans for Tax Reform	www.atr.org/	Conservative
Arizona Democratic Party	www.azdem.org	Liberal
AZConnect Community	getnet.com/azconnect	Neutral
Bob Dole as Obstructionist	www.ctyme.com/dole/obstruct.htm	Liberal
Californians for Justice	www.igc.apc.org/cfj	Liberal
Campaigning On-line	www.campol.com	Conservative
Capital Research	www.capitalresearch.org	Conservative
CapWeb: The Citizen's Guide to Congress	www.capweb.net	Neutral
Center for Civic Networking	civic.net/ccn.html	Neutral
Center for International Policy	www.us.net/cip	Liberal
Center for Public Integrity Homepage	www.essential.org/cpi	Neutral
Center for Voting and Democracy	www.igc.apc.org/cvd	Liberal
Cerebral Commentary Site	www.wavefront.com/~albert	Liberal
Christian Coalition	www.cc.org	Conservative
Citizens for Better Government	www.afn.org/~govern	Conservative
Citizens for Tax Justice	www.ctj.org	Rightist
Colorado Hemp Initiative Project Homepage	www.welcomehome.org/cohip.html	Conservative
		Libertarian

(Continued on next page)

(Table A.2, continued)

Site Name	Site Address	Ideology
Common Cause	www.commoncause.org	Liberal
Common Dreams	www.commondreams.org	Liberal
Concord Coalition at UW	weber.u.washington.edu/~freeman/CONCORD/	Conservative
Conservative Generation X	www.cgx.com	Conservative
Conservative Zone, The	www.soltec.net/~cknite	Conservative
CRY Home Page	www.wnx.com/~cry	Liberal
Democratic Capitalism Against Rush Limbaugh Economics	web.cetlink.net/~kellycm/	Liberal
Democratic Leadership Council -- Progressive Policy Institute	www.dlcppi.org	Liberal
Democratic Socialists of America Home Page	www.dsausa.org	Leftist
Doug's Political Essays	www.muscle.net/~doug/essays	Conservative
Empower America	www.empower.org	Conservative
Ethics and Public Policy Center	www.eppc.org	Conservative
Fair Housing Institute, Inc.	www.mindspring.com/~fairhous	Neutral
Federalist Society	www.fed-soc.org	Libertarian
Federation of American Scientists	www.fas.org	Liberal
Fight the Right Network Homepage	www.critpath.org/ftrn	Liberal
Flat Tax Home Page	flattax.house.gov/	Conservative
Fletcher Prouty Reference Site	home.xl.ca/fiasco/prouty/	Rightist
Florida Secession Home Page	hubcap.clemson.edu/~mwsmith/fishpan/florida	Rightist
Golden Key Campaign for Private Communications Online	www.eff.org/goldkey.html	Libertarian
HYSN Home Page	www.pixi.com/~hinet	Neutral
Industrial Workers of the World	www.iww.org	Leftist
Institute for Anarchist Studies	members.aol.com/iastudy/Default.htm	Leftist
Institute for Policy Innovation	www.ipi.org	Libertarian
John Birch Society	www.jbs.org	Rightist
Journal X	www.journalx.com	Neutral
League of Conservation Voters	www.lcv.org	Liberal

(Continued on next page)

198

(Table A.2, continued)

Site Name	Site Address	Ideology
League of Revolutionaries for a New America	www.mcs.com/~jdav/league.html	Leftist
Learning Logic Foundation Think Tank	pw2.netcom.com/~think/tank.html	Neutral
Let America Speak!	www.rtk.net/las	Neutral
Liberals and Libertarians	www.batnet.com/liberty/liberal/	Libertarian
Libertarian Party	www.lp.org	Libertarian
Log Cabin Republicans of Austin	www.bga.com/~labinski/512top.htm	Conservative
Motorcycle Riders Foundation	www.mrf.org/	Libertarian
Myth of the Magical Bureaucracy	www.house.gov/hoekstra/myth/home.html	Conservative
National Center for Policy Analysis	www.public-policy.org/~ncpa	Conservative
Natural Resources Defense Council	www.igc.apc.org/nrdc	Liberal
New Democracy Home Page	members.aol.com/newdem/index.htm	Leftist
New Party	www.newparty.org	Leftist
NY Transfer	www.blythe.org	Leftist
Official Reform Party Home Page	www.reformparty.org	Conservative
Patrick Henry On-line	www.clandjop.com/~mlindste	Rightist
Pennsylvania Association for Government Relations	www.pagr.org	Neutral
Policy.Com Home Page	policy.com	Neutral
Political Chat!	www.4-lane.com/politicalchat/	Neutral
Political Distortions	www.ibsnet.com/ndl/distortions/political.html	Neutral
Power to the People	ourworld.compuserve.com/homepages/americani	Rightist
Presidents of the United States	www.ipl.org/ref/POTUS/	Neutral
Prince William County Young Republicans	www.princewilliam.com/pwcyr	Conservative
Public Access Project	members.aol.com/paccess593/index.htm	Neutral
Puerto Rican Political Prisoners	members.aol.com/baileme/theprisoners.htm	Leftist
Puerto Rico Statehood Website	www.puertorico51.org/english/index2.html	Neutral
RAND Corporation	www.rand.org	Conservative
Reason Foundation	www.reason.org	Libertarian
Repper Garcia Online -- Tampa Bay Politics	www.repper.com	Neutral

(Continued on next page)

(Continued on next page)

(Table A.2, continued)

Site Name	Site Address	Ideology
Republic of Texas	www.republic-of-texas.com/	Rightist
Rick Tompkins for President	www.nguworld.com/rick96	Libertarian
Rutherford Institute	www.rutherford.org	Conservative
Santa Barbara Democrats	www.sbdemocrats.org	Liberal
Save Our Skies	www.scican.net/~sos	Liberal
School of the Americas Watch	www.derechos.org/soaw/	Leftist
Secret History of the United States 1962-1996, The	w3.one.net/~conspira/Welcome.html	Leftist
Sempervirens Fund	reality.sgi.com/employees/ctb/sempervirens/	Liberal
Sheet Metal Workers International Association	www.smwia.org	Liberal
Socialist International	www.gn.apc.org/socint	Leftist
Student Space Awareness Virtual Headquarters	www.seds.org/ssa	Neutral
Third Parties '96	www.envirolink.org/greens/3rd-p96	Liberal
Third Parties '96	sunsite.unc.edu/spc/tp96	Liberal
Town Hall	www.townhall.com	Conservative
United States Freedom Fighters Home Page	usff.com	Rightist
Unofficial Rush Limbaugh	www.rtis.com/nat/pol/rush	Conservative
Unofficial Traci Topps for Prez Page	www.geocities.com/CapitolHill/9194/	Conservative
USS Liberty	www.halcyon.com/jim/ussliberty	Neutral
Vox Pop	www.voxpop.org	Neutral
War Criminal Watch	www.igc.apc.org/wcw	Liberal
Whitewater Estates Home Page	biz.arkansas.net/whitewaterestates/	Conservative
Woodstock Institute	online.nonprofit.net/woodstock/	Liberal

Bibliography

Abramson, Jeffrey B., F. Christopher Arterton, and Gary R. Orren. 1988. *The Electronic Commonwealth: The Impact of New Media Technologies on Democratic Politics.* New York: Basic Books, Inc.

Beck, Paul Allen. 1974. "A Socialization Theory of Partisan Realignment." In *The Politics of Future Citizens,* ed. Richard G. Niemi. San Francisco: Jossey-Bass.

———. "Voters' Intermediation Environments in the 1988 Presidential Contest." *Public Opinion Quarterly* 55 (Fall 1991): 371–94.

Bonchek, Mark S. 1995. "Grassroots in Cyberspace: Using Computer Networks to Facilitate Political Participation." Paper presented at the 53rd annual meeting of the Midwest Political Science Association, Chicago.

———. 1996. "From Broadcast to Netcast: The Internet and the Flow of Political Information." Ph.D. dissertation, Harvard University.

Boone, Peter. 1994. *Politics and the Effectiveness of Foreign Aid.* London: London School of Economics.

Campbell, Angus, Phillip Converse, Warren Miller, and Donald Stokes. 1960. *The American Voter.* Ann Arbor: The University of Michigan Press.

Carmines, Edward G., and James A. Stimson. "The Two Faces of Issue Voting." *American Political Science Review* 74 (March 1980): 78–91.

Chaffee, Steven H. 1986. "Mass Media and Interpersonal Channels: Competitive, Convergent, or Complementary?" In *Inter/Media: Interpersonal Communication in a Media World,* ed. Gary Gumpert and Robert Cathcart. New York: Oxford University Press.

Connolly, Terry, Leonard M. Jessup, and Joseph S. Valacich. "Effects of Anonymity and Evaluative Tone on Idea Generation in Computer-Mediated Groups." *Management Science* 36 (June 1990): 689–703.

Diamond, Larry. 1992. "Economic Development and Democracy Reconsidered." In *Reexamining Democracy: Essays in Honor of Seymour Martin Lipset,* ed. Gary Marks and Larry Diamond. London: Sage.

Diamond, Larry, Juan Linz, and Seymour Martin Lipset. 1988. *Democracy in Developing Countries.* Boulder, Colo.: Lynne Rienner.

Diener, Ed. 1980. "Deindividuation: The Absence of Self-awareness and Self-regulation in Group Members." In *The Psychology of Group Influence,* ed. Paul B. Paulus. Hillsdale, N.J.: Erlbaum.

Easton, David, and Dennis, Jack. 1969. Children and the Political System. New York: McGraw-Hill.

Edinger, Joyce A., and Miles L. Patterson. "Nonverbal Involvement and Social Control." *Psychological Bulletin* 93 (January 1983): 30–56.

Finifter, Ada. "The Friendship Group as a Protective Environment." *American Political Science Review* 68 (June 1976): 607–25.

Forsyth, Donelson R. 1983. *An Introduction to Group Dynamics.* Monterey, Calif.: Brooks/Cole.

Frederick, Howard. "Computer Communications in Cross-Border Coalition-Building: North American NGO Networking against NAFTA." *Gazette* 50 (March 1992): 217–42.

Gallupe, R. Brent, Lana M. Bastianutti, and William H. Cooper. "Unblocking Brainstorms." *Journal of Applied Psychology* 76 (February 1991): 137–42.

Gastil, Robert. 1985. "The Past, Present, and Future of Democracy." *Journal of International Affairs* 38 (Spring 1985): 161–79.

Graber, Doris. 1992. *Public Sector Communication: How Organizations Manage Information.* Washington, D.C.: Congressional Quarterly.

Hauben, Michael. 1996. *The Netizens and the Wonderful World of the Net: an Anthology.* Available at *http://www.columbia.edu/~hauben/netbook/*.

Herbst, Susan. 1994. *Politics at the Margin: Historical Studies of Public Expression outside the Mainstream.* New York: Cambridge Press.

Hill, Kevin A., and John E. Hughes. "Computer-Mediated Political Communication: The Usenet and Political Communities." *Political Communication* 14 (March 1997): 3–27.

Hiltz, Starr Roxanne, Kenneth Johnson, and Murray Turoff. "Experiments in Group Decision Making: Communication Process and Outcome in Face-to-Face Versus Computerized Conferences." *Human Communication Research* 13 (Winter 1987): 225–52.

Huckfeldt, Robert. "Political Participation and the Neighborhood Social Context." *American Journal of Political Science* 23 (August 1979): 579–92.

———. "Political Loyalties and Social Class Ties: The Mechanisms of Contextual Influence." *American Journal of Political Science* 39 (May 1984): 1025–54.

Huckfeldt, Robert, and John Sprague. "Networks in Context: The Social Flow of Political Information." *American Political Science Review* 81 (December 1987): 1197–216.

Huckfeldt, Robert, Paul Allen Beck, Russell J. Dalton, and Jeffrey Levine. "Political Environments, Cohesive Social Groups, and the Communication of Public Opinion." *American Journal of Political Science* 39 (November 1995): 1025–54.

Huntington, Samuel P. 1991. *The Third Wave: Democratization in the Late Twentieth Century.* Norman, Okla.: University of Oklahoma Press.

———. "Will More Countries Become Democratic?" *Political Science Quarterly* 99 (Summer 1984): 193–218.

Internet Freedom Network. 1996. *Meeting Summary, May 13, 1996.* Available at *http://www.cdt.org/internat/960513_IFN_mtg.html*

Intertrader. 1997. *How Large Is the Internet?* Available at *http://www.intertrader.com/netstats.html*

Kaplan, Roger. 1994. *Freedom Review.* New York: Freedom House.

Kedzie, Christopher R. 1995. "A Brave New World or a New World Order?" In *Research Outposts on the Information Highway,* ed. Sara Kiesler. Hillsdale, N.J.: Erlbaum Associates.

Kiesler, Sara, Jane Siegel, and Timothy W. McGuire. "Social Psychological Aspects of Computer-Mediated Communication." *American Psychologist* 10 (October 1984): 1123–43.

Krauss, Robert M., William Apple, Nancy Morencz, Charlotte Wenzel, and Ward Winton. "Verbal, Vocal, and Visible Factors in Judgements of Another's Affect." *Journal of Personality and Social Psychology* 40 (February 1981): 312–20.

Lenin, Vladimir. 1905. *What Is to Be Done?* Moscow: Progress Publishers.

Lerner, Daniel. 1968. *The Passing of Traditional Society: Modernizing the Middle East.* New York: Free Press.

Liklander, J. C. R. 1962. "On-Line Man Computer Communication." Memorandum, Massachusetts Institute of Technology, Department of Computer Science. Available at *http://www.isoc.org/internet-history/#JCRL62*

Lispet, Seymour Martin. "Some Social Requisites of Democracy: Economic Development and Political Legitimacy." *The American Political Science Review* 53 (March 1959): 69–105.

Lispet, Seymour Martin, K. Seong, and Juan Torres. "A Comparative Analysis of the Social Requisites of Democracy." *International Social Science Journal* 136 (September 1993): 155–75.

McColm, R. B. 1992. "The Comparative Survey of Freedom 1991–1992: Between Two Worlds." In *Freedom in the World: Political Rights and Civil Liberties, 1991–1992,* ed. Freedom House Survey Team. New York: Freedom House.

Meherabian, Albert. 1971. *Silent Messages.* Belmont, Calif.: Wadsworth.

Moe, Terry. 1980. *The Organization of Interests: Incentives and the Internal Dynamics of Political Interest Groups.* Chicago: University of Chicago Press.

Neuman, W. Russell, Marion R. Just, and Ann N. Crigler. 1992. *Common Knowledge: News and the Construction of Political Meaning.* Chicago: University of Chicago Press.

Olson, Mancur. 1968. *The Logic of Collective Action.* Cambridge: Harvard University Press.

———. "Dictatorship, Democracy, and Development." *American Political Science Review* 87 (June 1993): 567–76.

Owen, Diana. 1996. "Who's Talking? Who's Listening? The New Politics of Radio Talk Shows." In *Broken Contract: Changing Relationships between Americans and Their Government,* ed. Stephen C. Craig. Boulder, Colo.: Westview Press.

Panos. 1995. *The Internet and the South: Superhighway or Dirt-track?* Available at *http://www.oneworld.org/panos/panos_internet_press.html*

Parenti, Michael. 1993. *Inventing Reality: The Politics of News Media.* New York: Saint Martin's Press.

Pew Research Center for the People and the Press. 1996. *News Attracts Most Internet Users.* Washington, D.C.

———. 1995. *Americans Going Online. Explosive Growth, Uncertain Destinations.* Washington, D.C.

Putnam, Robert. 1994. *Making Democracy Work: Civic Traditions in Modern Italy.* Princeton: Princeton University Press.

Rash, Wayne, Jr. 1997. *Politics on the Nets: Wiring the Political Process.* New York: W. H. Freeman and Company.

Rheingold, Howard. 1993. *The Virtual Community: Homesteading on the Electronic Frontier.* Reading, Mass.: Addison-Wesley.

Rosenstone, Steven J., and John Mark Hansen. 1993. *Mobilization, Participation and Democracy in America.* New York: Macmillian Publishing Company.

Rowen, Henry S. "The Tide Underneath the 'Third Wave.'" *Journal of Democracy* 6 (Winter 1995): 52–64.

Schenk, David. 1997. *Data Smog: Surviving the Information Glut.* New York: Harper-Collins.

Schifter, Richard. 1994. "Is There a Democracy Gene?" *The Washington Quarterly* 17 (Summer 1994): 121–27.

Schwartz, Edward. 1996. *Net Activism: How Citizens Use the Internet.* Sebastopol, Calif.: Songline Studios, Inc.

Siegel, Jane, Vitaly, Dubrovsky, Sara Kiesler, and Timothy W. McGuire. "Group Processes in Computer-Mediated Communication." *Organizational Behavior and Human Decision Processes* 37 (April 1986): 157–81.

Toffler, Alvin, and Heidi Toffler. 1994. *Creating a New Civilization: The Politics of the Third Wave.* Atlanta: Turner Publishing.

Truman, David. 1951. *The Governmental Process.* New York: Alfred A. Knopf.

Vanhanen, Tatu. 1997. *Prospects of Democracy: A Study of 172 Countries.* New York: Routledge.

Wald, Kenneth, Dennis E. Owen, and Samuel S. Hill, Jr. "Churches as Political Communities." *American Political Science Review* 82 (June 1988): 531–48.

Weber, Max. 1995. *The Protestant Ethic and the Spirit of Capitalism.* London: Roxbury.

Wilson, James Q. 1961. *Political Organization.* Cambridge: Harvard University Press.

Index

About the Authors

Kevin A. Hill is assistant professor of political science at Florida International University. **John E. Hughes** is assistant professor of political science at Monmouth University.